Rethinking the South

Michael O'Brien

RETHINKING THE SOUTH

Essays in Intellectual History

The Johns Hopkins University Press

BALTIMORE AND LONDON

© 1988 The Johns Hopkins University Press
All rights reserved
Printed in the United States of America

The Johns Hopkins University Press
701 West 40th Street
Baltimore, Maryland 21211
The Johns Hopkins Press Ltd., London

The paper used in this publication meets
the minimum requirements of American
National Standard for Information Sciences—
Permanence of Paper for Printed Library
Materials, ANSI Z39.48-1984.

LIBRARY OF CONGRESS CATALOGING-IN-PUBLICATION DATA

O'Brien, Michael, 1948–
  Rethinking the South.

  Bibliography: p.
  Includes index.
  1. Southern States—Intellectual life. 2. Romanticism
—Southern States. 3. American literature—Southern
States—History and criticism. I. Title.
F212.024 1988   001.1′00975   87-32482
ISBN 0-8018-3617-4 (alk. paper)

FOR JONATHAN STEINBERG

Contents

Illustrations

Acknowledgments

Essays written over some fifteen years bear the mark of many influences, and the help of several institutions, which it is right to acknowledge. I have received advice, criticism, and encouragement from Daniel Singal, Richard King, Eugene Genovese, David Moltke-Hansen, Steven Stowe, Jane Pease, William Pease, Mills Thornton, Lacy Ford, Lewis P. Simpson, Fred Hobson, Dewey Grantham, James Meriwether, Thomas Bender, Clyde Wilson, Ella Puryear Mims, Catherine Mims, Laurence Goldstein, C. Vann Woodward, David Sloan, Elizabeth Payne, John Thompson, and many others. My most consistent and valued counselors have been Richard Lounsbury and Patricia O'Brien. The plan of this volume was greatly helped by Henry Tom at the Johns Hopkins University Press and benefited from the shrewd and generous observations of Bertram Wyatt-Brown.

Research and publication over the years have been facilitated by grants from the Department of Education and Science in Britain, the American Philosophical Society, the Arkansas Endowment for the Humanities, and the Fulbright College of the University of Arkansas and by the philanthropy (unsought but welcome) of Catherine and Ella Puryear Mims and Willard B. Gatewood. At various times, I have received the patronage of the University of Cambridge and colleges therein, the University of East Anglia, Homerton College, the Michigan Society of Fellows, the Southern Studies Program of the University of South Carolina, the University of Alabama, the University of Arkansas, and Miami University of Ohio. I am in debt to many libraries and librarians, of which these have been most important: the Cambridge University Library, the Harlan Hatcher Graduate Library in Ann Arbor, the Mullins Library in Fayetteville, the Southern Historical Collection, the Joint University Libraries in Nashville, the

South Caroliniana Library (especially Allen Stokes), and the South Carolina Historical Society (particularly David Moltke-Hansen and Gene Waddell).

For permission to republish these essays, I am obliged to the following: for chapter 1, the University of Arkansas Press and the Board of Trustees of the University of Arkansas; for chapter 2, the *Journal of American Studies* and the Syndics of the Cambridge University Press; for chapter 3, the University of Tennessee Press; the chapter 5, the *Historical Journal* and the Syndics of the Cambridge University Press; for chapter 6, the *South Atlantic Quarterly* and Duke University Press; for chapter 7, *Perspectives on the American South* and Gordon and Breach, as well as the *Michigan Quarterly Review;* for chapter 8, the *Journal of Southern History* and its managing editor; for chapter 9, the *American Historical Review;* and for chapter 10, the University of Alabama Press and William D. Barnard.

This book is dedicated to Jonathan Steinberg, to whom I owe a debt that cannot be discharged by so simple a gesture. When I became an undergraduate at Trinity Hall, he was both my director of studies and supervisor: later he became a friend, who in the bleak days of academic recession helped to find me refuges in which I might continue an interest angular to the practice of Cambridge history. I doubt that my vocation would have survived without his efforts, and I know I would have been intellectually impoverished by the absence of his guidance. He was the model of an imaginative and cosmopolitan historical intelligence, sympathetic and critical. I hope he will accept these essays as a small gift, and a report at (what for my work may be regarded as) the end of the Michaelmas term.

Rethinking the South

The Endeavor of Southern Intellectual History

THERE HAS been some interest, over the last decade or so, in the intellectual history of the American South. During those years, I have had occasion to write essays whose revision and republication here may help to establish a perspective upon the endeavor of Southern intellectual history. That endeavor is a new one, and a little troubled by the charge of illegitimacy. Those engaged upon it are vexed by the suggestion that they spend their time among phantom documents and people, and ruminate on thin air. For it has been familiarly objected that the South has no intellectual history, or one so etiolated that the effort is misguided. To writing on the twentieth-century South this objection is mild, since the standing of the Southern Renaissance in critical estimate is great. To writing on the Old South the objection is weighty, enough to make the endeavor seem quixotic. Knowing and disbelieving these objections, I have permitted these essays sometimes to be betrayed into necessary polemic. When an axiom is in error and needs detonation, a little violence may be in order. Here, however, it is right to stress that the recovery of the history of the Southern intelligentsia should be regarded as a modest enough proposal, too long adjourned.

Nonetheless, experience indicates that to say there is such a history can excite alarmed reactions. Is it claimed, the scandalized inquire, that the mind of the Old South is equal to that of New England? To which the answer is no, because such questions of stature are only mildly useful, and best as an agreeable parlor game. A reader who opens this volume to find the verdict of a cultural hanging judge will be disappointed. A culture is not a candidate for tenure and cannot be

A few sentences in the latter part of this introduction have been borrowed from "Clio as Medusa," *Southern Review* 16 (January 1980): 249–55.

expunged because it did not write enough, publish in the best places, or influence others who have received tenure elsewhere. A culture is there, for good or ill, for better or worse, and there is an obligation to understand it.

Understanding is not easy, for reasons that will be adduced below. The greatest enemy of the endeavor of Southern intellectual history is the premise of social organicism, just as paradoxically the same premise has initiated the endeavor. W. J. Cash made much of the idea that one Southerner is much like another. It is a misguided notion, and pernicious when translated to studying the life of the mind. An illustration may help to make the point. At a recent historical convention Southern intellectuals were under discussion. Some were praised, others rebuked, which might be thought the ordinary process of historical criticism. But members of the audience were restless. How can it be, it was asked, that one can speak slightingly of the merits of William Gilmore Simms, while recommending the virtues of Hugh Legaré? The implication seemed to be that if one Southern thinker was weak, they were all weak; if one was strong, they were all strong. But parallel cases diminish the implication. The case for Emerson is not weakened if a successful indictment is brought against Margaret Fuller. One need not think the less of Voltaire because one doubts Montesquieu. Rather, is it not an obligation of the historian to look as steadily as possible upon the individual thinker before he constructs a social portrait of the intelligentsia? Unfortunately we have been much prone to the reverse, to imposing a social analysis that has posited the mindlessness of the South, with the result that minds have gone unnoticed and unassessed.

So it may suffice to say here, by way of perspective, that the South has had an interesting intellectual culture, and a provincial one. It has had a number of subtle intelligences, and a great many dull ones. But all cultures are provincial; that is, their ideas are indigenously fashioned for local usages, however much they may be influenced by importations. Some cultures get into the exporting business, as Europe transmitted ideas to American shores from the time of Jamestown to that of Henry James, and as the United States has sent ideas to Europe in the twentieth century. The South, except insofar as it contributed to the definition of American political thought in the late eighteenth century, has not been much in the export business until the names of the Southern Renaissance became resonant in the 1930s in Boston, Paris, and London. Hence many of the names that the reader will come across in these essays, though they may ring a distant bell, are unlikely to be his constant companions, unless (as is probable) the reader is a Southerner. I am perverse enough to think this makes the venture no less worthwhile. To say we should only write about those who have exercised cross-cultural hegemonies (however interesting and important that subject is) is another way of saying that we should only be interested in the mechanisms of domination. Feminists have hazarded firm words on this matter, and they are worth heeding. As someone who has spent his adult life passing from one provincial culture, England, to another, the South, I find this passion for domination deadening to curiosity. I have never seen why I should think the less of the television criticism of Clive James because he was not syndicated in Chapel Hill, or of the irony of John Wade because his name never comes up at gatherings in Hammersmith.

Then, too, it is said, as a way of dismissing the endeavor, that the South is an anti-intellectual culture. So it is. But so are most Western cultures, with the possible exceptions of France and Germany. England has been relentlessly philistine; indeed it was an Englishman, Matthew Arnold, who coined the term. The United States, too, has been inhospitable to intellect, as the generations of Americans who abandoned Main Street for the Boulevard Montparnasse have testified. The cant of commencement addresses aside, there is distressingly little reason why a utilitarian society should be other than anti-intellectual, given that most intellectuals write on unintelligible matters in an unintelligible manner and have been growing more inaccessible since the late eighteenth century. Intellectuals are by nature scavengers, whom society is wise to mistrust even when useful services are rendered.

Anti-intellectualism has been worse in the South than many other places. Southern thinkers have felt lonely, been criticized, dismissed from jobs, and made miserable. The record is undeniable. But before we join too energetically in the lamentations of W. J. Cash, a little perspective might help. No Southern intellectual has been banished to a Gulag, none (to my knowledge) even lynched, which is the punishment Southerners have reserved for those they regard as serious enemies. It is well to remember, when hearing those lamentations, that intellectuals are incorrigibly voracious for praise. Unless society regularly hands over prizes, money, and fame, intellectuals are very prone to maudlin complaints about neglect. This is as true of an academic who has just failed to get a Guggenheim fellowship as it was of Simms in Charleston in 1850, when the locals failed to buy his latest novel in sufficient quantities. Intellectuals like to have simultaneously the dignity of alienation and the reward of belonging, which, like any demand to have one's cake and eat it, is a recipe for discontent. An intellectual abused by society is a melancholy sight. But an intellectual rewarded by society can sometimes be worse, as anyone who has been in an Oxford senior combination room will testify.

This sounds anti-intellectual, but is not. Rather it is intended to stress that the intellectual historian must respect or doubt ideas and thinkers for their own sake and not rest his case upon social utility. In the negotiations that have gone on recently between intellectual historians and the new social history, much has been profitably exchanged. But two camps have developed: those who study ideas and need to find their social context, the school of Pocock and Skinner; and those who study society and see ideas as part of its fabric, the way of the Annalistes. Both agree on the necessity of text and context, but for the former, intellectuals and their products are the text, and society is the context, and for the latter the matter is reversed. This is not an ominous schism, and it has been fruitful in its tension. But it helps in clarity to declare allegiance. In this matter, not just for tribal reasons, I stand with the two gentlemen from Cambridge.

Such cultural history is open to the accusation of elitism. The writings of Perry Miller have been vilified for neglect of popular *mentalité*. This lesson has been learned, and the intellectual historian knows now with sharpness that he writes, not on the mind of the South, but on the minds of Southern intellectuals and their collective discourse. Driven back, he needs a last ditch, lest he be reduced to a servant at the feast of social history. For me that ditch is the belief that, within the discourse, thinkers and their ideas merit scrutiny and do not require justification from the great roar of society and social historians that stream past the study window, however often those intellectuals have gone out into the street to roar themselves.

I stress this point because of a delicate matter of chronology in the development of Southern intellectual history. The arguments about elite culture and social history were thrashed out in the European and American traditions, where social history had to prune an arrogant history of ideas that seemed to suggest that Plato and Aristotle, Jonathan Edwards and Thomas Jefferson, defined social thought. The battle for social history was won, the head of Arthur Lovejoy duly displayed in preface after preface. Unfortunately, to transfer that battle to the South poses a difficulty. It is premature to repudiate the Perry Millers of Southern history before those historians have come to exist, especially as such a repudiation will prevent their emergence. So the matter is peculiar. The scholar of "high culture," elsewhere Banquo's Ghost, must ask leave in Southern history to dine in the flesh before he is dispatched and can return to haunt.

THE TEST of legitimacy will be the essays themselves, about which a few words. It will be obvious that the vision is selective, comprising merely those topics that initially attracted my attention and fitted my competence. At a time when writing history and introductions has become like running for the presidential nomination of the Democratic party, an exercise in placating constituencies poised in outrage, it may be necessary to observe that I have written mostly about Southern white males, all of them (from my standpoint) foreigners. A resident alien perspective has meant a crookedness of vision, as a critic of these studies was shrewd enough to remark. The reader will find the transatlantic dimension of Southern thought better understood than the indigenous, the secular better than the religious, texts better than contexts. Two overriding themes will be apparent, one historical, the other historiographical.

It is contended that beginning in the early nineteenth century and continuing into our own day, Romanticism has been peculiarly powerful as an influence upon the Southern life of the mind. This contention is both a general one about the shape of European and American thought and a particular one about the South. It rests on the proposition that Romanticism has provided an analytical glue that has held in agreed category the underlying heterogeneity of social life in the Southeastern United States. Since historians are ever alert for "central" themes in Southern history, it is fair to warn that this is offered as no central theme, on the strict understanding that a history can have no central theme. But I do think that Romanticism—along with slavery, race, wealth, honor, poverty, among many other things—has had a role in shaping Southern culture, and we have erred in underestimating its formative power. Along with this has gone the corollary that Southern thought has been more in and of the outside world than has usually been thought. This is not a denial of Southern distinctiveness but a suggestion that some of the raw materials of that distinction have been borrowed and adapted. Intellectual Southerners have chosen their culture knowingly, not in ignorance. This is the unsettling prerogative of an ex-colonial culture. In the comfort of hindsight and our own Treasury of Virtue, to use Robert Penn Warren's phrase, we may deprecate or celebrate the choices they made for themselves and their culture, but the dead are not interested in our curses or eulogies.

Nonetheless, the mixed record of Southern experience—its hideousness and attractiveness—is a standing reproof to the shallowness of the Whig interpretation of history. This is one reason why it has drawn so many vexed historians in recent years, when American culture has been obliged to reconsider the shallowness of the American dream, which is Whiggery run amok.

The second theme has to do with the problem of canons, about which there is now much discussion among literary theorists.[1] Both sections of this book, "Old South" and "New South," have essays that attempt to ask why we have read one set of texts rather than another, and how this came about. In those essays, it is argued that our view of the Old South has been distorted by the anachronistic analytical premises developed by the New South, and that little progress will be made until the blinkers put on, chiefly in the 1930s, are taken off. In turn, it is suggested that we might reconsider the canons the critics of the Southern Renaissance imposed upon their contemporaries and successors. In both cases an attempt is made to disentangle the endeavor of Southern intellectual history from those who hitherto have been its chief guardians, the literary critics. This has led to an extended quarrel with Allen Tate, who above all has formed the dominant interpretation. Since this act of dissociation will seem ungrateful, it is proper here to stress that my own debt to those guardians has been great; indeed, they formed my own introduction to the problem of the Southern mind. I hope that the drift of these essays will not destroy the relationship between "literature" and history, not make Southern literary criticism an adjunct to an imperial intellectual history, but help to reconstruct that relationship.

When C. Vann Woodward acknowledged, in *The Burden of Southern History,* that the historians of the 1950s should make a bow towards the writers of the Renaissance, he spoke justly. Most of the creative energy in Southern culture from the 1920s to the 1950s issued from novelists and poets, who in turn were imaginatively and faithfully represented and celebrated by Southern literary critics. But times change. It is my strong impression, diffidently advanced, that recent Southern literary culture is rather stuck on the themes of 1930, still recycling Faulkner and echoing Tate. While there are fresh voices, such as Walker Percy, their originality consists in the skepticism with which they use the old themes. But old themes they remain.

By contrast, Southern historiography, so pale and miserable in the 1920s, is now vibrant. Western history, once dominant under the aegis of Frederick Jackson Turner, has been shunted into a sidetrack, and for two decades and more the South has been central to the writing of American history. There has been a torrent of new history and historians, many of them Southerners, some non-Southerners, such that a new compendium, *Interpreting Southern History,* feels obliged to open with the remark, "Probably no field of American History has been more transformed by recent scholarship than the study of the South."[2] The Southern Historical Association, in the 1940s a private gathering, is now a cosmopolitan convention. Indeed it stands in mortal danger of becoming intellectually fashionable, the regrettable consequence of what is otherwise admirable, a willingness to entertain fresh ideas and evidence.

This outburst seems to have made little impact upon Southern literary criticism, which with a few exceptions seems to potter along with the history it glancingly learned in the 1950s. This would matter little if most Southern literary critics were deconstructionists or semioticians or even rigorous New Critics. But the tradition has, peculiarly, taken history seriously, so it is of great moment that its version of Southern history is now painfully ill-informed and dated. In short, the relationship between history and literary criticism, without which a humane Southern culture is impossible, needs reconstructing. For a while the critic needs to listen to the historian, just as once the historian needed to listen to the critic. And the urgency of this resides in the belief that history, the novel, poetry, and criticism are at bottom the same venture, all branches of literature.

In these matters the situation of the intellectual historian stands close to that of the literary critic. He, too, has been obliged to keep up with this torrent of writing from political, social, and economic historians, and try to consider where it leaves him. Hence there is a good deal of discussion, in these essays, of other historians, by way of making sense of the transformation. As Tate once found, new times mandate alertness, discrimination, winnowing, that the heterogeneous be made intelligible and usable. This may help to explain why this book is not reluctant to be blunt. In the deluge, he who admires everything is lost. It is the business of the critic to criticize, just as he expects and hopes in turn to be criticized; this is, partly, the conversation of ideas. Clive James has diagnosed the critic's obligation: "The first duty of the intellect is to extend, or if it cannot extend at least protect, the area of common reason." But Kenneth Tynan has expressed the critic's mood: "Although some of it was written in fury, the best of it was, I think, written in gratitude."[3]

The historian becomes the historiographer at his peril, and it is useful, though difficult, to keep the roles distinct. Hence the anthology *All Clever Men, Who Make Their Way,* the introduction to which is included here, was intended as an intervention in the critical discourse of modern historians. But *A Character of Hugh Legaré,* from the research for which another essay is drawn, eschews such issues. Historiography, except as a species of intellectual history, can degenerate into gossiping with one's peers, when it should be a ground clearing for the dialogue between the historian and the past. When an undergraduate in 1966, I heard J. R. Pole observe that one of his first impressions upon being translated from the University of London to Cambridge was that teaching the subject matter of the past had become overwhelmed by discussing the historians. No one talked about the Constitution of 1787; everyone talked about Charles Beard on the Constitution. Pole, as an influence on that most inert of creatures, the Historical Tripos, greatly contributed towards diminishing that emphasis. But as Pole's essays have demonstrated, the categories of historiography and history are not tidily exclusive.[4]

THIS INTRODUCTION has sounded rather positivist, as though all that is needed for the clear light of history to dawn is to throw away a few mistaken premises and read a few disused texts. This is not my understanding of the historical enterprise, which I take to be a literary endeavor of the most exacting discipline. The historian of Romanticism, more than most critics, has the obligation to denote standpoint, especially if it is one idiosyncratic among those usual to modern historians. That standpoint is Romantic irony, whose first definer was Friedrich von Schlegel: by this is meant the belief that while historical reality is incoherent, narrative is cohering, and the narrator has an obligation, by means of his voice, to denote awareness of this vitalizing incongruity.[5]

Yet a species of positivism was a doctrine learned in apprenticeship at Cambridge. The Historical Tripos assumed that there are such things as pieces of historical knowledge, discoverable by right application, effort, and a little flair, and that the way one talks about historical knowledge is less important than the knowledge itself. Words merely convey the reader to the knowledge that the historian, as researcher, has wrested from the coprolites of the past. Philosophy, as the Tripos viewed it, was political philosophy. The undergraduate read Hegel's *Philosophy of Right,* which is philosophy about political action, rather than his *Phenomenology,* which is philosophy about the nature of thought. And perhaps the Tripos in its hoary majesty was right to exercise this censorship. It can be a dangerous business to meditate too long on these things. Herbert Butterfield, sensible North country man that he was, managed, anchored as he was in a brisk Christian faith. But some of his disciples, frailer men, went half-mad with it and cluttered up Peterhouse for a generation or more with their melancholy brooding and literary indigestion. They were swept aside by the optimistic positivism of others, such as J. H. Plumb, who declaimed the faith of progress. Somewhere in the rear came furrow-browed Quentin Skinner, who told the rapt undergraduate that while there was a doubt about the reality of historical knowledge, he was thinking it through. His preliminary report indicated that probably we could sleep safely in our beds, without the ghost of epistemological insanity disturbing us.[6]

History, as Lord Acton implied in his inaugural address as Regius Professor, was a thing greater than the historian: "There is virtue in the saying that a historian is seen at his best when he does not appear." Douglas Southall Freeman, in the preface to his biography of Robert E. Lee, remarked: "A biographer, like a dramatist, has no place on the stage. When he has made his bow to his audience and has spoken his prologue, telling what he will try to exhibit, it is his duty to retire to the wings, to raise the curtain and to leave the play to the actors."[7] The image seems plausible, until it is remembered that when the curtain goes up, the historian as dramatist is still there, perched on a stool, reading to his audience with more or less mimetic skill.

Until the late eighteenth century there was no distinction between history and literature. History, the novel, poetry, epic, were all branches of literature, distinguished only by their subject matter and rhetorical techniques. Literature was merely the business of writing. The classical discipline of rhetoric instructed the writer in the modes by which he could adjust subject and means of expression, with the two coequal, matched to the expectations and knowledge of a clearly perceived audience. In the course of the nineteenth century, history and the novel, history and poetry, began to go separate ways. Rhetoric began its long decline in popular understanding from its supremacy as a center of understanding and expression to a term of abuse applied to fustian parliamentarians, and its ancient role as the iron hoop that bound all the branches of literature together rusted away.

Classical and eighteenth-century theories of history assumed that the facts of history were, as Aristotle argued, necessarily heterogeneous and confused. Coherence lay in the mind of the historian, which was why the means of expression were so central, and formed an important part of the historian's training. Art lay in communicating a vision to the mind of the reader, and the reader was expected to be interested not only in the matter of history but in the matter of the historian. If the reader was not so interested, the failure lay with the historian's lack of distinction in prose and, since prose was the measure of mind, in mind. It is important to note that this was hedged with no suspicion of egotism. Self, as the eighteenth century saw it, was inescapable, and Acton's claim that the historian could somehow not appear in his own historical narrative would have been viewed as inherently absurd, as indeed it is.

The nineteenth century was, intellectually speaking, a great furniture auction of the mind of the eighteenth-century country house, in which rooms were broken down into small lots and sold off separately. The pieces of furniture were placed in very different settings. Poetry went, as it were, into garrets. History went into solid middle-class homes, into the North Oxford villas of dons, into the well-padded residences of Cambridge, Massachusetts. These were homes in which the self-assurance of Gibbon came to seem improper, a little pushy, lacking in a proper respect for form. In Gibbon's case, the sin of presumption was compounded by that of irreligion, in a man who impudently denied the individual's subjection to a general scheme of Providence. Self had become egotism, which in the auction had been given to the poets and novelists to indulge. And poets especially were oddly respected for plying their self-centered trade, because they were thought to risk fearful psychic dangers, to play with fire, risk madness, go to live in Paris, or wear long beards like that nice Mr. Tennyson. Poets were permitted to be egocentric, even obliged to be, to refine their personalities along with their words, to experiment with their lives, to get drunk night after night, to get the clap, in order to improve their verse. Lord Acton would have been severe with any historian who got syphilis in order to improve his contribution to historical narrative. What Acton, author of a series of lectures upon the French Revolution, would have thought of Richard Cobb, whose celebration of Thermidor vies in his narrative with the record of his bibulations, scarcely bears contemplation. It would have been a majestic explosion.

One must not forget that expositors of much nineteenth-century historical philosophy, such as Ranke, posited from a religious standpoint the abnegation of self in the historical narrative. The rejection of self was a religious decision, and a tense imperative. Precisely the closeness of these philosophers and historians to the instabilities of Romantic thought, with its insight into individual psychology, precisely their elevation of the Reformation as the liberator of the individual conscience, precisely this made them careful to build walls around the self, to remind themselves and their readers that self was expressed in an identification with the general, with the state or with culture. Particularly for Ranke, religion was important and vexatious. As a young man in Leipzig he had agonized over its objectivity or subjectivity. Later he came to insist on the historian as a priest, with the documents as the bread and wine of his mass before God, whose obligation in devotion was "to keep in mind only the object itself and nothing more, in all its impartiality."[8] The fact was the footprint of God. What has been left, by the secularization of Ranke, has been just the reality of the fact.

Aesthetic counsel for historians survived the nineteenth century, if only just. But advice became increasingly displaced from the historian to the historical narrative. It was not the historian whose aesthetic identity was to be educated, and therefore the narrative, but just the narrative. G. M. Trevelyan, between brisk afternoon walks from Trinity College, used to think he defended the old ways. He fought the heresy of J. B. Bury, Acton's successor as Regius Professor, who entertained the delusion that history was a science. But in what did Trevelyan's counsel consist? This is Trevelyan on art in history, in an essay called "Clio, A Muse," an attempt to refute the notion that she had become a laboratory assistant, merely passing chemicals and test tubes to the historian: "To my mind there are three distinct functions of history, that we may call the *scientific*, the *imaginative* or *speculative*, and the *literary*. First comes what we may call the *scientific*, if we confine the word to this narrow but vital function, the day-labour that every historian must well and truly perform if he is to be a serious member of his profession—the accumulation of facts and the sifting of evidence. . . . Then comes the *imaginative* or *speculative*, when he plays with the facts that he has gathered, selects and classifies them, and makes his guesses and generalizations. And last but not least comes the *literary* function, the exposition of the results of science and imagination in a form that will attract and educate our fellow-countrymen. . . . Writing is not . . . a secondary but one of the primary tasks of the historian."[9]

Most practicing historians, while they may not act upon such counsel, would regard this as proper advice. His idea that literature is difficult, that what is "easy to read has been difficult to write," is sound enough, though narrow, for it excludes as good prose the Baroque, the hard labor and satisfaction of a Tacitean style. But, for the rest, the advice is mischievous, because Trevelyan saw the means of expression as something added to the humdrum tasks of the historian. You did this, then you did that, then you wrote it up. All Trevelyan urged was that you write it up well, trippingly on the pen. This was not a repudiation of scientific history but its gilding. Lytton Strachey probably had Trevelyan in mind when he wrote in 1909 in a review: "When Livy said that he would have made Pompey win the battle of Pharsalia, if the turn of the sentence had required it, he was not talking utter nonsense, but simply expressing an important truth in a highly paradoxical way—that the first duty of a great historian is to be an artist. The function of art in history is something much more profound than mere decoration; to regard it, as some writers persist in regarding it, as if it were the jam put around the pill of fact by cunning historians is to fall into a grievous error."[10]

Both Trevelyan's and Strachey's examples have miscarried. Trevelyan is doubted because it seems less plausible that it is the function of the historian to promote a Gladstonian national welfare, to bond together ordinary citizen and intellectual elite, or to celebrate great men like Garibaldi, and because the style itself now seems cloying. Least of all is it plausible that history is a former of character, like rowing and long Alpine walks. Strachey has been little emulated for more complicated reasons. His rebellion against Victorianism was too successful for his own good. His act of demystification has been carried sufficiently far beyond him that his own writing, like Trevelyan's, ironically, now reads a little sentimentally—not perhaps in *Eminent Victorians* and certainly not in his real masterpiece, *Portraits in Miniature,* but in *Queen Victoria* and *Elizabeth and Essex.* Then, too, the battle he fought against pomposity and obscurity is still being fought, and there are always more ranged against than for him. The advice that his contemporary F. M. Cornford once gave to the young academic, on a path to a reputation for sound learning, is still usable: "If you should write a book . . . be sure that it is unreadable."[11] But Strachey had grave faults, of which the greatest was a narrowness of range. He was a master at understanding individual psychologies, but he did not understand politics save as personal and dynastic drama, and he worked exclusively from published works. Economics, sociology, political science, all were beyond or beneath him. If Strachey, like Gibbon, claimed that his history should be the image of his mind, one comes away from a reading with the feeling that the mind was not various and rich enough to sustain the claim.

Trevelyan represented a dying creed in several senses. He believed that history itself was literature, which is the oldest of creeds. But he also tended to believe that good prose was something one could learn about from the novelists, which was something newer. In the division of spoils in the early nineteenth century, Walter Scott was thought to have defined *how* to write, while historians merely provided the subjects about which to write. And when historians now are given aesthetic counsel, as often as not they are told to read novelists. And there's a rub. It is too late now to write like Scott. Would a historian be willing to update his models? It may be too late for James Joyce, as literary modernism has aged. If the historian should choose to enrich his sensibility in this way, where would he look? Would we be condemned to a succession of stream-of-consciousness histories, absurdist histories, antihistory histories. Must we see E. P. Thompson transformed into Thomas Pynchon before our incredulous eyes? The thought is instinctively abhorrent. Why? Because in our culture the historian has become the great apostle of common sense. The poet and the novelist might each choose to become the guardian of our aesthetic insanity, to explore and objectify incoherence, but the historian is condemned to be the guardian of metaphysical innocence and practical hope.

The novelist and the poet have, more than any others, defined for us the philosophical confusion of modernism. It is through Joyce, Eliot, or Virginia Woolf that most of us begin to feel the force of modernism in our bones: the disruption of time sequences, the variety of standpoints and meaning attributable to actions and thoughts, the location of meaning everywhere and nowhere. This is, as these essays will suggest, nineteenth-century Romanticism run to bleak seed. Romanticism conceded the necessity of alienation, but it went on to insist that the philosophical mind could transcend alienation and fragmentation, could find its way on to a higher level of meaning, stamped with the experience but restored, whole. Literary modernism has abandoned this hope and left us with the alienation. History, it is important to observe, has not. Historical narrative is, with very few exceptions, precisely about coherence, finding synthesis, imposing order. The assumption of order, common ground to most literary practitioners of the eighteenth century, has grown a peculiarity of the historian. He can go back to a manual of rhetoric like that of Hugh Blair and find more familiar and usable doctrine than could a modern novelist, poet, or literary critic. The historian would find, for one thing, this familiar and comforting advice: "The first virtue of historical narration is clearness, order, and due connexion. To attain this, the historian must be completely master of his subject; he must see the whole as at one view; and comprehend the chain and dependence of all its parts, that he may introduce every thing in its proper place; that he may lead us smoothly along the track of affairs which are recorded, and may always give us the satisfaction of seeing how one event arises out of another. Without this, there can be neither pleasure nor instruction, in reading history."[12]

Here is an important paradox. The more the philosopher or novelist has urged the instability of things, the more the historian has clung stubbornly to his sense of coherence, his sense that he, the historian, is not coequal with history itself, that it is greater. The more the novelist has insisted that understanding is private but fragmented by our own psychological changes, contingent experiences, broken memories, the more the historian has denied the privacy of his own vision. There are those who would argue that this is symptomatic of naïveté in the historian.[13] This may be true. But it does the social role of the historian an injustice. He is performing an honorable role in the division of spoils. Romantic social thought survived because it was a subtle philosophy designed to explain and cope with an unprecedented pace of social change. It offered two things simultaneously. There was the vision of disappointed hope, Carlyle's French Revolution with men gone mad, De Quincey's opium reveries, Hawthorne's bleak hand of the Puritan past, Dostoevsky's philosophical murderers. And there was the vision of aspiration fulfilled, Wordsworth at Tintern Abbey gratefully musing on the still, sad music of humanity, Keats asserting the supremacy of beauty, Michelet bringing his narrative of the French Revolution to a triumphant conclusion, Herder insisting on the fraternity of the *Volk* in language. In Poe's story "A Descent into Maelstrom" the unhappy hero falls into a whirlpool, sees his boat break up, sees his brother disappear, is consumed with horror and awe at his approaching end, until he deduces by observation that large objects descend slower than small, spherical objects slower than the irregularly shaped, cylinders slowest of all. He straps himself to a wooden cask and survives. It is an allegory of Romanticism as a philosophy of survival, survival rooted in thought and emotional temerity but a survival not worthy of respect unless dearly bought.

So the bleak side of Romanticism was given into the hands of the novelists and philosophers, the optimistic side to the historians. This point may be subject to misunderstanding. In the lessons they may inculcate, in temperament, many modern historians (including some discussed herein) are exceptionally depressing: wars, famine, morgues, racism, social oppression. There is enthusiasm at every discovery of a bread riot, rising levels of abortion, bulging penitentiaries, packed madhouses. But if one listens not to what they say but to how they say it, the case is otherwise. With the possible exception of Michel Foucault, narratives remain models of pristine coherence. Fact follows fact, footnote succeeds footnote, deduction leads to conclusion. Beginnings, middles, ends. No one would be admitted to the guild of historians who did not have them. There must be order, or there is no history. And it is a communitarian order. Historians write for the community of historians; prefaces, footnotes, acknowledgments, all speak to this. Friedrich Schiller's declaration at Jena in 1789 that there is a universal history, a coherent story, a *Cambridge Modern History* in the sky, to which each historian contributes his mite, is no longer explicitly believed by historians. But their narrative structures say otherwise.

It is in this that one must look for the diminution of the literary responsibility of the historian. History is, after all, myth. It is written for us, by us, for the location of meaning in the past, with implications for the present. History is a very large myth in our culture, one that has been getting larger since the eighteenth century at about the same pace as it has been growing inelegant, for reasons that may be obvious. The faster the speed of change, the greater the need for the explaining myth of change. If the past has become a crucial deity in our society, vital to our sense of social purpose and sanity, the historians, the acolytes and priests of the deity, are the more reverent if they tremble, stumble awkwardly around the altar, believe that the past is real, and can come and strike them down with a thunderbolt. The secular myth of modern society is not very old. Historians are still primitive priests to a young religion. We have not yet got to the eighteenth century of our myth, to Gibbon smiling at the folly of it, to Talleyrand as bishop of Autun going sardonically through the motions of the Mass.

Part I · OLD SOUTH

CHAPTER I

On the Mind of the Old South and Its Accessibility

VERY FEW are disposed to grant any vitality to the mind of the Old South. That it was superficial, unintellectual, obsessed with race and slavery, enfeebled by polemic, is a ruling assumption of American scholarship. The explanation for this is well worn. The humane eclecticism of the Enlightenment, it is said, was displaced by the focused narrowness of a Calhoun. The planter class, which dominated the region, withdrew from its former cosmopolitanism, grew out of touch with modern intellectual developments, when once it had led them, became frantic with worry or guilt over the place of slavery in the Union, was isolated on remote and supine plantations far from the invigoration of urban life. Skepticism became displaced by the emotionalism of evangelical religion. Thought had become prejudice.

Wilbur Cash, on this as on many things, summed it up dashingly: "Leaving Mr. Jefferson aside, the whole South produced, not only no original philosopher but no derivative one to set beside Emerson and Thoreau; no novelist but poor Simms to measure against the Northern galaxy headed by Hawthorne and Melville and Cooper; no painter but Allston to stand in the company of Ryder and a dozen Yankees; no poet deserving the name save Poe—only half a Southerner. . . . In general, the intellectual and aesthetic culture of the Old South was a superficial and jejune thing, borrowed from without and worn as a political armor and a badge of rank; and hence (I call the authority of old Matthew Arnold to bear me witness) not a true culture at all."[1]

This essay was first published as the introduction to *All Clever Men, Who Make Their Way: Critical Discourse in the Old South* (Fayetteville, Ark., 1982), 1–25. I have eliminated only such features as mark it firmly as an introduction to the texts of that anthology; however, I have added to the footnotes, in square brackets, references to subsequent scholarship and a few extra thoughts. A few infelicities have been amended.

Now I suspect that this judgment is seriously mistaken and that we stand in our understanding of antebellum Southern thought where the study of colonial New England stood when Perry Miller came to revise the orthodoxy of Brooks Adams. That is a large claim, I am aware. But beginnings are being made elsewhere, in books by the likes of Drew Faust, Robert Brugger, and E. Brooks Holifield, that make the claim begin to seem plausible.[2] Here it is necessary to provide the structure of an explanation of why Cash's judgment came to be stated, is still believed, and should no longer be believed. The mind of the Old South has come to seem uninteresting and inaccessible, come to be worth studying only for the proslavery argument or for picking out from its literary dross the solitary gold of Poe or the tarnished silver of Simms. Why?

It helps to begin with a brief social portrait of the antebellum Southern intellectual and the institutional structure of his discourse, although only part of the explanation is intrinsic to the Old South itself. The term *intellectual* must, of course, be used with reluctant caution, for it has acquired in our century an air of professionalism. We have come to see the intellectual as someone who lives by and for the understanding, dissemination, and judgment of ideas. By this modern and anachronistic definition, there were few antebellum Southern intellectuals in the period between Jefferson's decline and the Civil War. Instead there were a great many men, and a very few women, who were interested in ideas and might be described by Coleridge's term, the clerisy. A very few, such as Simms, lived by the pen, but most read and wrote in the midst of lives otherwise engaged. They were lawyers, politicians, clergymen, planters, diplomats, teachers, newspaper editors, sometimes several of these simultaneously or serially. Most lived in cities and small towns rather than on plantations. Some owned plantations, it is true, but most moved within the penumbra of urban life. They might live part of the year in the country, but the house in Charleston or the visit to Richmond usually offered the impulse to set thought to paper. Editors were vigilant for literate visitors who could turn their reading of Eugene Sue's latest novel into an essay for a periodical such as the *Southern Quarterly Review*. Urban life itself offered modes of discourse. In Charleston there was the Conversation Club, which met every few weeks for papers to be read and madeira to be consumed. In small towns were similar if less imposing literary, historical, and debating societies. Colleges, agricultural societies, religious meetings, political occasions, generated their own thought and printed expression. Nothing was more usual than this editorial preface to an 1856 *De Bow's Review* essay: "An intelligent gentleman at the South sends us the following article, which we insert without change. In his letter, he says: 'I herewith send an article written by an intelligent gentlemen, for you to publish all, a part or none, as to you may seem proper. The views which it expresses were first presented to me in a conversation, and I was so impressed with their truthfulness, in the main . . . that I suggested to him to write them out, and submit them for publication.'"[3]

This was casual, not in itself inimical to thought but ill-designed to produce professional men of letters. Such a loose structure created, most of all, criticism expressed in periodical literature. George Tucker of Virginia considered the periodical the typical expression of the American mind of his day.[4] It was certainly that of the South. Even then some thought this a mistake. William Grayson observed in 1863, "It is reversing the natural order of production to begin a Country's literature with a Quarterly Review. We should begin with books to be reviewed."[5] But anyone who has read the journals of the nineteenth century, whether issued from Edinburgh, Boston, or Charleston, will know that their definition of criticism was generous. Sermons, orations, and addresses were reprinted. Essays independent of any book to be reviewed were used. Articles purportedly reviews were often, perhaps usually, not so. Who now remembers what book prompted Macaulay to write on Chatham? It is doubtful that Macaulay himself cared overmuch. "Look at the Reviews which now form so striking a feature in our general Literature," George Frederick Holmes, then of South Carolina, noted in 1845 in just such a review. "They are no longer expressions of opinion upon the merits of new books, but independent essays upon all subjects under the sun."[6]

As has been observed often enough, such journals did not always prosper. William Gilmore Simms buried as many of them as he did children. It has been usual to put this down to the indifference of the reading public, though as often it was the result of feckless editing. Simms liked to blame his readers. His readers as often blamed him, and with equal justice. Such instability was not, however, confined to the South, the impressive and subsidized solidity of the *North American Review* aside. From 1828 to the Civil War the region always had one major review. In the late 1840s and early 1850s it had three doing tolerably well, despite the endemic and too often cited laments of ambitious and necessarily harassed editors: the *Southern Literary Messenger,* which lasted for thirty years; the *Southern Quarterly Review,* which carried on for fifteen; and *De Bow's Review,* which went on for twenty.

The first and the last of these were only stopped by the Civil War itself. On top of these were innumerable more specialized journals, such as the *Southern Presbyterian Review* and the *Southern Agriculturist*.

Into such periodicals the intellectual energies of the region were liberally poured. In them, that energy has been frozen and lost to an indifferent posterity. And the fault has lain partly with journals that observed the convention of an author's anonymity. Not only do *we* not know the identity of many contributors, Southerners themselves were often ignorant. This usage was not peculiar to the South. It was sanctioned by Francis Jeffrey and the elder Stephen Elliott alike. Nor was the secrecy perfect: occasionally a name was attached to an article, sometimes by mistake or stealth, or initials might offer a delicate hint. Neither was secrecy always intended to be perfect. Periodicals were often products of, and spoke to, small local elites, and few doubted that readers might guess authorship and offer proper congratulations. It is doubtful that anonymity betokened a contempt for writing, let alone ideas, and that to be known as an author made one ineligible for polite society.[7] If that were so, a remarkable number of the most prominent Southerners were pariahs. Poe was not received, for reasons quite other than his association with the *Messenger* and inkwells: being unable to hold even a small drink has always diminished a man's social circle, if drunkenness precipitated roaring abuse to one's host. To write was respectable. *Only* to write was less so. To advertise was vulgar, and the prefix of one's name to an essay was a form of self-aggrandizement. In a society whose authors did not usually depend upon payments for words, it was not only vulgar, it was superfluous.

The consequences of anonymity, however, have been immense, not alone for precipitating our own ignorance. The South lacked a robust book-publishing trade (not to be confused with a printing industry— every Southern town had its printer), and the conjunction of this with the convention of anonymity meant that the transition from essay to book was not often made. There were few publishers who clamored to turn the casual author into the creator of a folio volume. The great merry circle that is modern authorship—the book, the review of the book, the book of the reviews, and so on, round and round, all eased by the public knowledge of and demand for an author freely acknowl-edged and promoted—this circle was seldom closed in the Old South. Books as such form a smaller part of its intellectual culture than else-where. This, it is true, impoverished its critical mind. Its discourse was fragmented. Thought did take place and was expressed, but the bar-riers between author and reader, author and other authors, periodical and book trade, inhibited synthesis and reconsideration.

It was a point that George Frederick Holmes well understood. "As long as it was necessary," he wrote in 1853 of the loosely comparable British situation, "to purchase and peruse the expensive and extensive series of the Edinburgh or the London Quarterly, in order to possess and become familiar with the modern master-pieces of English criticism and speculation;—as long as we were compelled, even then, without special initiation, to remain ignorant or doubtful of the authorship of the articles most admirable for their grace, ingenuity or depth;—it would have been unreasonable to anticipate, except in rare instances, that the ablest of them should continue to possess any general interest, or should exercise any durable influence on literature and scholarship. The practice of republication . . . affords a great convenience to the anxious student, and revives, with a fresher interest and under more favorable auspices, the pleasure and profit which might have previously attended the cursory perusal of any striking articles. . . . we may now make them the intimate associates of more sedate studies, and we may consort with the ablest productions of recent times, with an assured confidence in their excellence, and without undergoing the tedium of winnowing the sound grain from . . . endless amount of chaff."[8] This was an observation that prefaced Holmes's own oblivion, for there was no collected edition of Holmes essays.

New England periodicals, of course, observed the same tradition of anonymity. But that region was smaller and more integrated than the South, and it had a lively publishing trade. The South, by comparison, had at least three foci of thought and periodical distribution, radiating from Richmond, Charleston, and New Orleans. The half-secret names would not carry such distances. Even so distinguished a name as Hugh Swinton Legaré, immediately spotted in South Carolina by the literate cognoscenti, could be referred to by the *Messenger* as "little known" in Virginia.[9] But most crucially, New England won the Civil War, and the postbellum generation thought it proper to memorialize the ideological authors of that famous victory. As Perry Miller has observed, "Scholars diligently hunt out the earliest scrawls of Emerson, Hawthorne, Thoreau; the slightest stirrings of intelligence in New England became part of the national record, for here, the assumption runs, began the problem of the mind in America. The reason is, of course, that New England, by its peculiar coherence, not only presents to the country a body of literature which even those who resent the hegemony have to salute, but that New England scholars have taken care of their own."[10]

If one examines the chronological pattern of reputations objectified in the great multivolume sets of Emerson and Lowell issued by the

Riverside Press, if one peruses the biographies by sibling Nortons and Cabots that fixed irrevocably in the American mind the weight and importance of the antebellum New England tradition, one finds books dated in the late nineteenth century.[11] Turn from the bibliopoles of Park Street to the heirs of Legaré in Charleston, turn to a Paul Hamilton Hayne, who had as high a regard for Legaré as Octavius Brooks Frothingham harbored for Emerson, and it is pathetically clear why the postwar Southern generation had neither means nor motive to commemorate the intellectual achievements of their forebears.[12] Look later, and the New South is writing essays praising James Russell Lowell and damning Charleston for the curse of slavery. Poverty is a catafalque for fame.

Hayne, fond as he was of the dying fall and romantic about the South Carolina of his youth, could see in 1870 how it might happen. "The great names of the South are dying out. For want of an adequate record, men, whose genius the whole country honored in their lifetime, are beginning to sink into obscurity. With the decay of the present generation, the passing away of all contemporary evidences, all familiar memoranda, of their ability, services and *personnel,* we must lose forever those means whereby fresh and vivid portraitures of character are secured, and be forced to content ourselves with such meagre, and imperfect, if not distorted, likenesses, as the hand of the future biographer can draw, with the hesitating aid of Tradition, and the dry details of official documents." This was sentimental, as was always the case with Hayne, but prescient. He wrote this in preface to a biographical sketch of Legaré based upon the two volumes of Legaré's *Writings* published in Charleston in the mid-1840s. He judged them as botched by their editor, as indeed they were: execrable in arrangement, binding, annotation, incomplete. "We never take the disjointed volumes in hand," he wrote, "without involuntarily regarding them as a species of sepulchre in which the bright genius of Legaré lies buried!"[13] He tried to interest others in a new edition, but failed. And Legaré, ironically enough, was one of the luckier Southern intellectuals. Most never achieved a collected edition, however mangled. Twenty years later William Trent ratified the dust on Legaré's *Writings*. "I have to confess that I laid down the two thick volumes of his works with a sigh of relief and regret. Of relief, because I had discharged the duty I owed to one of the few classic writers of my section; of regret, because I could not but acknowledge that here was another instance of the fact that great industry and great learning cannot of themselves make a man a great writer."[14]

Apart from the arid filiopietism of compendia such as the *Library of Southern Literature,* the neglect continued until the 1920s and the recovery of the Southern mind itself. H. L. Mencken, it is true, offered his usual swingeing dissent. Prefacing his bastinado of the New South with kind words for its superseded predecessor, he observed that the Old South was "a civilization of manifold excellences—perhaps the best that the Western Hemisphere has ever seen—undoubtedly the best that These States have ever seen. Down to the middle of the last century, and even beyond, the main hatchery of ideas on this side of the water was across the Potomac bridges. . . . The Ur-Confederate had leisure. He liked to toy with ideas. He was hospitable and tolerant. He had the vague thing we call culture."[15] Mencken said this and may even have believed it; but he was aware that few others would grant his premise and was glad of it.

In fact the years of the Southern Renaissance saw a considerable reevaluation of the antebellum mind. The first to lift the dust were the literary critics. Vernon Parrington's *Romantic Revolution in America* (1927) was surprisingly thorough. The Jeffersonian considered John Taylor, John Marshall, William Wirt, Beverley Tucker, William Alexander Caruthers, John Pendleton Kennedy, Poe, Calhoun, Alexander Stephens, Francis Lieber, William Grayson, William Crafts, Legaré, and Simms. Parrington was interested in the relationships among economics, politics, and literature. This eclecticism and standpoint were not to prove characteristic of the new indigenous school of literary critics.[16] They have taken as their patron saint—for we are still living in the midst of that school[17]—not Thomas Jefferson, but Allen Tate. Lewis P. Simpson opened a gathering of Southern literary critics a few years ago with the remark that there is "a particular version of the Southern literary reaction that has prevailed widely among us—although not by any means with doctrinaire uniformity. If this version can be attributed to a single person, we may say that it is probably Allen Tate, whose brilliant critical work is so central to the field of Southern literary studies that we cannot imagine it without him."[18]

I will try to assess this aspect of Tate later in this book. Here it is enough to observe that his achievement and influence lay in reversing the implicit question of Parrington. The Jeffersonian had asked, What literature has helped to foster a humane society? The New Critic insisted, What society has helped to create a great literature?[19] Reversing the polarities established a new theory about the role of Southern social history in creating favorable or unfavorable contexts for "creative writing." The Old South took its place in a general theory of Southern literature that has two dimensions.[20] The literary side of the equation between literature and society has, it is said, an ascending theme. The literature of the Old South is deemed inferior, that between the Civil War and the First World War is a shade better but flawed, that of the 1920s and 1930s is an admired "Renaissance," and—here the consensus weakens—that since the Second World War is less impressive. This faltering crescendo is related to a descending theme of social history. The Old South is viewed as a coherent community of values, religion, face-to-face personal relationships—a premodern Gemeinschaft culture. The Civil War is said to have strengthened the community of values by the shared experiences of defeat and poverty. But the war permitted the industrial transformation of the New South, which undermined this coherence, shattered the values, and left the Southerner perilously subject to an urbanized mass society, left him with recourse only to an atomistic existentialism or that resistance to fragmentation that is conservative modernism. At the moment when these two themes crossed, the literary music was most harmonious. That moment was the "Renaissance."

A conundrum was basic to Tate's viewpoint. Both a coherent and a shattered society produce indifferent literature, flawed by excessive complacency or random skepticism. Great literature happens in the delicate moment of transition. Louis Rubin has adapted this doctrine with his customary energy and applied it to the Old South. In *William Elliott Shoots a Bear* he has set the hunting sketches of Elliott—antebellum South Carolinian, sea-island planter, politician, and author—beside Faulkner's "The Bear" so that the unflattering comparison might stand as a metaphor for early impoverishment and later riches in Southern literature. Why is Elliott a bad writer? Rubin asks. Because he was laboring under the neocolonial delusion that significant materials for literature happened, not in the South, but elsewhere, usually in Europe, and a long time ago. Thus Elliott penned an uninspired play about political intrigue in Renaissance Genoa but failed to see the latent opportunity for writing about his own backyard. Mostly the social grip of slavery on the Southern imagination was crippling. Elliott "could not ground his writing in what he knew, the life of a planter and sportsman in the Low Country of South Carolina, because the result would have been a searching scrutiny of a social structure all too flawed in its design and grounded upon an attitude toward a certain segment of the population that involved grave injustice and inhumanity. . . . [T]his would have been . . . the inevitable direction in which imaginative fiction would have led him, and no doubt certain others as well—others like him, men of education, refinement, talent, possessed of a deep involvement in the life of their time and place. Thus it was that antebellum southern literature remained an affair of surfaces." This theory of alienation—unkind, it must be said, to Jane Austen's domestic comedy of manners, Shakespeare's Italian plays, and, not least, that intelligent author, William Elliott—has been endorsed by Hugh Holman, a closer student of the Old South: "We would probably all agree that a great writer always transcends his region and is more than a voice of his region, and probably that a great writer is always in some way or other in an antagonistic posture toward the world around him. . . . [O]ne of the things that happened to the antebellum southern writers, the men of talent . . . was that they were at home and had at least ostensibly accepted, or thought that they had accepted, the terms of life in the region."[21]

Lewis P. Simpson has argued similarly but with more sophistication. The Old South, he says, chose to defy history by forging the image of an integrated pastoral society, a dream world no less messianic for being conservative. Thereby it lost contact with the mainstream of Western literature. "The South's lack of distinguished literary accomplishment in the nineteenth century . . . can be attributed to its being cut off from the literary sensibility of the larger world, the culture of alienation. . . . The antebellum Southern writer . . . was cut off from what affected the general stream of literary culture because of the involvement of the Southern man of letters in the politics of slavery." All this is an elaboration of Tate's central claim, that antebellum Southern literature was bad because it was "hagridden with politics."[22]

Such critical insights belong, of course, to a particular school of literary criticism. The discussion of the historical nature of Southern literature has been oddly engrossed by an ahistorical aesthetic doctrine. The recent South has had its T. S. Eliot in Tate but no Edmund Wilson to compete.[23] It has few Marxist critics, next to no structuralists. It has had the New Criticism, dealing incongruously with history. This has led to confusion. Cleanth Brooks has protested that, as his studies of William Faulkner demonstrate, he is not uninterested in history. But he lacks, and wishes to lack, an essential element of the historical vision: the past must be allowed to define its own terms.[24] The Southern version of the New Criticism has worked within history but not for it. It has given the literary critic a shopping list of the ingredients for a great literature, and he has wandered up and down the face of Southern history to find the market that best fills his requirements. His recipe contains: alienation, but not the capacity for habit-

ual skepticism; a sympathy for religious values and an "organic" society; a hierarchy of literary forms, with short poetry at the apex, the
novel further down, and social analysis and polemic at the bottom; a
nicely developed sense of irony and "tension"; a vision of literature
that is not "relativist, arbitrary, materialistic, but absolute, unswerving, spiritual"; priorities that place the "imaginative artist" above the
"limited view of the scientific historian."[25]

The historian may be chagrined at being relegated to the dungeons
of literature, if not only for himself, then at least for Gibbon. But what
matters here is that such ahistoricism goes hard upon periods with differing preconceptions about the life of the mind. It happens that the
Old South lay in just such a period. Now, it is true that the roots of
the modernist theory of alienation lie partly in the antebellum years.
Poe was part of the chain that led from Coleridge to Eliot and from
Eliot to Tate. Simms had some sense that his novels or his romances
were superior to his political orations.[26] But on the whole, the Old
South saw differently. The attempt of the New Criticism to narrow
the definition of literature to a mysterious thing called "imaginative
literature"—chiefly the poem and the novel—would have made little
sense to John Pendleton Kennedy, who did not think he had ceased to
practice literature when he moved from *Swallow Barn,* a novel, to
Quodlibet, a political satire, and on to his biography of William Wirt.
Charles Gayarré would have been haughtily amused to learn that his
History of Louisiana would be disregarded as nonliterary. Few citizens
of Charleston and Richmond would have thought a political imagination fatal to literary accomplishment. Antebellum intellectual culture
moved with no sense of disjuncture between genres that modern criticism has sundered.

Given such perspectives, Southern literary criticism has been most
zealous in resurrecting "imaginative literature." Poe was the first and is
still the most important beneficiary of this. But the researches of literary critics have given us many Simms novels, George Tucker's *Valley of
the Shenandoah,* Beverley Tucker's *Partisan Leader,* and so forth. But
their textual endeavors have been aimed at answering and illustrating
their literary theory, and so the agenda they proffer has been limited.
Thus we are not given for perusal in modern editions Simms's history
or political thought, George Tucker's *Essays on Various Subjects of Taste,
Morals and National Policy,* or Beverley Tucker's lectures on legal theory. We are offered Legaré's essay on Byron but not his reflections on
D'Aguesseau or Demosthenes.[27] Most of the agenda of the intellectual
historian has been absent: theology, philosophy, political theory, social criticism, history, classical scholarship, rhetoric. This is not an ac-

cusation but a fact. There is no reason why the modern literary critic should have done these things, given his sense of what is literature. But it does mean that his archaeology of Southern literature has taken us only a short distance into the resurrection of the Southern mind.

The second major development in promoting study of the mind of the Old South has lain with the political and social historians. Three intertwined subjects have fascinated recent historiography: race, politics, and sectionalism. We know far more and subtly about the social organism of the plantation, the nature of slave culture, the character and motives of proslavery and antislavery movements, and the complex relationship between local and national politics. In the midst of this some intellectual history has been written. Where the literary critic has fled at the very mention of politics and slavery, the eyes of the historian have lit up. Political polemic and racist ideology have become central considerations. Eugene Genovese has written on George Fitzhugh, George Fredrickson on the racist anthropology of Josiah Nott.[28] Yet this has been as partial a shopping list. Historians have wished to explain the great facts of slavery and the Civil War, and they have culled the mind of the Old South for these purposes. Some believe that Southerners thought seriously *only* about these subjects. Slavery and politics are supposed to be sufficiently inclusive of the antebellum Southern mind. Others, less extreme, concede the existence of more but insist upon its unimportance.[29]

Hanging between the literary critic and the political historian has been the work of William R. Taylor, whose *Cavalier and Yankee* remains the most thorough attempt to understand thought in the Old South. His achievement and limitation was to ask the historian's question of the literary critic's agenda of texts. How can we understand the coming of war and the growth of intersectional mythologies by looking at the novels and poetry of Simms, Grayson, and Caruthers? It was an important question, making a vital conjunction, yielding many insights, and rightly celebrated. But Taylor was an exponent of the American Studies methodology of Henry Nash Smith, a school never very happy with intellectual history. It disliked formal philosophy, because it was absorbed in the quest for an American national character, a will-o'-the-wisp thought to flee at the mention of epistemology or ontology. It disliked manuscript research and preferred the literary critic's contemplation of the text. It was not adverse to second-rate literature as a guide to the popular mind and was, indeed, incorrigibly democratic in its ideological commitment. Abstruseness suggested elitism, and that was to be avoided.[30]

As for the explicators of abstruseness, the American intellectual historians, their record has been a sorry one. In the historiography of the colonial and revolutionary generations this is less true. Southern names of the seventeenth and eighteenth centuries are there mingled freely with considerations of a wide variety of intellectual problems. The emphasis rests still most heavily upon New England but not cripplingly so.[31] But the first half of the nineteenth century is a different matter. The South is singled out for separate and brief treatment, the clichés of the literary critics and political historians are indifferently stated, and the matter is hastily dropped for more interesting matters: the survival of the Puritan mind, the philosophy of transcendentalism, the emergence of professionalism, the cultural relationship between America and Europe.[32] Does the Old South have a relevance for any of these and more? Apparently not. There is a recent book, a manifesto of the younger generation, entitled *New Directions in American Intellectual History*. The directions are many, everywhere but below the Potomac. Not a word is breathed about the Old South. (Not a word about the New South either, but that is a different complaint.)[33] And so it is with most new works in American intellectual history; the student of the Southern mind proceeds with hardened skepticism to their indexes, looks for the word *South,* looks for the names of Southern intellectuals, finds little or nothing, is absurdly pleased to find the merest reference, however botched. He mutters defiantly, I can summon spirits from the vasty deep, and the American intellectual historian seems sardonically to reply with Hotspur, So can any man. But will they come when you do call for them? It is a fair question. It would be wrong to rail too severely at the less than thorough contributions of literary critics, political and social historians, or American intellectual historians to the study of the antebellum Southern mind. "The South," as I have argued elsewhere, has long functioned as an excluding system of discourse.[34] It is little wonder that other scholarly modes of discourse should have dealt inadequately with it. If Southern historians themselves have not summoned the spirits and produced convincing evidence of an interesting intellectual culture in the Old South, no one else can be expected to do it for them.

This is where we stand. The picture is gloomy. It is only justice to add, however, that in very recent years a few books have trickled forth to hint at the emergence of a Southern intellectual history. It is not a self-conscious trickle. There are no bands of malcontents that gather at historical conventions and declaim the virtues of their subject, foundations are not besieged to finance conferences in agreeable spots, newsletters are not issued to eager Young Turks steeped in the lesser writing of Albert Taylor Bledsoe. A quarter of a century ago, Clement Eaton declared, with that Turnerian turn of phrase so beloved of the American historian, that the "new frontier in Southern historiography . . . is destined to advance into the area of intellectual history."[35] Only a very few wagons have set out.

Some of the most recent prairie schooners, however, have been of hearteningly sound construction. We have now good biographical studies of Beverley Tucker, George Tucker, and George Frederick Holmes, as well as an intriguing collective study of an improbable "Sacred Circle." James Henry Hammond's speeches have been reprinted, and Edmund Ruffin's diary published. Aspects of Southern theology have been analyzed. Somewhat earlier, George Fitzhugh's life was studied by Harvey Wish, and Clement Eaton tried to fulfill his own prophecy.[36] Such books, and more articles, have been helpful. Yet somehow this research has not cohered in and influenced the American historical imagination. Some of it is too recent to make a prediction of miscarriage altogether convincing. Yet the precedents are not encouraging. Why is this?

I suspect that the central reason, waving aside the vexing matter of the South's place in American intellectual life even now, is that the Southern intellectual historian—like any such historian—has a twofold responsibility, part of which is being neglected. He has a duty to narrative synthesis, he must write intellectual biography and analysis, he must trace with all proper deference to social history the changing force of ideas. He must, as Quentin Skinner has forcefully restated, reassemble the context.[37] But he must make available the text itself. For the Old South this has not been done.[38] It is as though we were obliged to study the French Enlightenment through biographies of Voltaire and Montesquieu and could not read *Candide* and *De l'esprit des lois* save by expeditions to a rare books room. Southern literary critics have long understood this, and that is one reason why their version of the antebellum mind is so dominant.

For to study the Old South is rapidly to learn a central fact: one can read *about* a George Frederick Holmes, but one cannot read Holmes himself without elaborate effort. One can, it is true, go to the bibliography in Neal Gillespie's biography, jot down the essays that Holmes published anonymously and prolifically, proceed to the appropriate volume of the *Southern Quarterly Review* or the *Methodist Quarterly Review*, if one's library has it, and read Holmes. The hardiest student might choose to risk the hazards and inconveniences of interlibrary loan. He or she may or may not care to peer into the gloom of a microfilm machine. It is easier to read Emerson. Life is short, and scholarship long, to waste upon an intellectual culture that all agree is scarcely worth a nod.

What is true for Holmes is true for most of the names that one might plausibly assemble as a Who's Who of the antebellum Southern mind: Beverley and George Tucker, David and Louisa McCord, James Warley Miles, Hugh Swinton Legaré, Stephen Elliott, Thomas Dew, Thomas Cooper, Henry Nott, Robert Henry, James Henley Thornwell, Hugh Blair Grigsby, Frederick Porcher, William Grayson, and many others, known and obscure. They are inaccessible. The orthodoxy argues that these are obscure because they deserve to be. I am not sure this is true. The orthodoxy's case is weakened, after all, because it shows little evidence of having read these people.

The problem of this culture's stature is, of course, a real one, but it is one that needs evasion for the moment. I doubt that the present state of scholarship permits a convincing answer. As these writers cannot be read without surmounting formidable barriers, the dissonance of opinion and rebuttal has never swirled around them to create an answer—or rather answers—on the matter of stature.[39] I could airily pronounce Holmes's essays exceptionally interesting. The reader could not make an informed response. He has not read Holmes. He could, of course, make an uninformed response and well might, but Holmes would remain my critical prisoner. Now, this is always somewhat true of the relationship between a historian and a very dead author, but the measure is modified in the case of a Thoreau because one can expect the literate to have read Thoreau independently. If I say absurdities about Walden Pond, an informed skepticism can be expected. But I could pronounce a series of idiocies about Holmes—that he was a closet abolitionist, that he once raped his daughter and this explains his abomination of Herder, that he wrote with purple Bollandist ink lives of the saints—and need only await chastisement from Holmes's biographer, a small audience.

In short, many scholarly tasks remain unaccomplished. Only the *Southern Literary Messenger* has had its contributors systematically identified, a consequence of the rediscovery of Poe.[40] Without such spadework, much Southern history, not only intellectual, is rendered ghostly and faceless. Historians constantly refer, when they utilize original sources, to a fiction called "a Southern commentator" or "a writer in the *Southern Quarterly Review*."[41] This is disabling to our understanding. The source is made to stand alone, untouched by the specifics of authorship, place, or circumstance. Is the "commentator" a

Virginian or a Louisianan, a Methodist or a Roman Catholic, a Whig or a Democrat, an enthusiast for Lamartine or Dugald Stewart? The quotation sits upon the page, indifferently representative of all Southerners, when in all logic it speaks for only one, if we but knew who he or she was. Surely we are past the point when one Southerner is believed to be much like another.

How much more intriguing would have been the quotation in George Fredrickson's discussion of Southern attitudes to race that he attributes to "a writer in *De Bow's Review*"—a quotation that curdlingly reads: "the brutish propensities of the negro now unchecked [following any possible emancipation] there remains no road for their full exercise . . . but in the slaughter of his white master, and through the slaughter, he strides (unless he himself be exterminated) to the full exercise of his native barbarity and savageness"—if Fredrickson had known that the initials cited in his footnotes stand for Louisa McCord, the daughter of Langdon Cheves. Would not such a feminine outburst usefully have counterbalanced the gentler remarks on slavery by McCord's friend Mary Chesnut, whose views reside so conveniently in paperback?[42] What nonsense is made of Rollin Osterweis's agreeable metaphor for the influence of European Romanticism upon South Carolina nationalism, the assertion that David Flavel Jamison was both a student of Herder and president of the 1860 secession convention, when one knows that Jamison did not write the 1844 essay.[43] Even the student of these matters is easily misled. I find, looking into the matter, that when I cited earlier an observation in the *Southern Literary Messenger* upon the obscurity of Legaré in Virginia, I was quoting William Gilmore Simms: a South Carolinian upon a South Carolinian, and not, as I inferred from the provenance of the periodical in Richmond, a Virginian upon a South Carolinian.[44]

This is not the place to attempt a full discussion of the Southern mind and its appearance once scholarly tasks are accomplished: authors identified, collected and usable editions provided, biographies and critical studies written. It is the burden of my argument that we do not know. But I am persuaded a portrait of the Southern intellect will look very different, not least because Southern social history has been recently rewritten, and that alone incapacitates half the logic of the traditional historiography. What Allen Tate believed about the Old South is believed by very few historians now. At least five props of the conventional wisdom have badly slipped, and they are worth a cursory notice.

The first is the proposition that the isolation of plantation life discouraged opportunities for intellectuality. This idea has faltered, not so much because the plantation has been proved especially hospitable to spreading thought, but because the planter himself did not occupy a central place in the region's intellectual elite. Very few writers were planters. Most were ministers, lawyers, college teachers, city or small-town dwellers. This is not to say that they were not unconnected with the planter class, just as the modern university intellectual is mated to the mechanisms of corporate capitalism. But most Southern intellectuals had as little to do with planting cotton as the *New York Times* book reviewer has to do with the sweatshops of Wall Street. Their friends might have been obliged to be planters, their relatives equally so, but the young professionals of the Southern mind were urban. Recent economic studies have shown how swift and pervasive was the pace of urbanization in the antebellum South.[45] Outside of the northeastern United States and England, the South was the most urbanized culture in Western society and did not much repine at the fact.

The second doubtful assertion is the obsession of the Southern mind with slavery. There is little question that slavery was a central concern of Southerners. No amount of revisionism could disturb that assumption. But that does not mean a debilitating obsession. If one surveys, for example, the first *Southern Review*'s contents, one finds that only about 10 percent of its essays were concerned with either slavery or, indeed, any kind of politics, despite its span coinciding with the heat of the Nullification controversy in South Carolina. For the *Southern Quarterly Review,* deeper into the years of sectional controversy, the proportion was about 20 percent. In years of particular stress, under an editor like Simms of markedly political instinct, the share would rise. In 1851, it went as high as 35 percent as the arguments for separate secession were thrashed out. It is for such years, of course, that most political historians have looked into such periodicals, precisely to explain the crisis. The *Southern Literary Messenger,* cultivating belles-lettres but starting in the mid-1830s, fell somewhere between the *Southern Review* and the *Southern Quarterly Review.* Its leading piece for its first several issues was a history of Tripoli. *De Bow's Review,* on the other hand, was peculiarly dedicated to the study of economic and political matters and hence of slavery and dealt only perfunctorily with philosophical and literary matters. So its proportion was the highest of all. The popularity of *De Bow's* as a source for historians has perhaps helped to foster the legend of obsession.[46]

The third proposition, that the South was debilitated by the enthusiasms of an anti-intellectual evangelicalism, is a half-truth. There is no doubt that the deism of a Jefferson or the materialist atheism of a

Thomas Cooper grew less common. But a recent study has pointed to a large urban influence upon Southern theology, an influence characterized by a search for a rational theology and not by emotional panache.[47] And it may be a logical error to imagine that because the terms of the debate had shifted—from disputes between deism and belief to arguments within orthodoxy—any less weighty intellectual endeavor went on. It may be just that historians have found the debates less dramatic and less accessible. That most learned of Presbyterian elders, James Henley Thornwell, ranged far and wide to find philosophical errors whose repudiation might strengthen the Westminster Confession of Faith. In the process he kept many extremely well informed about the unorthodox.

The fourth element in the old case, that the South's consensus on the propriety of slavery undermined freedom of thought, seems the most vulnerable to objection. Many did, of course, suffer from dissent on this matter of racial ideology. But it is only a sentimentalism about the seamlessness of freedom and culture, a belief so characteristic of the American passion, that imagines all thought must cease because in one matter consensus, latterly demonstrated pernicious, was strong. Southerners could still think about Coleridge or Vico or whether statues should be naked or clothed without bearing too closely upon the matter of slavery. Racism itself, of course, elicited discourse. But there is little evidence that Southerners argued less with each other on most things because they agreed with one another on a single thing, however important. Periodicals were clamorous with dispute, mostly of Southerner with Southerner.[48]

The last proposition, that the South was out of touch with innovations in thought, is the most important and the most mistaken. The misunderstanding is at least as old as William Trent. He wrote in 1892 of Charleston: "Most of the elegant gentlemen forming those circles were still living, in imagination at least, in the time of Horace. If they had come down the centuries at all, they had certainly stopped at another Augustan age,—that of Pope and Addison. Not a few private libraries in the South will be found, upon examination, practically to have stopped there."[49] The misconception is at least as recent as William R. Taylor, who has observed: "During the first half century of national experience. . . . The South gradually lost touch with Europe at the very time that intellectual leaders in the North, and especially in New England, were establishing new cultural contacts abroad." Taylor contrasts the unintellectual Grand Tour by William C. Preston with the cultural pilgrimage of George Ticknor. He examines the catalog of Legaré's library published in 1843 and finds only six "roughly contemporary writers"—Coleridge, Channing, Goethe, Schiller, Thomas Moore, and Herder.[50] Such evidence, I fear, is unpersuasive even in these particular cases, and more so in the general instance of the antebellum Southern mind.

The contrast between Preston and Ticknor is a pleasant conceit that proves little. It merely demonstrates that if you compare Preston and Ticknor, the intellectual advantage would seem to lie with Ticknor. Of the South and New England, the abstractions lying behind the image, it adduces but one partial piece of evidence. Even on the score of Preston it is probably unsound. William Campbell Preston was a man of no little learning who liked to appear the casual Hotspur. His *Reminiscences,* upon which Taylor bases his case, are both incomplete and not intended as an intellectual autobiography.[51] If one looks into Preston's correspondence, one finds something else. One finds, for one thing, an 1824 letter to George Ticknor thanking the Bostonian for passing along a recent edition of the *North American Review*—which contained a letter of Preston's upon the tariff—and praising the *North American Review* as a valuable influence upon public opinion. And this is not surprising. George Ticknor, William Preston, and Hugh Swinton Legaré had, after all, been friends together in Edinburgh in 1819.[52] Nor is there anything intrinsically unintellectual about a Grand Tour. Gibbon, at least, would have been surprised to hear of it. It was possible, after all, to learn something outside of a German university. It was sometimes difficult for Americans to learn anything inside one.[53]

As for Legaré's library, the evidence is quite otherwise. There are, in fact, two catalogs of the library. The first, of 1843, was used by Taylor; the second, of 1848, was not. The second is itself sufficiently damaging to Taylor's case. It would, indeed, be easier to list "roughly contemporary writers" who are not represented. Even to cite the most obvious names in the catalog would be taxing the reader's patience. These, at least, are worth mentioning: Jomini, Tocqueville, Henri Saint-Simon, Thierry, Michelet, Maistre, Thiers, Guizot, Lamartine, Balzac, Béranger, Dupin, Villers, and Villemain among French writers; August von Schlegel, Tieck, Heeren, Klopstock, Kant, Schiller, Niebuhr, Becker, and Grimm among the Germans; Paley, Hallam, Dugald Stewart, Allan Cunningham, Bulwer, Mackintosh, Bentham, and Nassau Senior among the British; Manzoni among the Italians; Webster, Jefferson, Hamilton, Washington, Henry Wheaton, Thomas Cooper, Thomas Grimké, and Jasper Adams among the Americans; and sets of the British Poor Law Reports and the American Congressional Debates and State Papers among official documents. Yet even Taylor's use of the 1843 catalog is curious. One can find even there the following:

Bentham, Nassau Senior, Grimm, Savigny, Tieck, Heeren, Creuzer, Kant, Schiller, Niebuhr, Wheaton, Dupin, Villers, Eichhorn, Schlegel, Klopstock, Webster, Jefferson, Hamilton, and Cooper. Moreover, while it is true that the library contained seventeenth- and eighteenth-century editions of the classics in abundance, it also harbored many of the best recent editions from Germany, France, and England.[54] And no one should underestimate the role that philology played in the Romantic movement. These were very modernized classics.

I dwell on this, not to malign an intelligent book, but simply to indicate that closer scrutiny may yield a different picture. One can, of course, find Southerners who continued to prefer Pope to Byron, Addison to Disraeli. That is not the point. In general, the Southern intellectual was as likely as his Northern contemporary to be *au courant*. The South was slumbering in no Augustan twilight. We have, it seems, gravely distorted the balance between North and South on this score: as Carl Diehl has recently suggested, it is easy to exaggerate the impact of German thought on New England; it has certainly been easy to underestimate its force in the South.[55]

The desire to identify the modernization of nineteenth-century thought with New England and to deny the same title to the South has doubtless proceeded from honest and worthy motives. It has seemed hard to call a slave society progressive. But recent historiography has been moving to an appreciation of the Old South as far from premodern, precisely because our sense of the flexibility of industrial modernity has increased as the phenomenon has spread far beyond its original homes in Manchester or Lowell. In Japan industry has fastened upon older forms of paternalism. In India it has not proved inimical to the caste system. In Korea it has not led to significant democratization. We must entertain the real possibility that the South's peculiar institution did not doom the region to anachronism, that the Old South was a different and evolving version of what an American modernity might have come to look like. I suspect that a history of antebellum Southern intellectual life, when seriously undertaken, will betray a similar image; it may possibly show a modernity more marked in the South's intellectual elite than in even its social structure, contemporary and potential. Liberalism and conservatism were the twin children of the years after 1776 and 1789. In the century of Mazzini and Bismarck, Michelet and Fichte, Emerson and Beverley Tucker, there was nothing old-fashioned in the South's movement to cultural and political nationalism. It was all too modern.

CHAPTER 2

The Lineaments of Antebellum
Southern Romanticism

IT IS A curiosity of modern scholarship that the only general work on antebellum Southern Romanticism is Rollin G. Osterweis's *Romanticism and Nationalism in the Old South*, which has been in print since 1949, is still read, and still—if only for want of a competitor—used. Yet much has changed in understanding of the social and intellectual history of the Old South, and even more of the phenomenon of Romanticism. These changes, natural enough over the span of two intellectual generations, have made many of that book's presumptions questionable; so a second look at the problem seems worthwhile, to clear the ground and to indicate fresh directions. For Osterweis wrote within the assumptions of the 1940s about the nature and shortcomings of Romanticism. He was guided by Irving Babbitt, who scorned Romanticism as a puling and exaggerated passion instigated by Rousseau, a disaster for rational men: at best silly, as with the jousts of antebellum Virginia; at worst dangerous, as with the secession convention of South Carolina. But Osterweis was Babbitt with a difference. While Babbitt and, more weightily, Ernst Cassirer had thought Romanticism had led the world astray and it was still astray, with Hitler the avatar of Hegel as chilling evidence, Osterweis cheerily regarded Romanticism as a movement that had expired with the nineteenth century, a fossil safe to mock. To this perspective, largely adopted from Jacques Barzun's *Romanticism and the Modern Ego* (1943), Osterweis added the view of Arthur Lovejoy, who had insisted that Romanticism, while possessing a core notion of diversity and flux, should

An earlier version of this essay was read at a meeting of the Southern Historical Association in 1984, where it benefited from the criticisms of T. J. Jackson Lears, John McCardell, and Drew Gilpin Faust. It was then published under this same title, in the *Journal of American Studies* 20 (August 1986): 165–88.

most safely be regarded as multiple: there were Romanticisms, not a Romanticism.[1]

Thus, for Osterweis, Romanticism was dead, foolish, and multiple. These perspectives he engrafted onto the vision of the Old South that he had learned from Ulrich B. Phillips at Yale, summed up (at least for Osterweis) in seeing the region as quasi-feudal, premodern, and static. The nature of Southern Romanticism, that is, the form Romanticism took in the South, was explicable by the synthesis of imported ideas and local circumstances: Europe provided the supermarket of ideas, while Southern society dictated the purchasing. So while Romanticism in Europe and the North had many ideas that catered to change, the South could assimilate only the most static and reactionary aspects of the movement. The greatest of these, and the most comic, were the medieval romances of Walter Scott, formative of antebellum culture even as they bequeathed the most lasting monument of the Old South to the New: the Lost Cause, Jacobitism transformed. After Scott, the most influential importation was Thomas Carlyle, the Tory philosopher and critic of industrialism. Here, then, was a paradox, to which we must return: that Osterweis thought a dynamic philosophy relevant to explaining a static culture. As for dating, Osterweis thought the turning point to be the Virginia Convention of 1831–32, because it was thought to have begun the "Great Reaction" of proslavery conservatism. Hence he drew his evidence almost entirely from sources after 1832, notably the three leading regional periodicals, the *Southern Quarterly Review* of Charleston, the *Southern Literary Messenger* of Richmond, and *DeBow's Review* of New Orleans.[2] Let us consider how such theses have worn.

Most transforming is the recent assessment of Romanticism. Babbitt used Romanticism as a style or typology, available to any era but characteristic of certain ones. In this he was faithfully echoing the ideas of the Schlegels themselves, who had meditated upon the distinctions between classic and Romantic in ancient Greece, in Rome, in the Middle Ages, and who used Shakespeare as the archetype of the vigorous angularities of the Romantic manner.[3] Very few now prefer this usage. Rather, Romanticism has been confined to the period usually beginning decisively in the 1790s, though occasionally pushed back to Goethe's Sturm und Drang phase of the 1770s. There were once squabbles over precursors, over something called pre-Romanticism, by which was meant the eighteenth-century cult of sentiment, the pastoralism of James Thomson, the Gothic novels of Horace Walpole, or the theory of sublimity examined by Edmund Burke or Hugh Blair.

This debate has lessened recently. Quentin Skinner's strictures made us all nervous about the anachronism of a theory of precursors, and a closer examination of the so-called precursors had tended to show that they used objects also used by the Romantics later, but differently.[4] Horace Walpole and Jules Michelet both may have written about medieval fortresses, but the Castle of Otranto and the Bastille present contrasting views to the reader. There is a gulf between amusement and passion, between the shepherdesses of the Petit Trianon and the shepherds of Wordsworth. But these debates over antecedents were a necessary transitional stage in the establishment of the more important point, that it makes no sense to speak of a Romanticism before 1770. Only art historians cling to the old, ahistorical usage.[5]

The closing date of Romanticism is subject to greater dispute. Some critics, such as M. H. Abrams, Frank Kermode, and Morse Peckham, think that we still live largely within its assumptions and that modernism is a schismatical sect within the religion. Others are persuaded that modernism marks as profound a shift as Romanticism itself did in its relationship to the Enlightenment.[6] On both sides, however, the tone of criticism has shifted palpably, in a way that bears upon the ageing of Osterweis's analysis. The need for polemic against the Romantics has lessened, and a case has been made, if not universally accepted, that they were the first moderns, the creators of habits of thought we still use. Not all, perhaps, would go so far as Victor Brombert, who recently observed: "The fact of the matter is that a bond links us with the great Romantics: we communicate with them through anguish and irony."[7] But certainly the genres of the Romantics linger: the autobiography, the psychological novel, the self-scrutinizing poem, the historicist narrative. Their emphasis upon alienation we assume. Few now read Irving Babbitt with other than discomfort. It is not that we are stuck with an unthinking admiration for the Romantics, with a mirror image of Babbitt; it is that the movement commands serious respect, so that we may make our discriminations within the corpus. So Osterweis's assumption that Romanticism is both idiotic and dead strikes us as certainly condescending on the first score and probably mistaken on the second.

It would be too much to expect a strict new consensus, for Romanticism has become eclectically useful for many disciplines, each with a private logic. The word means different things to art historians, literary critics, architectural students, and philosophers. Nonetheless, interdisciplinary lines are less firm than a generation ago, with intellectual historians sensitive to literary and philosophical texts and literary critics renouncing the ahistoricism of the New Criticism. Indeed, the guiding light of the new interpretations, M. H. Abrams, began in *The Mirror and the Lamp* by providing a historical explanation for Symbolist aesthetics, thereby both methodologically and explicitly challenging the presumptions of the New Criticism, just as *Natural Supernaturalism* stands as a reproach to the semioticians who have attempted both to praise and to bury him.[8] Influenced by Abrams, who has defined a "high Romantic argument," recent scholars, though they concede multiplicity, are more willing than Lovejoy to stress a core doctrine, the distinctiveness of which lay in the combination of a sociology of community with a psychology of alienation. Both have to be borne in mind. Much confusion has followed when attempts have been made to separate the two, to make the dialectical simple, to stress a sense of belonging, whether to nation or race, at the expense of alienated self-consciousness or alienation at the expense of belonging; the tension was what mattered.

A consequence of the growing agreement upon chronology has been that Romanticism has become a historical problem. That is, historians are more comfortable with a now firmly historical concept, and it has become imperative to fashion a grounded historical explanation for the origins and course of the Romantic movement. So far, except in isolated studies such as Henri Brunschwig on Prussia, this has not been done.[9] We know what happened; we do not know why. It has been a very great temptation to argue that Romanticism is the epistemological solution to the social crisis of industrialization, that its subtle emphasis upon change, alienation, and invented community was the natural counterpart to the strains of change; this is the argument of Raymond Williams.[10] It is a temptation not entirely to be resisted. But the chronology is not quite right, and we should be suspicious. Goethe, when he looked upon Strasbourg Cathedral in 1770 and first contemplated the unclassical merits of German culture and the Gothic, had never seen a dark satanic mill. Herder began to put together his notions on language and nationality in Riga and Bückeburg, just as most of the formative ideas of German Romanticism were propounded in small German towns that had not changed much economically since the seventeenth century and would not see an industrial revolution of any major consequence for another century.[11] One finds, indeed, that often Romantics rather liked factories, as evidence of innovation and energy, as institutions that would break the mold of traditional culture. In the South, too, Romanticism was important before there was an indigenous industrialization to mistrust or fear, though one can do something with the fact that the South formed a crucial peripheral region in the new international capitalist system.[12] To make sense of the social origins of Romanticism, a firm distinction must be drawn between origins and persistence.

The origins of Romanticism do not lie chiefly in industrialization, but in a congeries of local social and political crises, of which the French Revolution was the greatest but not the only one. Because of these, the Enlightenment collapsed as an explanatory system. Theory and reality became dissonant, young men could no longer read Gibbon or Condorcet without a sense of disjuncture, and a new explanation was required. Romanticism, which made such room for the wanderer, the alienated, and the untraditional, naturally appealed to a generation who felt the immediate past unnourishing, the present unreliable, the future unpredictable. But the reason Romanticism became so powerful, so much more than an intellectual fashion destined to evaporate with the generation of 1810, who first systematically articulated it, does lie in the permanent crisis of modern industrial society. For those coming of age in 1850 or even 1890 who did know what a factory looked like and began to understand its consequences, Romanticism remained resonant.[13] The particular crises of the early nineteenth century generated a system of thought that, partly by accident, explained the different general crisis of modern industrialism. Thus it becomes very important for the historian, interested in origins, to be careful and specific. It will not do to say that philosophical change occurred in Germany and spread to France, England, and the United States, like ripples on a pond into which Immanuel Kant had thrown a stone. We must deal with specific social and political crises, mated with epistemological change and influence, in each culture where Romanticism became important. In this sense, the South is not a footnote to the history of Romanticism, the last link in a chain that winds from Weimar to Tuscaloosa, but deserves scrutiny as a case study in a historical process where no one case or culture is definitive.

Movement, flux—these were the indispensable motifs of Romantic literature and philosophy. It was a conundrum in Osterweis's analysis that such a vision should have been deemed important to a Southern culture that he thought was static. Here the researches of political and social historians of the Old South have transformed the context in which the intellectual historian must work, by tentatively reassessing the role of modernization, by showing the Old South to have been very much a part of the anxious and rapidly changing political economy of the early nineteenth century, its slavery a part of the modern world, its population mobile, its politics democratizing, its elites insecure, its cities respectably influential. Eugene Genovese's theory that the Old South was essentially premodern has found many critics.[14]

Most striking for the intellectual historian is that social historians, largely oblivious to the issue of Romanticism, have empirically identified a shift in the early nineteenth century to the centrality of emotion and introspection that mirrors the sensibility of the Romantic movement. Jan Lewis's delicate and sensitive book *The Pursuit of Happiness: Family and Values in Jefferson's Virginia* delineates a transition of emphasis from the public to the private sphere, the development of an individualism that painfully counted the emotional cost of sentimental attachments and evangelical commitment. Virginians came to reject the Jeffersonian values of harmony, balance, restraint, and the distancing of emotion. Instead they began "to prize emotion," to reject "the conventions of restraint," to become enraptured by "enormous grief." This occurred, Lewis argues, because of a generational crisis in the political economy of postrevolutionary Virginia.[15]

The especial crisis of the revolutionary tradition in Virginia was echoed elsewhere in Southern culture, just as the catalyst and failure of the French Revolution led to the disappointment of hopes and the bifurcation of ideology that fed into Romanticism in Europe. As Carlyle once said to Froude, "I should not have known what to make of this world at all, if it had not been for the French Revolution."[16] Similarly, the ageing of the American Revolution had a crucial bearing upon the origins of Romanticism in the South. The cultural ambitions of David Ramsay, springing from the extravagant political claims of 1783 that George Washington, like Saturn in the Fourth *Eclogue,* might begin a new order, had begun to look rather barren by the mid-1820s. It was not working out, and the intellectually honest and acute knew it. Even the deliberately eulogistic, such as William Wirt writing of Patrick Henry, sensed it.[17] The theory of man's Fall into eventually redemptive self-consciousness, which M. H. Abrams has identified as the "high Romantic argument," was resonant for Americans who felt that Cincinnatus gone, the world was peopled by underlings who could only wrangle.[18] For Southerners, this melancholy was exacerbated by the continual politics and debate enforced by the slavery controversy. But more, the melancholy bore closely upon the intertwined question of the fate of republicanism and the country ideology of the commonwealth tradition.

As Britain became more notable as the home of the Industrial Revolution than as that of Lord North, the view of Great Britain as the corrupt demon of the body politic was transferred almost wholesale from being a critique of mercantile politics to being a criticism of industrial free-labor society, first of Britain, second of New England. This parallels what Carlyle did to the Scottish eighteenth-century tradition in fashioning his thunderbolts against the Great Wen of London, but Carlyle's influence was not required for the transmutation in the South. It is exactly summed up in the "Address to the People of the United States by the Convention of the People of South Carolina" in 1832: "South Carolina now bears the same relation to the manufacturing states of this confederacy, that the Anglo American Colonies bore to the mother country."[19]

Moreover, the republican tradition's emphasis upon the growth of corrupting luxury and the consequent need for vigilance obliged the patriotic slaveholder to be uneasy. Tradition made him grateful for the opportunity of ritual cleansing, usually in politics, which might renew the stoic virtues of republicanism and refute the self-accusation of declension from the standards of the Founding Fathers. This taste for symbolic purgation is a major reason why the Burkeanism of Southern thinkers, otherwise so striking, was so compromised and a more important reason than the Lockeanism of which Louis Hartz has written. The conservatism of a revolutionary tradition is a paradox in any stabilized culture with an honored revolution in its past, and it can be traced in Burke and Macaulay when they write of 1688 as readily as in Hugh Legaré.[20]

For it is inadequate to say that only the conservative dimension of Romanticism made it to the South. If by this we mean socialist ideologies such as Saint-Simonianism, the point is well taken, though it would not be difficult to argue that the vision of the plantation in the proslavery argument was as utopian as that of the phalanstery of Fourier. But it is important to remember that compared with European versions, Southern Romanticism was not especially conservative, because Southern political culture was comparatively liberal. A conservative Southerner translated to Prussia or Paris or the Papal States would have found himself in prison for his sentiments, just as a bourgeois liberal such as François Guizot would have made a fervent anti-Jacksonian in Georgia. For Southerners had inherited the gentlemanly chiliasm of the republican tradition, which was to detonate at Fort Sumter, just as they had helped to define in Jacksonianism one of the most egalitarian of Western political ideologies, which can still cause unease to the European. The radicalism of the South did not need importation; it was indigenous. This consideration is important: though European and Southern Romanticism often shared perspectives, by dint of having a different context, the former usually became a criticism of conservative social order, while the latter was often a criticism of too rapid social change.[21]

Similarly, antebellum Southern theology was both radical and explicable largely by reference to local intellectual evolution. Southern religion, like Southern politics, had its fear of declension and sin and its ambition to cleanse. Emotion, kept at a distance in the political theory of Madison, had long since found a place in Southern religion, and Carlyle, the Calvinist intellectual ranter, was preaching to the converted in the South, and in a tone that must have made more sense to a backcountry North Carolinian than to a Londoner, accustomed to the gentle, undemanding voice of Anglicanism. The Pietist sources of German Romanticism, so evident in Herder, were paralleled by a rich indigenous tradition of Southern evangelicalism, more than ready to see the utility of a "natural supernaturalism" and understand the frantic dilemma of the "everlasting no" and the "everlasting yea" resolving itself by faith into stern action and belief.[22] So while it is interesting and important that James Warley Miles spent time in Berlin and fashioned a transcendentalist theology after Schleiermacher, it is more crucial to an account of Southern thought, because more typical, that James Henley Thornwell was an old-school Presbyterian whose theology embraced an awareness of the perils and virtues of rationality that, often in matters away from formal theology, habituated Southerners to seeing merit in the Romantic dialectic of passion and reason, to accepting the double vision of alienation and community.[23]

This congruence between evangelicalism and intellectuality as it bore on the proslavery argument has been delineated by Drew Faust and Jack P. Maddex. But the meshing is of wider significance for the South's intellectual culture than just in the context of the proslavery argument: evangelicalism was a crucial precondition not so much for the initial articulation of Romanticism as for its general acceptance. In a figure such as Thomas R. R. Cobb of Georgia, the sweet agonies of the evangelical conscience flowed easily into the convictions of Southern Romantic nationalism, into a belief that the Confederacy and religious separatism might redeem men's social and private souls. Beverley Tucker found that a conversion to evangelicalism impelled Romantic modes of thought. For evangelicalism shared with Romanticism a conviction of the necessity and possibility of human and social regeneration. Indeed, the survival of evangelicalism is a reason for the unusual longevity of Romantic habits of thought in the region, beyond even the civic religion of the Lost Cause, to which Charles Reagan Wilson has drawn our attention.[24]

The psychological individualism that Jan Lewis has delineated and the evangelicalism that Thomas R. R. Cobb represented flourished

amid social contradictions. Such conflicts are reminders that socially
and intellectually, the antebellum South was neither a single nor a con-
tented culture. Before the Civil War, state loyalties were more important than regional affiliations to almost any important Southern
thinker. It mattered much more to Thomas Dew that he was a Virginian than that he was a Southerner; indeed, for him, as for most of his
Virginian contemporaries, the South was everything below Virginia.
As Alison Freehling and Dickson Bruce have made more clear, Dew
on slavery was firstly Dew on slavery in Virginia.[25] Likewise, Simms
was a South Carolinian first, a Southerner later. This ordering was
most marked in the older seaboard South, which had inherited identi-
ties from the eighteenth century, least marked in the western South,
where Romantic dogma was coincident with statehood and where
one finds the least skeptical of Southern Romantics, men like Alexander Beaufort Meek of Alabama and Albert Pike of Arkansas, who
played Byron on the edge of the prairies.[26] The idea that Charleston
was the natural cultural partner of rural Mississippi was not self-
evident, least of all to those who lived in Charleston and rural Mississippi, the one disdaining the rural boor, the other mistrusting the un-
godly city.

The periodicals of Charleston, Richmond, and New Orleans, if
only for reasons of circulation, were inclined to invent a Southern
market. They took the names *Southern Literary Messenger* and *Southern Review*, not the more accurate titles *Richmond Literary Messenger* or
Charleston and Columbia Review. But their circulation lists and, more,
their lists of contributors (insofar as we know them) show that this
was a largely unfulfilled ambition. Yet there was some interregional
penetration, which makes it proper to speak of these journals as certainly advancing the theory and somewhat advancing the fact of Southern solidarity. But the tradition of anonymous contribution made this
interregionalism curiously abstract, especially in social theory. Novels,
originally serialized, were usually republished under their authors'
names; social criticism, with the exception of proslavery writing, almost never. The irony became that the South often did not know the
identity of its own ideologists, unless they were politicians. But the
point to be reiterated is that we should err if we wrote a unified history of Southern intellectual life before 1860, because Southern nationalism was then a hypothesis, not a fact. We would do better, as
Osterweis did, to write of smaller regions, of (to use the modern
phrase) communities of discourse.[27]

Where are those communities? We need more research to speak

with confidence, and we badly need a subregional analysis of Southern intellectual life to preserve us from the standing vice of Southern historiography, synecdoche, a vice that political historians have been more successful in reforming of late. George Fredrickson has pointed the way with suggestions about the differing versions of the proslavery argument of the eastern and western South. That his analysis has been criticized does not diminish the general utility of such distinctions; it only increases the need for more precision. Mark Kaplanoff has speculated upon the distinctions between political economy as elaborated by Virginians and as elaborated by South Carolinians in the early nineteenth century, but the contrast is more deep-seated.[28] The Romanticism of Virginia is lusher, more fanciful, less urban and *au courant* than that of South Carolina, as exemplified by the greater susceptibility of the Virginians to the Cavalier myth.[29] Both Virginia and South Carolina produced more remarkable legal theory than did the rest of the South, though perhaps only South Carolina matched that legal sophistication in theology. North Carolina and Alabama elaborated a more democratic, less hierarchical political theory than either South Carolina or Virginia, just as Alabama produced a sprightlier school of humorists. Much of the western South formed a social and cultural diaspora from Virginia and South Carolina, but much lay beyond their influence. It is obvious, though little studied, that a French intellectual tradition, with the faltering survival of French as a literary language, profoundly affected the nature of intellectual life in Louisiana in ways that only the etiolated Huguenot strain in South Carolina can begin to match. Little is known of Florida and the Spanish. As Randall Miller and Jon Wakelyn have reminded us, Roman Catholic culture in the South has been too little examined, or as in the case of Bishop John England of Charleston, it has been studied by Catholic historians not especially interested in the Southern context.[30]

Our narrowness is great, but we may know enough to hazard this, which might be offered as a tentative criticism of Drew Faust's interesting book *A Sacred Circle: The Dilemma of the Intellectual in the Old South, 1840–1860.* Faust suggests that we think of Southern intellectuals as in widespread interstate communication, discontented because they subscribed to a Romantic theory of genius, taking on the politics of proslavery as a solution to their alienation. That is, her image is of a horizontal division, the intellectuals belonging more to each other and the region than to their locality, which becomes important to them as an implication of their intellectuality. I am not sure this is right. It is my impression that the links among Southern intellectuals are very fragmented, as likely to come about for political or family reasons as for ideological ones, and that their connections (to use an apposite eighteenth- and nineteenth-century word) are initially and finally more with their locality than with the incipient class of the intelligentsia. I infer, perhaps wrongly, that Faust sees her sacred circle as the prototype of a modern intelligentsia, though going badly wrong in electing proslavery, when I suspect that they are much more like the civic and local cultural elites of the eighteenth century, much more like the Edinburgh of the *Edinburgh Review* than the Bloomington of the *American Historical Review*.[31]

But much of this is guesswork, because there is as yet no intellectual map of the Old South. Faust has shrewdly indicated the utility of defining networks of friendship, sympathy, and influence, and we need to nail these down more precisely and elaborately, to plot the strengths and weaknesses of such lines of communication. There is interstate and even intrastate intellectual commerce to be inventoried, as evidenced by the fierce arguments of Tidewater and western Virginia in the constitutional convention of 1829–30 over not just practical politics but also political philosophy. In plotting such a map, we will find much variety.

But there is also need for a fresh map of the intellectual trade between Europe and the United States that helped traverse the line between Enlightenment and Romanticism. Osterweis argued that the lines of influence ran from Europe to Britain and thence across the Atlantic. This was why he thought Carlyle—the Carlyle who wrote on Goethe and Richter for the *Foreign Review* and the *Edinburgh Review*, who translated the philosophy of phenomenology into the bizarre reveries of *Sartor Resartus*, who adumbrated a conservative historicism in *Past and Present*—so important to his thesis. It helps also to explain why Osterweis thought Southern Romanticism occurred so late, because it required time for German thought to be digested in England before being belatedly transmitted to the South. Neither the structure nor the chronology of this thesis bears up under close examination.

Cassirer and Lovejoy and, even later, Isaiah Berlin were insistent upon the primacy of Germany in the development of Romanticism.[32] Broadly speaking, one would not wish to disturb that assumption, but there are crosscurrents that complicate the picture. Recent work on the social thought of the Scottish Enlightenment makes clearer, not that Edinburgh developed a coherent version of historicism, but that much was intimated by Scotland which flowed both into German thought, from, for example, Adam Ferguson to Herder, and into later English and Scottish thought. Carlyle was the heir, not just of his reading in German literature, but of his Scottish forebears. Consequently, the United States and its Southern provinces had available a body of thought that tilted independently towards Romanticism. How deeply Scottish thought ran in Southern thought is only just being plumbed, but we know that to receive a college education in the Old South was to be grounded in Adam Smith, Lord Kames, Dugald Stewart, and Thomas Reid. Indeed, in intellectual matters the South of 1820 is almost more Scottish than English. Yet, save for a few evasive and general essays by David Hume, the Scots gave Southerners a social and not a political theory. Politics had not been safe in the century of Culloden. As Nicholas Phillipson has made clear, the political fact of a contested union with England explains the apolitical emphasis upon the merits of sociability that characterize the writings of the Scottish Enlightenment.[33] The Adam Smith of *The Theory of Moral Sentiments* was as important to the pedagogy of Southern colleges as the Adam Smith of *The Wealth of Nations*. Community, wealth, and virtue were the visions of Edinburgh, and they became the ambitions of Southerners.

In addition, Osterweis's insistence on the United States as an intellectual colony of Britian, as a culture unable to assimilate Romanticism until Britain had done so, is much exaggerated. There were lines of communication between the South and the continent of Europe that never touched English soil. The first doctoral degree granted to an American was granted to Philip Tidyman of Charleston at Göttingen in 1800, only shortly after Coleridge had spent the academic year of 1798–99 there. Joel Poinsett was in Germany in 1804. Hugh Legaré was writing on August von Schlegel contemporaneously with the Scotch Reviewers.[34] Many Southern thinkers knew of Continental writers, not from the English, but from reading the Continental writers themselves.[35] It is true that German was a scarce linguistic skill in the United States. But so it was in Britain and France, which long maintained the eighteenth-century prejudice that German was a barbaric and hideous tongue and that Germans were possessed of a negligible literature worth notice only for the occasional hymn or Christmas carol. For his contemporaries the achievement of Coleridge in the *Biographia Literaria* was not merely grasping what Schelling had said but reading German at all.[36] As with the English, there were a few Southerners—Jesse Burton Harrison, Hugh Legaré, Thomas Caute Reynolds, George Henry Calvert, Basil Gildersleeve—who mastered or essayed the language, but more got their German philosophy through French, the language almost all cultured Southerners knew.

Thus the picture of patterns of influence is complicated. Influence runs from the Scots to Germany and from the Scots directly to the United States; flows from Germany directly to the United States; moves from Germany to England and on to the United States; goes from Germany to France and then in two independent streams to England and the United States; descends from one generation of Scots to a successor generation of Scots and Englishmen, thence to the United States. On top of that, there were independent intellectual developments within the United States itself; indeed, the single most influential study of antebellum Southern thought, William Taylor's *Cavalier and Yankee,* has been found plausible, though it mentions no exotic intellectual influences. There were as many permutations as there were cultures and generations. In short, Osterweis's pattern of influence is both too belated and too simple. We have instead a series of intellectual communities, with Germany as the core, that traffic and interact. For it is important to stress that the United States and the South are not especially belated in these interchanges, nor markedly crude in their discriminations.[37] Romanticism in America all but predates that of France, if we take Victor Hugo's preface to *Hernani* (1830) as the beginning of a full-blown French Romantic tradition, and is earlier than that of Russia. This would be clearer if the students of Romanticism were not so provincially Europocentric. And in noting the precedence of German and English Romanticism we too often forget the very stubborn reargued action of obdurate neoclassicists. Germany and England had their own William J. Graysons, puzzled why anyone should prefer Wordsworth to Pope or Chateaubriand to Fénelon. Goethe himself repented of *Werther* and scorned the Romantic as "weak, morbid, and sickly."[38] Romanticism was a disputed sensibility in England well into the 1840s, and the English were perhaps more stubbornly insular than the Americans, as a reading of Matthew Arnold's polemics will affirm.[39] Indeed, I am inclined to think that the United States, certainly the South, became a Romantic culture more quickly and more abruptly than either Britain or France because Romanticism had special appeal for those who felt themselves on the periphery. Only the Russian intelligentsia swallowed Romanticism with such eagerness, with Belinsky as its Simms, energetic and somewhat indiscriminate.[40]

The South shared a characteristic with other Romantic cultures, even or especially the instigating Germans: it was a provincial culture anxious to invent and legitimate itself.[41] To call it provincial is not to insult, for any Romantic sensibility honored itself by the adjective. The indigenous always mattered. The attraction of Romanticism was precisely the dignity it gave to the local. Romanticism was the doctrine of the outsider, its pattern a sense of unjust denigration swelling into a proclamation of self-worth. This is the shape of German Romanticism: the progress from the Gallicism of Frederick the Great to the assured independency of Goethe, to the populist gaiety of Herder, eventually to the almost absurd cultural egocentricity of Hegel. It is the shape of Scottish Romanticism: the shift from the embarrassment of David Hume for speaking English with an ineradicable Scottish accent, a North Briton writing a history not of Scotland but of England, to the pride of Walter Scott in retailing his *Tales of a Grandfather*. Even in England we find how often Romanticism was the ideology of the English provincial, resentful of London, rusticating by choice or birth in Porlock or Grasmere. This provincial emphasis explains why Romanticism came so slowly to France, which had had centuries of thinking herself the core of civilization, and why when it did come, the archetypal figure of French Romanticism was a provincial like Julien Sorel in Stendhal's *Le Rouge et le noir*.[42]

Southern literature, too, as William Taylor has documented, was full of outsiders—of orphans, Hamlets, Hotspurs[43]—because often written by parvenus, the migrant, the odd: Kennedy the son of Irish immigrants, Simms the half-orphan, Holmes the wandering Englishman, Caruthers the failed doctor, Chivers the disgruntled, Wilde the expatriate, Timrod the invalid, Hammond the proud diffident, Legaré the disappointed, Poe the ecstatic rationalist.[44] They are not a happy crew, on the whole, and the predominant tone of antebellum Southern Romanticism is melancholy, *Manfred* rather than *Don Juan*, the anticipations of delicious failure. As Drew Faust has shown, one merit of intellectuality in the Old South lay in its potential to preserve and reform a world always thought to be poised upon disaster. This grim pleasure may indeed be one of the Old South's chief legacies, for no one caught the mood with more ingenuity and discipline than Poe, "the planet out of orbit," who gave it to Baudelaire, thereby clarifying the sentiment of the *fin de siècle*.[45] Certainly few cultures have been better prepared ideologically for the disaster of war. Ruins are vivid in Southern thought long before Columbia was reduced to ashes. For Mary Chesnut, both as a woman and as a Southerner, adversity was an old antebellum friend.[46]

In the South the grievances of politics, slavery, and trade, the flux that preconditioned Romanticism, created the case for provincial self-justification. This is abundantly documented, whether we look at the Revolutionary novels of William Gilmore Simms, the proslavery and

regionalist analyses of Thomas Roderick Dew, or the booster essays of
J. D. B. DeBow. Just as elsewhere defense became attack, inferiority
was transmuted into superiority, and the guess that the survival of
civilization resided as much on the periphery as in the core became
Fitzhugh's messianic doctrine of Southern culture as the savior of civilization.[47] But in the South, presenting this case meant hard work. The
federal union had no London or Paris against which to rebel, the
feeble powers of Van Buren being a poor substitute for the despotisms
of Napoleon or Coleridge's William Pitt and the power of the Southern political elite being so great and independent.[48] So it became necessary, by force majeure, to invent a core against which to rebel. By
the 1850s the cultural answer became Boston, conveniently the center
both of abolitionism and of Ticknor and Fields, which Southerners
made into the London they could repudiate. By 1860 this was a gross
overestimation of the cultural power of New England to mold American opinion, but it was a necessary invention.

If intellectual influences mattered, it is vital that we do not miscon-
strue those imported. As in much antebellum Southern history, it is
necessary to disentangle what the late nineteenth and early twentieth
centuries came to think had happened from what, in the first place,
did happen. Three influences will be illustrative: Walter Scott, Samuel
Taylor Coleridge, and Madame de Staël.

It is a considerable irony that Osterweis echoes the diminution of
Scott's reputation begun by Carlyle, advanced by Walter Bagehot, and
polished by Leslie Stephen, wherein Scott became close to children's
literature, escapist, fantastic, something for the young to pluck off the
shelves of grandparents' libraries to amuse themselves on long summer
evenings.[49] This view of Scott, the view of William Alexander Percy's
generation, has long since been abandoned by literary critics and historians, with the opening blows coming from David Daiches in 1951
and Georg Lukacs (in the first English translation of *The Historical
Novel*) in 1962. Since then there has been a steady supply of critical re-
assessments of Scott from such as Duncan Forbes, Avrom Fleishman,
A. O. J. Cockshut, Alexander Welsh, David Brown, and Graham
McMaster.[50] Their net result has been to see Scott as great if flawed,
more important for and effective in his Scottish novels than his medieval (the latter the product largely of his frenetic attempts to pay his
debts), an imaginative and subtle contemplator of the problem of survival in a progressive and unsettling world. Behind this reassessment is
the thesis that Scott was firmly rooted in the Scottish Enlightenment
and had been trained within the world view of Adam Smith, John

Millar, and Dugald Stewart but had fashioned narratives that made explicit the previously implicit tensions of that ideology. As Daiches has put it, the Waverley novels "attempt to show that heroic action is in the last analysis, neither heroic nor useful, and that man's destiny, at least in the modern world, is to find his testing time not amid the sound of trumpets but in the daily struggles and recurring crises of personal and social life."[51] Those who think Scott was a celebrator of medievalism should read the joust scene in *Ivanhoe*, where they will find a deeply unsympathetic account, a delineation of senseless butchery. Scott did accept the characteristic typology of the eighteenth-century Scottish tradition, the theory of stages, which did so much to instigate historicism. But his achievement, the reason why we can justly regard Scott as having stepped over the line between Scottish rationalism and Romantic alienation, was that he understood the price men paid who stood at the breaking points of history.[52] Jacobites, Scottish chieftains, knights, and squires were men doomed by history, but men worthy of compassion nonetheless. On balance, Scott thought his own world—of the New Town of Edinburgh, of commerce, of urban civility, of the comfortable Gothicness of Abbotsford—better, but he thought it right to remember and shed a gentlemanly tear. This is why even Carlyle conceded that Walter Scott was "one of the *healthiest* of men," an adjective that carries extra weight when we recall all that the Victorians meant by the word *healthy*.[53] Scott was by temperament a practical and moderate man, and if transplanted, he would probably—Mark Twain to the contrary notwithstanding—have voted for John Bell in 1860. After all, the burden of the eighteenth-century Scottish tradition was the insistent message that we must compromise and make this Union work.

We do not have the research that will accurately tell us about the reception of Scott in the Old South (and it is extraordinary that this is so, given how much Scott's name has been bandied about),[54] but there is reason to think that antebellum Southerners read Scott better than did Rollin Osterweis, that they, too, found his Scottish novels superior to his medieval, that they knew he had weaknesses of characterization, that he was often hasty.[55] But they found him congenial because his standpoint so matched their own situation, buckling down to modernity while shedding a tear for the old ways. In short, Scott was resonant, not because he justified a static quasi feudalism, but because on balance he endorsed progress, and Southerners unquestionably felt themselves to be living in a progressive society. More than we realize, Southerners knew when Scott spoke to real issues, when he permitted himself nostalgia. The falconry scene in *Swallow Barn* is burlesque, be-cause John Pendleton Kennedy presumed that his audience under-stood the difference between romance and reality.

By comparison with Carlyle, Coleridge's influence on the South has been neglected. Yet he was more important and earlier as an inter-preter of German thought than Carlyle and at the more fundamental level of philosophy. There is much evidence of his acceptance in the region. Hugh Legaré and Jesse Burton Harrison, the one reluctantly, the other almost with idolatry, had absorbed the lessons of the *Biogra-phia Literaria* by the late 1820s. Coleridge was central to Poe's theory of literary criticism; and Poe described him, not very accurately, as "the man to whose gigantic mind the proudest intellects of Europe found it possible not to succumb." Simms could write to Philip Pendleton in 1841 of Coleridge as a settled intellectual influence.[56] The *Biographia Literaria* was a manual of the new-fangled German philoso-phy adapted to persuade those reared in the English literary tradition by offering a gloss on the new poetry of Wordsworth. More even than Scott, Coleridge was often taken with a grain of salt, especially the younger Coleridge, barely emerged from his flirtation with Unitarian-ism in the 1790s. But the utility of knowing Coleridge lay partly in his private reenactment of the ideological lesson of the French Revo-lution, the movement from radicalism to conservatism. Indeed, the ghost of Coleridge in Southern thought does much to explain the bored tone of Southern reaction to Emerson, who seemed unneces-sary because what he offered was just an inferior repetition of old themes: indifferent Wordsworthian poetry, secondhand Coleridgean transcendentalism, and a plea for national intellectual independence that Hugh Legaré had articulated in the 1820s. But more important, the knowledge that Coleridge had thought his way through to the conservatism of *On the Constitution of the Church and State* made Southerners impatient with what they saw as Emerson's jejune radicalism.[57]

Coleridge was a notoriously difficult writer, mystic and obscure. Madame de Staël was the very model of lucidity, the preeminent popular commentator upon Continental literature and philosophy. Like Scott, she appealed to those who were aware of new currents, did not yet grasp them, and needed an intellectual Baedeker. More than Coleridge, she was available in cheap American reprints, though even in French she was accessible enough. And because of her exile by Napoleon, she belonged to the English-speaking world almost as much as she did to the French, a community emphasized by her insistent enthusiasm for English and American liberties. Like Coleridge, she offered a translation of German thought, though *De l'Allemagne* is far stronger as literary than as philosophical criticism, better on Goethe than on Kant. But her popularity in the South does much to explain the interest that was to express itself in Southern students going to German universities before the Civil War and in the "Teutomania" of Basil Gildersleeve of Charleston and Göttingen. She gave dignity and prominence to German culture, though she was often (especially early in her career) a skeptic of Romanticism, a neoclassicist puzzled but interested by the new schools, notable for a cheerful nonpartisanship that informed the reader of the new currents without demanding allegiance.[58] Southerners took her elegant exuberance, the tone of *Corinne,* more seriously than her caveats and especially adopted her explications of the nationalist sociology of literature. Like Sismondi, whose histories of the Italian republics and the literature of Southern Europe were widely read, she gave a glamor to the South, that is, to Italy (and, very secondarily, to Spain), that was to form an important, if rather confusing, part of Southern self-perception. Like Shelley and Keats, Southerners trooped off to Florence and Rome to find themselves, and by the theory of their time with more plausibility, coming as they did from one hot climate to another. But in this enthusiasm, as in much else, Southerners were torn between the logic of heredity, which made them northern Europeans, and the logic of circumstance, which made them southern, almost Mediterranean.[59]

Particular influences are important, but the final significance of Southern Romanticism resided in its offering the framework of a self-conscious cultural hypothesis, the shared hypothesis of Southern culture. Those who have argued that the origins of the South lie in the special patterns of colonial and antebellum social structure, or in the sectional undertones of Revolutionary conflict and constitutional settlement, or in the catalyst of abolitionism have not so much missed the point as failed to complete it.[60] For these arguments beg a central question: What do we mean by a culture? *Culture* is supposed to be a synthetic and descriptive term that presupposes a self-conscious relationship among the components that make it up. One cannot have a culture until one has a theory of culture, a consent that the thing described is thus describable. Republicanism, slavery, and political competition were components, but Romanticism was preeminently the agreement to describe. Its dispersal as a mode of thought was the act of synthesis, the step that brought components into a relationship that the Southerners of 1840 agreed to call Southern culture. It is an agreement that survives to the present day. But that agreement was, it is important to reiterate, stateless, the outsider in the institutional life of the United States and necessary because of the failures of that institutional life politically, economically, psychologically. The psychology of alienation had generated the sociology of community, the breeding ground and dogma of Romanticism. Yet that Romanticism was plausible because its flexibility accommodated the tension not merely between North and South, but among differing Southerners. Romanticism had contributed, not merely themes and tone, but the crucial consent to debate; it could not legislate the willingness to agree.

CHAPTER 3

Politics, Romanticism, and Hugh Legaré: "The Fondness of Disappointed Love"

Rootedness is a vexatious and prominent issue in the eschatology of Southern history. In the legend of Southern place Charleston has loomed large, oddly for a city in a myth so agrarian. In that same legend Hugh Swinton Legaré has held a small but strategic place. He is a prime witness for the debilitations of excessive and unreflecting loyalty, "the great cham of Charleston literature,"[1] planted in a brocaded drawing room with a full glass of Old Carolina Madeira in one hand, a volume of Dryden in the other, declaiming pompously and obscurely to unreflecting admirers, a bar to younger doubting voices.

For the plausibility of this Augustan nightmare, one assumption has been vital: the loyalty of Legaré to Charleston and of Charleston to Legaré. And there is evidence to the effect. Almost the first critical assessment of Legaré, that by William Campbell Preston less than five months after Legaré's death in 1843, declares it: "Though his bosom was inspired by a real love of country, in the broadest sense of patriotism, yet it was warmed with a more genial glow for his own State, and cherished a romantic passion for his native city of Charleston. It was to him a dear and beloved impersonation, of which he never spoke but with a sort of filial devotion. All its inanimate objects had a living interest to him. He felt its rebukes as those of a parent, and cherished its manifold kindnesses with the most grateful affection."[2] The impression was strengthened by Legaré's own letters, printed by his sister Mary in the collected *Writings* of 1845–46, where he could be found to observe Charleston as "a happy state of things—a society so charming and so accomplished," even though ravaged by the divisions of Nullification, that he had to pray, "I ask of heaven only that the

This essay was originally published in Michael O'Brien and David Moltke-Hansen, eds., *Intellectual Life in Antebellum Charleston* (Knoxville, 1986), 123–51.

little circle I am intimate with in Charleston should be kept together while I live,—in health, harmony and competence; and that, on my return [he was writing from Brussels], I may myself be enabled to enjoy the same happiness, in my intercourse with it, with which I have been hitherto blessed."[3]

Legaré's first postbellum biographer, Paul Hamilton Hayne, intensified this belief in the complicity of Legaré and Charleston. He remarked, for example, that Legaré, upon leaving South Carolina College in 1814, "repaired without delay to his mother's home in Charleston, then, as always, both to his eyes and to his heart, the brightest spot on earth. About the city itself his deepest affections were entwined. Wherever the needs or duties of his subsequent career carried him, he would watch from afar its progress, and the progress of the State, with an almost painful solicitude." But it was William P. Trent, in his 1892 biography of William Gilmore Simms, who most fully articulated Charleston's reciprocal reverence. "The death of Crafts," he observed, "had left an especially good opening [for a new Southern writer]. But in the opinion of the Charlestonians, this opening could be filled by one man only, Hugh Swinton Legaré, whose prodigious performances at the new state college were still remembered."[4]

The evidence seems solid—from the man himself, from his friend, from his heirs, from scholarship. Yet look more closely. Preston spoke in the final paragraph of a eulogy commissioned by and delivered to the city of Charleston. Was it not fitting that in honoring a son of the city, Preston should link the two in amity, and where better or more inescapably than in a peroration? Legaré's own letters seem an unimpeachable source. Yet note that his *Writings* contain a bare and bizarre sampling of his correspondence, edited watchfully by a sister eager to memorialize her adored brother and excise passages inconvenient to his reputation in Charleston. As for Hayne, he wrote of Legaré in filiopietistic vein, when Hayne himself had been driven by war, illness, and penury to rusticate in the nether regions of Georgia, there to mislay his prewar discontent with Charleston and invent a vanished Eden with Legaré at its center. "A brief half century ago," Hayne had imagined, "and culture, refinement, hospitality, wit, genius, and social virtue, seemed to have taken up their lasting abode therein. A constellation of distinguished men—writers, politicians, lawyers, and divines—gave tone to the whole society, brightened and elevated the general discourse of men with men, and threw over the dull routine of professional and commercial labor, the lustre of art, and the graces of a fastidious scholarship."[5] And William Trent, as is well known, was intent upon proving the rejection of Simms by a snobbish and Ciceronian Charleston.[6] Legaré, a snob and a student of Cicero, was more than convenient to the thesis.

So there are circumstantial doubts attachable to the case for Legaré's rootedness that turn to certainty of a contrary thesis for anyone surveying the whole corpus of his letters and essays. In fact, Legaré was alienated from his birthplace, the more so the older he grew.[7] The character of that alienation is especially illuminating not only of Legaré himself but of the social dynamics of the city's intellectual life in his generation, which came of age during the crisis of Nullification, and of the legacy of those years.

As a young man he had been close to the city, and the city to him. He came from a good, if not splendid, Huguenot family, impoverished by his father's early death and aided by the beneficence of his grandfather, Thomas Legaré. He was educated first at the College of Charleston, then upcountry at the Willington Academy and South Carolina College, last at the University of Edinburgh. His social position in Charleston was solid without being brilliant, sufficient to gain him access to the best circles without effort. His prominence came chiefly from his intellectual eminence, first at college, later as a lawyer, eventually as the most prolific and accomplished contributor to the *Southern Review*. This was matched by political advancement: a term in the state legislature from St. John's, Colleton, from 1820 to 1822; removal to Charleston which led to three terms for St. Philip's and St. Michael's Parish from 1824 to 1830; a prominent place upon legislative committees, first as an ally of George McDuffie, later as a spokesman for the William Smith faction, catalyst for budging South Carolina politics from nationalism to States' rights criticism of the American system; election as attorney general of the state in 1830. All this was almost by acclamation. With this rise came a deepening engagement in the city's affairs: as attorney for Stephen Elliott's Bank of South Carolina, as a member of the city council for the Fourth Ward in 1825, as a lecturer before the Charleston Forensic Club, as a member of the Book Committee of the Charleston Library Society, as a lawyer upon Broad Street.[8] Born to the city's upper class, he had made himself one of its elite.[9]

All this was satisfactory, especially as he seemed to move in sympathy with his times, nationalist turning sectional. He had always been ambitious for fame and influence. "I have been as deliberate, in embracing my pursuits in life," he told Francis Walker Gilmer in 1816, when just nineteen, "as if it were really a matter of consequence to the public."[10] It was the more satisfactory because he labored under physical disadvantages. As a child he had been inoculated for smallpox; the virus had turned virulent and confluent, nearly killing him. Recovering, he grew very little between the ages of five and twelve, then shot up suddenly, chiefly in the torso and head, less in the legs and arms. Benjamin F. Perry was to remember: "His bust was a noble one, and he appeared to a great advantage seated in his chair in the House of Representatives, but when he rose to speak, his legs were so short that he seemed dwarfed. . . . His head and face were very fine and striking. But in walking he was ungainly, and I noticed that he seldom walked to or from the State House in company with any one. He never married. He was very sensitive and morbid on the subject of his personal appearance. I have understood that he said he would give all his learning and talents for the manly and graceful form of Preston."[11] Thus sensitive, he warmed at the applause of his estate. While it was never quite enough to satisfy him, it came closest in the crescent years of his early manhood, honors sanctifying honor.

Turn to the mid-1830s, and one finds a very different Legaré. Removed to Brussels, where he was American chargé d'affaires between 1832 and 1836, he was advising his mother to sell her South Carolina property and himself toyed with abandoning the state permanently.[12] He developed a lament: Charleston was going to the dogs, its manners were deranged, its weather sultry and detestable, its streets dirty, its harvests unreliable, its cotton prices unremunerative.[13] By the late 1830s the lament had become a dirge. "My home [is] untenable," he observed in 1838. "I am disgusted with this place & must try my adverse fortunes elsewhere," he said in 1840. Charleston had become but "this hot & out of the way spot."[14] Seeing malaise, friends advised him variously. James Louis Petigru cautiously suggested the wisdom of leaving South Carolina. The younger Stephen Elliott tried to woo him to stay with flattering offers of an undemanding professorship at South Carolina College and the editorship of a revived *Southern Review*, defunct since 1832, while noting that Legaré was but "lingering upon the threshold of [his] Fathers."[15]

For the last eleven years of his life, Legaré was more often than not, and by design, a nonresident of Charleston. Going to Brussels, he had intended to stay only eighteen months to two years. Yet he remained for four years, perplexed about his probable fortunes in Charleston. "What should I do in Charleston, for heaven's sake?" he asked in 1833.[16] The answer, when he did return in 1836, was an unsolicited election to the House of Representatives. Duty in Washington neatly served his ambivalence, as he stood formally for the city yet was obliged to be much out of it. He traveled incessantly—in the winters to Washington, in the summers to Boston and New York and spas such as Saratoga and White Sulphur Springs. Indeed, he was defeated for Congress in 1838 partly because he had spent so little time in his constituency. His friends were discouraged by a candidate who dallied irritatingly in New England and Virginia, reading *Manfred* to ladies, when he should have been upon the hustings.[17] Defeat returned him to the bar and Charleston between 1839 and 1841, but he stayed away from society, rusticating on a John's Island plantation and still traveling, both for private amusement and to further the political ambitions of the Whigs and his own splinter Conservative party. When he received news of his appointment by John Tyler as attorney general of the United States in 1841, he was not in Charleston but in Newport, Rhode Island.[18]

Cabinet office in the insecure tented camp of Washington implied but did not mandate removal from home. Unlike many federal officials, however, Legaré made his residence permanently in the District, even moving his mother and sister to a house there in the spring of 1842. He looked, it might be inferred, to a life as a well-remunerated Washington and Baltimore lawyer, with a practice based upon his deserved reputation in cases before the Supreme Court, a life dotted with further spells of federal office, in perhaps the Paris or the London embassy, upon which he had long had an eye. It is a rhythm not unknown today along the Beltway and in Georgetown, though less common before the Civil War.

As with his political life, so with his intellectual life. In the last decade of his life, the old mainstay of the *Southern Review* wrote not for Charleston or Southern periodicals—offers from which he spurned— but for the *New York Review*.[19] Even in death he was migrant and expatriate. Dying in Boston, he was buried in Mount Auburn Cemetery. Not until 1858 were his remains exhumed and transferred to Charleston, where they were placed in Magnolia Cemetery beneath a white marble monument that proclaims his Unionism. When Preston declaimed his eulogy in Charleston in 1843, testifying to the amity of city and son, Legaré was a thousand miles absent.

What had propelled Legaré away? What had happened to a man who once had dubbed himself a "thorough-faced Charlestonian"?[20] There were a variety of reasons, a few idiosyncratic, many characteristic of his generation.

There was economics. The crisis of the South Carolina economy, apparent since the 1820s, had made many expatriate and left a deep impression upon Legaré that was not assuaged by the improvement of the 1830s. His essays for the *Southern Review* referred to Charleston as a city "mouldering away, in silence, amidst the unavailing fertility of nature" and were consistently gloomy about the intrinsic unprofitability of a slave economy.[21] His own financial situation, though never desperate, required constant effort and vigilance. He had a small estate from his grandfathers, by no means equal to Legaré's needs and wants and paltry beside the fortunes of many of the friends with whom he shared power but not magnificence. Apart from himself, he was obliged to sustain his mother, his unmarried sister Mary, and his elder sister Eliza (who was married to a man as unsound financially as he was otherwise energetic, giving her twenty-one children and an early grave). Financial exigencies drove Legaré to the bar, a business he found tiresome, and to a "dusty, abominable" Broad Street office.[22] While he took pleasure in the rhetorical challenge of the courtroom, much of being a lawyer was tedious minutiae, and Legaré's passion for the law was philosophical—the contemplation of the elegance of the civil law or the devious sociology of the common law. As for the bench, promotion to which was often suggested, economics again forbade. Money lay in the fees of advocacy and conveyance; judges earned nothing exorbitant but dignity.[23] And Legaré practiced law most when politics drove him from office. Thus the Charleston bar grew into a melancholy symbol of political defeat and the vulgar pursuit of money for its own sake. To flee Charleston was to embrace success and advancement in Brussels or Washington or New York, where such things had been his.

There were intimate concerns and tastes. Legaré was never to marry, which might have bound him irrevocably into Charleston society. The reasons are only partly clear. His sensitivity about a smallpox-distorted body and constant ill health were significant factors. Equally, his very suspension between Charleston and the world beyond made marriage problematical. If he married a Northern girl, could he take her to Charleston? If he married a Charleston girl, could he take her north?[24] Whatever the cause of his bachelorhood, the consequence was the freedom to travel, restrained only by the call of sisters and mother, pressing but not sovereign. And he did love to travel. As early as 1819 in Edinburgh he spoke of his "restless disposition." In 1832 he confessed himself a "great rambler."[25] He was to see much of the United States east of the Appalachians, England, Scotland, France, Holland, Belgium, the Austrian Empire, Prussia, Bavaria, and many of the lesser German states. He traveled for edification and amusement but also for his health to watering places such as Aix-la-Chapelle, Saratoga Springs, and Spa itself to imbibe sulphurous liquids and placate the ravaged bowels that were eventually to kill him. One of his chief delights in a modernizing world was the increased ease of communications. He would praise Macadam for leveling roads that in his youth had battered his weakened frame. He would dwell fondly upon the steam engine, which rushed him so astonishingly from Charleston to Columbia or from Washington to New York.[26]

There was the matter of friends. He had written to Isaac Holmes of his "little circle," whose survival he craved. By the late 1830s so many had died or become estranged. As a prodigy, he had, no doubt, mingled with men his senior, and their deaths were to be expected: Stephen Elliott, whom Legaré revered, found dead with an unfinished contribution to the *Southern Review* on his desk; Samuel Prioleau, who had written so engagingly upon the ravages of dyspepsia; Edward Rutledge, who beguiled the holidays of a sickly and half-orphaned child; Thomas Pinckney, who had introduced Legaré to the intricacies and cadences of Greek.[27] But others, Legaré's contemporaries, went prematurely, as he himself was to go: Henry Junius Nott, Edward Pringle, Elizabeth Pringle, all drowned at sea; Thomas Grimké, an intellectual opponent, eccentric and much loved; Joshua Toomer, who took his own life with unnerving deliberation and rationality; John Gadsden; Jennings Waring; Robert Hayne. By 1840, amid this wreckage, Legaré observed, "Another of *my* best friends gone! Charleston is becoming a dismal solitude to me."[28] To friends dead he had to add friends lost: William Drayton, who left South Carolina in the wake of Nullification; William Campbell Preston, the companion of Legaré's student days in Paris and Edinburgh, estranged by the politics of the 1830s, whom Mary Legaré was offended to see as her brother's eulogist;[29] above all, most poignantly, Isaac Holmes, the very man to whom Legaré had spoken in 1833 of his "little circle," and the closest of friends, to whom Legaré had addressed letters of unwonted gaiety and intimacy: dear dim "Ikey" Holmes, enlisted at the last moment by the improbable coalition of Calhoun, Poinsett, and Van Buren to defeat Legaré in 1838, poor Holmes who thought it might be nice to have a political standing equal to his wealth, poor Holmes who lisped that the subtreasury was "wital," poor Holmes the foot soldier—who crushed Legaré at the polls. "He has been," Legaré explained to his Virginian political ally William Cabell Rives, "for twenty years one of my most confidential & devoted friends, and contributed very much to place me where I am. I should have regarded his opposing me, under any circumstances, as a *moral* impossibility—but is there in this sinful world, any such thing? . . . I have *felt* this opposition very much. I am a being, you know, of exclusive habits & so condemned to few intimates at best, on whom I very much depend for sympathy & support. A cruel death—a double shipwreck—deprived me in poor Nott & Pringle of two of these, men who had grown up with me in perfect intimacy from childhood. Holmes was one of the survivors on whom I most counted, & here he is lending himself to my capital enemies. . . . You see that my griefs are not merely those of a politician.[30]

To friends lost in Charleston he could add friends gained elsewhere, the harvest of his travels. George Ticknor, whom Legaré had known since Edinburgh, urged that he come to Boston, "our Western Florence," where nothing would be easier than to make his fortune at the bar or in the lecture hall, nothing more congenial than dinner with William Prescott and Jared Sparks, no summers less sultry than those upon Cape Cod.[31] Joseph Cogswell, also known from Edinburgh, pleaded the opportunities of New York, and certainly Legaré had there many friends, up and down the Hudson, so many rich and getting richer.[32] Legaré the economist, the friend of Nassau Senior, knew that New York was crescent and Charleston faltering. He had known it for twenty years, at least since he had urged his mother in 1820 to buy property in New York or Philadelphia. And then Baltimore was pleasant, with friends like John Pendleton Kennedy and the baronial Carrolls, the city's bar prosperous and inviting.[33] Legaré would visit them all, complain of the vexations of Charleston, and they would smile and say, "Come to us." And he would be very tempted when he picked up a copy of the Charleston *Mercury* and saw himself damned at home. The Charleston press, in the heat of polemic, accused him of overrefinement, of too much learning, of being an overelaborate jurist, of dallying in the salons of Europe during the crisis of his times, of anything that came to hand, and Legaré would find himself saying that Charleston "never loved me," that his own class had proscribed him in 1838, that "they" had once chained him to the *Southern Review*. "You know how many nights & days of laborious thought I have given gratuitously to what *they* represented to me as a work necessary to the interests & honor of So. Carolina," he grumbled. "My sight was & is seriously impaired by those thankless vigils—& now they ask me tauntingly with what useful undertaking my name has never been associated."[34] It was very hard when he received a letter from Cogswell that spoke of Legaré's "glowing pen"; flattered with "If we could secure the aid of such men as yourself, if there are any more such in our country, we would make the New York Review every way equal to the London Quarterly & I think a good deal better"; and offered what was more than Charleston ever did, a handsome stipend per page. Little wonder that Legaré would complain, not with entire accuracy, "I have found my *studies in Europe* impede me at every step of my progress. They have hung round my neck like a dead weight,—and do so to this very day. Our people have a fixed aversion to every thing that looks like foreign education. They never give credit to any one for being *one of them,* who does not take his post in life early, and do and live as they do."[35]

Lastly, most importantly, there was politics. The political world of Legaré in 1830, of Legaré the acclaimed and rising man, was broken by the crisis of Nullification. From the ideologue of a consensus he became the orator of a Unionist party, badly organized, harassed from power, futile. From the tidy world that had advanced him so evenly, so pleasantly, he passed into another, slippery, ominous, apocalyptic. Friends split from friends, houses from houses. Conversations grew strained and divisive. The elite of Charleston, to which as politician and lawyer he belonged, found itself diminished of influence by mobilizing Nullifier voters and politicians. Legaré, opposing Calhoun, commended himself thereby to a Jackson administration eager to patronize the opponents of an erring former vice-president and found himself offered the mission to Belgium. Seeing little prospect of advancement in a Nullifying state, Legaré accepted exile. State politics became progressively closed to him; he would not go back to a state legislature he despised as a pandemonium. He had already been state attorney general, a position good enough for a rising man but not one risen. The governorship was unlikely and uninviting. He could not afford to be a judge. No Unionist could expect to be a senator in Calhoun's South Carolina. For much of Legaré's political course was plotted in reaction to the mysterious ways of Calhoun, who helped to drive Legaré out in 1832, assisted his election in 1836 to chastise Henry Pinckney for straying on the abolition petition issue, struck him down in 1838 when Legaré orchestrated opposition to the subtreasury scheme and displeased the fleeting alliance of Calhoun and Van Buren. Calhoun's firm grip upon state politics, combined with erratic and whirling political schemes, bred a high mortality rate among the state's many ambitious politicians, created a centrifugal disillusionment that drove many, among them Legaré, to seek a political constituency beyond Calhoun's depredations. In Legaré's case the refuge lay in federal officeholding. After 1838 a sanctuary was contrived by a venture into national presidential politics, by an alliance with William Cabell Rives of Virginia in support of the small but not unimportant Conservative party, and eventually into the Tyler Cabinet, that refuge of the political misfit.

For a man so dedicated to public affairs, Legaré labored under the disadvantage of being an indifferent politician. He had received preferment when it was convenient for others that he be preferred. He never commanded events. He understood, in the abstract, how politics worked, and few Carolinians analyzed it more acutely or better understood how it could be deflected by unreasoning accident and angular passion. But Legaré could not bring himself to labor day in and day out, to ferret out information, to influence, to cajole, to intimate patronage, to use the propaganda of the press, to set loose pluguglies and bullyboys. He had been genteelly appalled in 1831 when his brother-in-law had boasted of keeping gentlemen drunk for days in order to ensure their votes. Studying oratory, excited by its tense achievement, he conflated the power of words with the power of politics. Meeting opposition, he bridled and delivered a long, erudite, grand and subtle speech that annihilated his opponents intellectually but changed little politically. Seeing this, witnessing intellectual superiority untranslated into advancement, he limped back to his solitary learning, wrote acid letters, and waited in discontent until events—at the will of others— turned smiling upon him again. Gouverneur Kemble of New York, a real politician in a Jacksonian age that perfected the American craft, was to remember Legaré to Joel Poinsett and deliver the professional's verdict: "But for his inordinate vanity, he would have been a very useful man, but this rendered him continually the dupe of others."[36] He was the victim of Nullification's transformation of South Carolina politics, and he knew it. He wrote in 1839: "The South Carolina in which & for which I was educated has some how or other disappeared, & left a *simulacrum* behind of a very different kind—which I don't understand, neither am understood by it."[37]

Such was his alienation—deeper because incomplete. Legaré did, after all, love Charleston and never ceased to do so. Preston was intentionally fudging when he observed that Legaré never spoke of Charleston but with "a sort of filial devotion," but shrewd to add, "He felt its rebukes as those of a parent." The Legaré who complained of Charleston was the same who, hearing of the great fire of 1838, wept. Toying with moving to New York, he hesitated and hedged that he might go "if I did not see many reasons for *loving* Charleston."[38] Unlike

William Drayton, he never did formally make a break. There was much to hold him—the accumulated attachments of family and friends, however depleted. Molded by Charleston, he was never quite at ease elsewhere. Legaré was a marked victim of the truth that powerful cultures denote themselves by the capacity to make their citizens dislike them or love them, yet be held. Charleston society had a tone he had absorbed in youth, enjoyed in early manhood, and grieved for in maturity. Even in decline, it seemed sweeter than society elsewhere. And he had a taste for decline, a proneness to elegy. Hearing in Brussels in 1836 of the death of an old patron, he wrote: "You know some of our earliest childish recollections relate to Christmas holidays spent at St. Johns. They have been haunting me for some weeks past. The smallest incidents come back upon me with all that is sacred in the innocence & simplicity of childish thoughts and feelings. Mr. Rutledge & Richmond were so *very* characteristic of poor dear Carolina. Such a person and such a place could have existed no where else, & can't exist, even there, *long*. That is always the burthen of the song with me, you know." The bonds of Charleston snapped one by one, but there were many strands, and the thinning left still a formidable connection. For Legaré had that worst of loves: he did not love Charleston and South Carolina for themselves; he loved the idea of them. Commenting in 1833 upon the Nullification convention, he shrewdly observed of himself, "For my own part, I do confess that the insolent & mad conduct of the convention has almost entirely alienated me from the state— which I do believe I loved more than any body in it."[39]

Much in this estrangement was personal, but much was social, the plight of his generation. His alienation had its intellectual sources, to which I shall turn, but its main rhythm was political. Here is an important general truth: many of the Old South's intellectuals were engaged in politics; just as conversely and not often distinguishably, many of its politicians were interested in ideas. It has been argued that the necessary alienation of the intellectual life led to a self-conscious attempt to use the politics of slavery as a way to establish intellectual and social legitimacy.[40] This may be only half of the equation between politics and thought, and perhaps not the most important half. Politics could engender alienated intellect as much as alienated intellect engendered politics. In a small social world like Charleston and South Carolina, crowded with intelligent men ambitious for office and esteem, estrangement was intrinsic. In a culture that prized male friendship but faced politically divisive, volatile, and whirling tensions, alienation that cut to the marrow was everywhere. It was not just the politically dispossessed who felt it. William Campbell Preston, successful Nullifier and senator, perhaps the most important man in South Carolina politics after Calhoun (the lid on this seething mass of self-consciousness), felt it too. In old age Preston was to muse to his old ally Waddy Thompson on the cost: "Amidst the struggle of life while it was intense I met with many and most agreeable men at the bar[,] in the Senate, in the court, Scholars, orators, men of talents and of spirit, men with whom I thought I had contracted *friendship*. Where are they[?] It was seed sown by the wayside. I ask not of the dead but of the living, where are they? The fowls came and devoured them up. Where is Pettigrew and Butler, whom I met at the bar[,] Mangum and Crittenden whom I met in the Senate gone glimmering and off."[41]

POLITICAL CHANGE created the conditions for alienation without comprehending it. If thought and politics danced together, one must pause to consider the intellectual presuppositions that Legaré brought to the vexations of his world. For thought mutated with society, which has implications for our understanding of both Legaré and Charleston. Legaré had a poised sensibility, divided between the convictions of fixity and change. Part of him believed in the stability of things, part in their mutability; part was classic, part Romantic. This was a dilemma characteristic of his times, which gave him ample resources from which to ponder the tension. Legaré had been young in a South Carolina versed in the sensibility of the eighteenth century, but he was mature in a world that tampered, albeit gingerly, with that sensibility.

Romanticism was a new intellectual order of things to which Legaré committed himself very gingerly, giving much, holding back much. One can, for exposition's sake, isolate five areas of his commitment—historicism, nationality, law, religion, and language—before making the caveats Legaré himself was careful to elaborate.

Legaré possessed a marked historicist sensibility, caring how time and place varied, how context mattered. "There is not a more common error," he once observed of commentators upon Magna Carta, "than to ascribe our own notions to those who have gone before us, and to suppose that in politics, the same words always mean precisely the same thing."[42] The virtue of studying original texts lay not in asserting the similarities of ancient and modern but in measuring the distance. "Compare the knowledge," he asked, "which a scholar acquires, not only of the policy and the *res gestae* of the Roman emperors, but of the minutest shades and inmost recesses of their *character,* and that of the times in which they reigned, from the living pictures of Tacitus and Suetonius, with the cold, general, feeble, and what is worse, far from just and precise idea of the same thing, communicated by modern authors. The difference is incalculable. It is that between the true Homeric Achilles, and the Monsieur or Monseigneur Achille of the Théâtre Français, at the beginning of the last century, with his bob wig and small sword. When we read of those times in English, we attach modern meanings to ancient words, and associate the ideas of our own age and country, with objects altogether foreign from them."[43]

So Legaré went to great pains, in essays for the *Southern Review,* to jar his reader out of a modern complacent understanding so that he might instead see the past without anachronism. "We are quite in a new world," he wrote of ancient Greece. "Manners and customs, education, religion, national character, every thing is original and peculiar. Consider the priest and the temple, the altar and the sacrifice, the chorus and the festal pomp, the gymnastic exercises, and those Olympic games, whither universal Greece repaired with all her wealth, her strength, her genius and taste—where the greatest cities and kings, and the other first men of their day, partook with an enthusiastic rivalry, scarcely conceivable to us." Here he dissented from those eighteenth-century Scots, influential upon him both at South Carolina College and the University of Edinburgh, who, though they spoke of and wrote much history, were too absorbed in defining the principles of human sympathy to seek out and celebrate the discontinuities of time and cultures. On the other hand, it is not unsurprising that a man versed in the scholarship of the civil law should have had an instinct for historicism. The legal scholars of the French Renaissance, men such as Jacques Cujas and François Hotman, by meditating upon the mutations of Roman law in medieval France, by struggling with texts by ingenious philology, by adapting the traditions of Italian humanism, had arrived at an intimation of historicism flawed less by theory than by weak technical accomplishment. With these Legaré was very familiar, and he consistently paid tribute to their improvement and critical reinterpretation of a corrupted civilian tradition. The abbé Terrasson, a later exponent, he had occasion to observe, had been among the first to attempt a reconstruction of the Law of the Twelve Tables, an attempt to be perfected by Barthold Niebuhr in the nineteenth century.[44]

Changing between time and place was national character, the spirit of culture, whether expressed in literature, jurisprudence, or politics. Literature, especially among the Greeks, "springing out of their most touching interests and associations—out of what would be called, by German critics, their 'inward life,'" was itself a social force, not the inert classical learning of bookworms, but interwoven into the very frame and constitution of society.[45] For Legaré, the chief recommendation of recent scholarship was to transcend pedantic antiquarianism and come to terms with the "true genius and spirit of laws and institutions" in a way more satisfactory than "the random epigrams" of Montesquieu because more systematic and philosophical.[46] Political forms and systems were indeed influential and more than worthy of analysis, but they meant little beside the spirit that created meaning. For example, "Magna Charta was the means of bringing back the feodal aristocracy to its first principles—one of the worst governments upon the whole, as a practical system, that ever existed—yet, Selden and Coke and Hampden, regenerated the government of England by bringing it back to the principles of Magna Charta, as explained in an enlightened age. So pliable are all political forms—so absolutely do they depend upon the spirit which animates them, and the sense in which they are interpreted."[47]

So powerful was the spirit of national character that it could be expected to remold and reform political institutions, even after constitutional debacle. The civil compact should be distinguished from the constitutional compact.[48] Once, contemplating the possible breakup of the United States, he speculated that while the Union was perhaps "the cause of all our liberties" and "its dissolution would make their duration far more uncertain," all would not be lost. New England would retain its popular institutions; in other sections, given the "peculiarities in their situation," matters would be less clear. "But we have no reason to despair of any. The first, almost the only question in such matters is are the people prepared for free institutions. It is the national character that is to be looked to when we talk of constitutions—it is the national history that is to regulate our conjectures about the future."[49] So crucial was national spirit that patriotism amounted to a moral obligation. That Byron had been disloyal to England was one of the gravest charges Legaré could think to bring. "Except the admirable lines in Childe Harold, in which he describes England as the 'inviolate island of the sage and free,' we do not, at present, remember one syllable in all his works, from the *spirit* of which, it could be fairly inferred that he was even a citizen, much less a hereditary counsellor, lawgiver and judge—one of the privileged and honoured few—of that famous commonwealth." True to this, Legaré mistrusted his own pleasure in visiting Europe and reminded himself that expatriation was no virtue and that Byron's self-characterization as a "citizen of the world" betrayed vice.[50]

As a lawyer Legaré was most distinguished for his interest in the civil law. He had studied it at Edinburgh, where the structure of Scottish jurisprudence had long mingled the civil with the common law. From Lord Stair to Dugald Stewart, law in Edinburgh had been construed in the spirit of the rational philosophe, a thing grounded in the logics of human nature and social necessity, largely independent of time and place. For Scottish law, like the Scottish Enlightenment, had sprung from the Latin cosmopolitanism of humanism, transmitted from Leyden to the Canongate, its elementary text for generations the works of the Halle scholar Johann Heineccius.[51] Legaré had been aware even in 1818—sufficiently to have planned to study at Göttingen—that such an approach was under challenge from German scholars—from Niebuhr, from Savigny, from a swarm resurrecting and editing Justinian, Gaius, Ulpian, the Salic Law, the niceties of the Witenagemot, just as another swarm were presenting new and surprising critical editions of the classics. In the 1830s, by learning German, by visits to Germany, by private reading, Legaré had measured the challenge and found it just. In 1837 he cited with sympathetic approval an observation by one of the older generation of German scholars: "Hugo quotes a letter from a friend . . . in which, congratulating the present generation upon the change, he declares, that he had taken his degree of Doctor, before he knew who Gaius or Ulpian was—writers now familiar to all his *hearers;* and Hugo confesses as much of himself, in regard to Ulpian and Theophilus. Our own experience, fortunately for us, is not quite so extensive, and yet it is difficult to imagine a greater contrast than that which presents itself to us, in comparing this *Lehr-Buch* of Göttingen lecturer [Legaré was reviewing Hugo's lectures], with what we remember was the *course* of professor of the Civil Law in the University of Edinburgh, just twenty years ago. One who was initiated into this study, as we happened to be, under the old plan of the eighteenth century, with Heineccius for a guide, will find himself in the schools of the present day, in almost another world— new doctrines, new history, new methods, new text-books, and above all, new views and a new spirit." The import of the new doctrine was to make the law a historical and relativist study. "The great dogma . . . of the *historical school,* that, in the matter of government, 'whatever is, is right,' for the time being, and nothing so for all times; that positive institutions are merely provisional; and that every people has, *ipso facto,* precisely those which are best adapted to its character and condition" was accepted by Legaré as a "great fundamental truth, without a distinct perception of which, history becomes a riddle, and government impossible."[52] Thus Heineccius, who had sought to import reason into the law by metaphysics, was displaced by Savigny, who sought reason through history. In turn, it became Legaré's mission and interest as a lawyer—as Joseph Story was to remark—to engraft on to the common-law roots of American jurisprudence the historical relativism of a reconsidered civilian tradition, to set up a dialectic between civil and common law within the delicate balance of English precedent and reasoned invention that was American constitutional law.[53]

Interwoven with the law was Legaré's view of the imagination and man's capacity for access to the sublime, which it was not the business of education to stunt by narrow concentration upon utility. Education was meant, not mainly to produce "druggists and apothecaries, or navigators and mechanists," but "to form the *moral* character"; not to kill with "barren precepts," but to fashion the sensibility by "heroical models of excellence," warmly inspiriting. For what was the object of a liberal education but "to make accomplished, elegant and learned men—to chasten and to discipline genius, to refine the taste, to quicken the perceptions of decorum and propriety, to purify and exalt the moral sentiments, to fill the soul with a deep love of the beautiful both in moral and material nature, to lift up the aspirations of man to objects that are worthy of his noble faculties and his immortal destiny"? And what was poetry but "an abridged name for the sublime and beautiful, and for high wrought pathos[?] It is, as Coleridge quaintly, yet, we think, felicitously expresses it, 'the blossom and the fragrance of all human knowledge.'" Such poetry was pantheist, "spread over the whole face of nature." It lay in every human deed or passion that created "the deep, the strictly *moral* feeling, which, when it is affected by chance or change in human life, as at a tragedy, we call sympathy—but as it appears in the still more mysterious connection between the heart of man and the forms and beauties of inanimate nature, as if they were instinct with a soul and a sensibility like our own, has no appropriate appellation in our language, but is not the less real or the less familiar to our experience on that account."[54] These mysteries were important because moral, instructive by making man conscious of smallness in the scheme of things: they taught resignation and submission; they expressed ambition and made failure tolerable; they served, in short, many of the usual purposes of religion.

Religion itself played a small part in Legaré's cosmogony, an off-shoot of these mysteries rather than their cause. Religion was poetry, and so Legaré preferred Milton, whose verse he carried vade mecum, to the Scriptures. The Bible was of use in discussing whether Hebrew poetry could be made to fit modern critical theories, but theology was Whiggishly useful if intellectually limited: "Take this very principle of utility for an example. In the hands of Paley, it is quite harmless—it is even, in one point of view, a beneficent and consoling principle. It presupposes the perfect goodness and wisdom of God; for the rule of moral conduct, according to that Divine, in His will, collected from expediency. This—whatever we may think of its philosophical correctness—is a truly christian doctrine, christian in its spirit and its influences, no less than its origin and theory." Thomas Grimké had insisted that Christianity, especially that of the Reformation, had rendered the ethics of the ancients supererogatory, but Legaré was cagey. He quoted Grimké with sly parenthesis: "that in every department of knowledge, whether theoretical or practical, where thinking and reasoning are the means and the criterion of excellence, our country must, if there be truth and power in the principles of the Reformation, (and that there is, no man entertains so little doubt as Mr. Grimké) surpass every people that ever existed"; and he could suggest that disquisitions on the Garden of Eden were less than riveting, though they were becoming the stock-in-trade for Romantics, for whom the Fall was a potent allegory of man's alienation. The Huguenot could not cry havoc on Christ, nor would he have wished to. Did he not politely note that revealed religion was "by far the most serious and engrossing concern of man"? So Legaré conceded the point, with irony sufficient to indicate that the concession was something to keep his mother and sister happy. "We have always been accustomed to think, that if those [ancient] refined ages have left us anything, in any department of knowledge, of which the excellence is beyond dispute, it is (after the Greek geometry, perhaps,) their moral philosophy. We presume it will not be considered as derogating from their merit in this particular, that they did not by mere dint of reasoning, *a priori*, make themselves partakers in the benefits of the Christian Revelation. Neither do we conceive ourselves responsible for certain strange customs and heathenish practices, into which they occasionally fell, in their conduct and way of living. . . . We concede, therefore, to save trouble, that their morality—that for instance of Rome in the time of the first Punic war—would not be good enough to stand the *severe* censure of London, of Paris, or of New-York." "The grand idea of Religion," Alexander Everett was to marvel, "which lies at the bottom of the whole, does not seem . . . to have made any impression upon him."[55]

Yet religion hinted at mystery, as did poetry, the music of Meyerbeer, Gothic cathedrals, and great waterfalls, the more sublime for being inexplicit.[56] So Legaré found deism, the solution of the eighteenth century to the inadequacies of Christianity, not intellectually mistaken but emotionally thin. He spoke partly of himself—though only partly—when he wrote to the editor of the *Southern Literary Messenger* in 1838 and commented on a shared quality of modern writers: "They almost all *feel* the want of *faith,* as they love to call it—faith in religion, faith in morals—*faith* in political doctrine, faith in men & women. There are proud blasphemies, there are wild ravings, there is demoniac phrenzy & moonstruck madness, but they believe & tremble—or what comes to nearly the same thing, they tremble that they do not believe. There is a craving void left aching in the hearts of the present generation. They are rebuilding the temple which the 'march of mind' had demolished, & putting away their proud philosophy to become as little children before their long desecrated altars. . . . The age of sciolists, called Age of Reason, is past with them."[57]

This sense that reason merged emotion with rationality gave Legaré's social understanding an instability. Emotion, being mobilized, could be wayward. Politics could not, as David Hume had hoped, be reduced to a science. "The springs and causes which operate in human events are so mysterious, so multifarious, so modified by the slightest circumstances, the most subtile and shadowy influences, that nothing is more unsafe than a political theory. The test of accurate knowledge in matters of inductive science, is to be able to predict the effects of any given cause. . . . But a politician should avoid prophecy as much as possible. Hume exemplified this in the instance of Harrington, who thought he had found out the secret of all government in the arrangements of property, and, on the strength of his discovery, ventured to affirm most confidently that monarchy could never be re-established in England. The words were scarcely written before the prediction was falsified by the restoration." Little wonder that Legaré was fond of Edmund Burke and, like so many of his contemporaries, used the French Revolution as a great fund, illustrating the dangers of speculation and the vagaries of life.[58]

Legaré's intellectual generation gave him a great controversy on which to make these perspectives turn: the dispute between classicism and Romanticism. He followed the controversy with care and interest,

noting its origin and usefulness. He judged that its chief source was
Germany, in those days when one could with justice say (August von
Schlegel had immodestly made the claim himself), "The Germans are,
of all nations that ever existed, the fairest in their criticism upon
others. Their studies are too enlarged for bigotry, and excessive nationality has never, we believe, been numbered among their faults."
And he judged correctly both the motive and the nature of these studies in a passage worth extensive quotation: "Since the beginning of
that struggle, which resulted in the deliverance of German literature
from the bondage of French authority and a servile imitation of foreign models, a new order of researches, and almost a new theory of
criticism have been proposed by scholars. It has been discovered that
there is no genuine, living beauty of composition which springs not
spontaneously, if we may so express it, out of the very soil of a country; which is not connected with the history, animated by the spirit,
and in perfect harmony with the character and opinions of its people.
It has been found that all imitative or derivative literatures are in comparison of the truly primitive and national, tame, vapid and feeble—
that Roman genius, for instance, did but dimly reflect the glories of
the Attic muse, and that, even in the *chefs d'oeuvre* of the Augustan age
of France, replete as they are in other respects with the highest graces
of composition, the want of this native sweetness, this 'color of pri-
meval beauty,' is universally complained of by foreigners. The German
critics, therefore, and, after their example, many others have, within
the present century, busily employed themselves in tracing the history
of modern literature up to its sources, with a view to show its connection with national history and manners. The repositories of antiquarian lore have been ransacked for forgotten MSS. The oldest
monuments—the most scattered and mutilated fragments have been
brought to light, and collated and compared. The simplest traditions,
the wildest fictions, the superstitions of the common people, the tales
of the nursery and the fireside, legend and lay, and love-ditty and heroic ballad, have all been laid under contribution, to furnish forth such
pictures of national manners, and 'to show the very age and body of
the times' which produced them, 'its form and pressure.'" This was to
discriminate against the not inconsiderable claim of the Scots to have
been the progenitors of historicism.[59]

He read and pondered the latest literature and scholarship: Goethe,
Herder, the Schlegels, Savigny, Niebuhr, Wordsworth, Coleridge—
these and many others. He pondered as far as his taste would take him,
which was short of the most abstruse of German metaphysics; Schel-

ling, Fichte, Hegel, and even the precedent Kant were too cloudy for him. "Nothing is more possible," he confessed, "than that we are ignorant of the understanding of these writers, instead of understanding their ignorance, according to the distinction of an ingenious admirer of the philosophy of Kant [Coleridge, in the *Biographia Literaria*]. Be it so. We do, however, for our own part, cheerfully resign these thorny and unprofitable studies to those who profess to comprehend and to read with edification such things as the Theaetetus of Plato or the cloudy transcendentalism of the German school." And he added, in rueful footnote, "We really debated with ourselves a long time whether we should venture to encounter those awful personages, the Metaphysicians," and, by way of commentary, quoted from the *Aeneid* about the underworld, of "Gods whose dominion is over the Souls, Shades without sound, Void, and you, Burning River, and you, broad spaces, voiceless beneath the night." This indifference to epistemology extended even to Legaré's discrimination of the Scottish Enlightenment, for he was as uninterested in the formal psychology of common sense philosophy, exemplified by Thomas Reid, as he was absorbed by the social meditations of David Hume and Dugald Stewart. He was to react with irritation when the American legal commentator David Hoffman felt it necessary to preface law with metaphysics, a discipline "in the last degree unprofitable as a science." Yet this indifference, since it scanted an epistemology that struggled mightily with the problem of man's place in nature, meant also a neglect by Legaré of the racist anthropology that was sketched in the speculations of Lord Monboddo and Lord Kames and became so vital in Southern thought.[60]

The critic he heeded most was August von Schlegel, the accessible popularizer of German Romanticism. The poet he wrestled with, as casting most light upon modern times and upon himself, Legaré, was Byron. It was in an essay upon Byron, with a digression upon Schlegel, that Legaré most considered the controversy.

"The distinction," he began, ". . . originated in Germany. It was seized by Madame de Staël with avidity, as well adapted to her purposes of metaphysical, mystical and ambitious declamation, and it has since been entertained, with more respect than we conceive it deserves, in the literary circles of Europe. A. W. Schlegel, in his valuable Lectures upon Dramatic Poetry, makes it the basis of all his comparisons between the ancients and the moderns in that art." Both accuracy of scholarship and the German philosophical temperament in Schlegel induced, by the comparison of the Greek and the modern drama, a belief that "in all the arts of taste, the genius of modern times is *essentially* different from that of the Greeks, and *requires,* for its gratification, works of a structure totally distinct from those which he admits to have been the best imaginable models of the classic style." Schlegel explained the distinction by religion. The "gay, sensual and elegant mythology" of the Greeks "addressed itself exclusively to the *senses,* exacted of the worshipper only forms and oblations, and confirmed him in the tranquil self-complacency of the joyous spirit which the face of nature and the circumstances of his own condition inspired." But in Christianity, to quote Schlegel, "every thing finite and mortal is lost in the contemplation of infinity; life has become shadow and darkness, and the first dawning of our real existence is beyond the grave. Such a religion must awaken the foreboding, which slumbers in every feeling heart, to the most thorough consciousness that the happiness after which we strive we can never here obtain. . . . Hence the poetry of the ancients was the poetry of enjoyment, and ours is that of desire; the former has its foundation in the scene which is present, while the latter hovers between recollection and hope. . . . The *feeling of the moderns is, upon the whole, more intense, their fancy more incorporeal, and their thoughts more contemplative.*"[61]

To much of this Legaré was "disposed to assent. . . . We think that modern Literature does differ from that of the Greeks in its *complexion and spirit*—that it is more pensive, sombre and melancholy, perhaps, we may add, more abstract, and metaphysical—and it has, no doubt, been 'sickled o'er' with this sad hue, by the influence of a religious faith which connects morality with worship, and teaches men to consider every thought, word and action of their lives as involving, in some degree, the tremendous issues of eternity." But this was as far as Legaré was willing to go. "The *spirit* . . . is changed . . . but does this alter, in any essential degree, the *forms* of beauty? Does it affect the *proportions* which the parts of a work of art ought to bear to each other and to the whole? Does it so far modify the relations of things that what would be fit and proper in a poem, or oration, a colonnade, a picture, if it were ancient, is misplaced and incongruous now? In short, has the philosophy of literature and the arts, the reason, the logic . . . undergone any serious revolution?" Schlegel was convinced that it had, but Legaré was unsure.[62]

For one thing, Schlegel was inclined to compare like with unlike, ancient sculpture with modern painting, or ancient melody with modern harmony. In architecture, for instance, modern taste hinted at a preference for the Gothic. No doubt, Legaré admitted, "a Gothic cathedral has its beauties. . . . The origin of the style was in a dark age; but it has taken root, nor is it at all probable that, so long as Christianity shall endure, the modern world will ever be brought to think as meanly of these huge piles, as a Greek architect (if one were suddenly revived) possibly might. Still, there are very few builders of the present age who do not prefer the orders of Greece—and, even if they did not, how would that prove that future ages would not?" In so arguing, Legaré was disdaining to accept a central point of Schlegel, namely, that the classic had separated genres, while the Romantic had mingled them.[63]

One needed to distinguish between essential and accidental, between form and associations: "Suppose the object described to be twilight. If the pictures were confined to the *sensible phenomena,* it is obvious there *could not be* any variety in them, as any one who doubts what is obvious to reason, may convince himself by comparing parallel passages in the ancient and modern classics—e.g., Milton's lines, 'Now came still evening on, and twilight gray', Virgil's beautiful verses on midnight, in the fourth Aeneid, Homer's on moonlight in the eighth Iliad. The exquisite sketches . . . are all in precisely the same style, and if they were in the same language, might easily be ascribed to the same age of poetry." This was essence. There were, to be sure, contingent associations of ideas or circumstance that would make a very material difference. "For instance, Dante's famous lines on the evening describe it, not as the period of the day when nature exhibits such or such phenomena . . . but by certain casual circumstances, which may or may not accompany that hour—the vesper bell, tolling the knell of the dying day, the lonely traveller looking back, with a heart oppressed with fond regrets, to the home which he has just left—very touching circumstances no doubt to those who have a home or have lived in Catholic countries, but still extraneous, and it may be, transitory circumstances." Thus spirit and associations could vary, but "ideal beauty, with which human nature, that never changes, will rest forever satisfied," could not.

Yet it was a historical fact that the ancient and classical differed from the modern and Romantic. The classical had unity of purpose, simplicity of style, and ease of execution. The Romantic was the less as art for not having these qualities. "The superiority in their exquisite *logic* of literature and the arts . . . is, we fear, a lamentable truth, nor will it help us much to call our deformities, peculiarities, and to dignify what is only *not* art with the specious title of the 'romantic.'" In short, Legaré conceded the historical point to Schlegel but bridled at the implication that classic and Romantic might be coequal, or the Romantic superior.

Legaré applied this discussion to Byron. For "Lord Byron's speculative opinions in literature, were . . . all in favour of the classical models. His preference to Pope is owing to this. . . . But," and this was a crucial *but*, for Legaré as for Byron, "theory and practice are unfortunately not more inseparable in literature than in other matters, and of this truth there is no more striking example than the author of Childe Harold." Nothing better exemplified the conflict between theory and practice, classic and Romantic, than Byron's *Manfred*, which Legaré deemed to be the poet's flawed masterpiece. Manfred's situation was classic—the lone hero struggling with the Fates. Yet the treatment was Romantic, for the burden of Manfred's anguish was the internal demons of his moral imagination. "The *spirit* of Manfred is strictly modern or romantic. The air of abstract reflection, the moral musing, the pensive woe, which pervade it, are a contrast to the sensible imagery and the lively personifications of the Greek play [the *Eumenides* of Aeschylus]. Yet its *frame and structure* are strictly 'classical.'"[64]

As he confessed, *Manfred*'s special interest, for Legaré as for Goethe, lay in Byron's "conception of Manfred's character and situation." The effect was religious: "We never take it up but with some such feeling as we conceive to have possessed of old the pilgrims of Delphi and Dodona, or those anxious mortals, who, like Count Manfred himself, have sought to learn the secrets of their own destiny, by dealing with evil spirits. The book contains a spell for us, and we lay our hands upon it with awe." What satisfied Legaré's aesthetic ambitions about *Manfred* was classical. Yet what drew him to the poem was Romantic: the internal monologue, the tangle of remorse, "not self-condemnation for a mere crime or sin committed," but the exemplification of Byron's ruling idea. "That idea is that, without a deep and engrossing *passion*, without *love*, in short, intense, devoted love, no power, nor influence in the world, nor genius, nor knowledge, nor Epicurean bliss, can 'bestead or fill the fixed mind with all their toys'; and that a man may be completely miserable for want of such a passion, though blessed, to all appearance, with whatever can make life desirable." In this definition lay much of Legaré's melancholy, his struggles with ennui, his dissatisfaction with his own ambition even when it was fulfilled, his sense of "that dreariest of all solitudes, the utter loneliness of the blighted heart." And why should *Manfred* be more evocative for Legaré than *Childe Harold*? "The style of Manfred is more sober and subdued . . . is, indeed, remarkable for a degree of austere and rugged force."[65] It embodied a spirit of resignation and submission to untoward forces that Legaré felt himself to possess. For Byron usually lacked the morality of the disciplined and impartial spectator, that lauded by Adam Smith, which "instead of consecrating the absurd conceits of vanity, the bitter moodiness of despite, the wild sallies of vengeance, the spirit of rebellion against restraint; the pride, envy, hatred, and all uncharitableness, which are the accursed brood of this concentrated *égoisme* . . . inculcates upon the aspirant that there can be neither happiness nor virtue where there is not resignation, and that it is not more the lot, than it is the duty and the interest of man, to acquiesce in the order of nature and of society."[66]

Lastly, even in his aesthetic of style did Legaré flirt with Romanticism, particularly in the historicist typology that he adopted from Schlegel and Sismondi: "The first efforts of genius are . . . the spontaneous effusions of nature, uttered without any idea of rules, or pretentions to elegance, or fear of criticism. . . . This is the whole sum and substance of the rhetoric and poetry of rude ages." A little learning thereafter induces inhibition, formality, and pedantry. Later yet, "a still more advanced age generally brings back the simplicity of nature, because it restores the confidence of genius—the Ariostos and Machiavellis take the place of the Dantes and Boccaccios, and, making allowance for improvement in minuter matters, extremes in literature—the perfection of discipline and the total absence of it—may be said to meet." This is the archetypal Romantic rhythm: simplicity, then overrefinement, and finally restored but complex simplicity. It is the rhythm that justified the Whiggish medieval romances of Walter Scott and Legaré's own interest in the likes of Amadis of Gaul, El Cid, Geoffrey of Monmouth, the troubadours, and the romances that surrounded Charlemagne, whose tomb Legaré never failed to visit when in Aix-la-Chapelle. It is the rhythm by which the Germans medievalized the classics, making Homer the Beowulf of the antique, the Greeks primitive Germans who chanced to live in a warmer climate, the Romans pedantic imitators and militarists.[67]

Yet, balanced with, and in tension against, Legaré's Romanticism was his training in the suppositions of the eighteenth century. He admired not just Adam Smith's political economy but *The Theory of Moral Sentiments*. He echoed Hume in thinking human nature to be "the same in all ages." He owned of morality that "we are content to explain the phenomenon after the manner of the Scottish school of metaphysicians, in which we learned the little that we profess to know of that department of philosophy." He found the concept of "an original law of nature" appealing.[68] Hence, an attempt to explain Legaré by reference to Dugald Stewart, as Preston once hinted, would be almost as persuasive as a try by means of Schlegel.[69] Intellectual worlds collided in Legaré's mind, as is best exemplified in his straining attempts to come to grips with Byron. In this he was a child of his times. Legaré was of that generation, occurring at different times in different countries, of first-footing Romantics. Byron, Coleridge, the Schlegels, gave such rapt attention to alienation, sketched it so laboriously in their verse and philosophy, because it was so fresh to them, astonished as they were by the French Revolution or the younger Pitt or Hume's cheerful explosion of rational belief. So it was for Legaré. To be born in Charleston in 1797 was to inherit a stately pleasure dome, or so it seemed. Did it seem likely that Legaré would find himself propelled towards exile? Did it then seem probable that the Charleston of the Pinckneys would grow little? Yet limbs were stunted, friends died, politics were deranged, and Romanticism grew necessary and plausible.

INTELLECTUAL LIFE often flourishes past the moment of power. The Charleston of the Pinckneys was powerful without being subtle. The Charleston of Hugh Legaré was subtle without being powerful, compelled by doubts into self-awareness. His city had grown paradoxical. It had come to build railroads and canals and to pronounce boldly upon the potentialities of a dizzy economic and political future. This is Charles Fraser, Legaré's friend, writing in the early 1850s: "Amply has she [Charleston] realized the advantages to which her enterprize entitles her; for to the agency of steam is mainly attributable the prosperity she now enjoys. Since its introduction her local manufactures have been improved, her business relations have been extended, her educational, professional and charitable institutions enlarged, her municipal structures repaired or rebuilt with great architectural beauty, new streets opened and former ones improved, her limits enlarged, her banking and commercial capital increased, new business ventures established." And this is Henry Cruger, Legaré's friend, reviewing James Fenimore Cooper's Venetian novel, *The Bravo*, in the *Southern Review* twenty years earlier: "Beneath a southern climate and sunny skies, in a champain country, and with a choice harbour, the structures of [Charleston], as you approach from the water of Sullivan's Island, corresponding to the Lido, forcibly induce a mutual recollection— and when the moon has thrown its light around, as the solitary passenger, through the deserted and sepulchral streets of Charleston, meditates upon her time-worn, rusty and mouldering edifices, he is gloomily reminded of the blank, icy and desolate aspect of that other city afar; now manifestly "expiring into the slime of her own canals.'" Taken singly, each of these voices is unexceptional. Together, mingled as they often were in one mind, the texture was Charlestonian, later erected by William Gilmore Simms into a "Social Principle," denoting "the vast importance to civilization of a community, at once stationary, yet susceptible of progress." This was robust elegy, energetic melancholy.[70]

No one better defined this ambivalent tone than Legaré. At the meeting place of politics and intellectual sensibility he had fashioned an image of Charleston interwoven with South Carolina. The image is best known from a latter of Legaré to Isaac Holmes in 1833, quoted by Paul Hamilton Hayne and Vernon Parrington later and used by William Freehling as a motto.[71] Legaré wrote, "*We* are (I am quite sure) the *last* of the *race* of South-Carolina; I see nothing before us but decay and downfall,—but, on that account, I cherish its precious relics the more."[72] It is a famous sentiment, antediluvian in the midst of the freshet of Nullification and before the flood of civil war. From the standpoint of 1865 and Hayne, it came to seem prophecy, its subtle unease transformed into the sentiment of the Lost Cause, the leitmotif of the city's history. Yet its pain was that of a special moment and a particular part of Charleston society, latterly annexed to a greater moment and wider culture. Its original context, apart from the special tension of Nullification, was a sense of declension from the Revolutionary generation. As early as 1828, Legaré was writing to Jesse Burton Harrison, "You complain of the downfall of Virginian prosperity & reputation. Alas! Sir, I know how to sympathize with you & have the very same sort of objects to excite my feelings: decaying *chateauxs,* once magnificent gardens & groves dilapidated & grown up in weeds & festive old elegance & hospitality departing. We have just this morning committed to the grave the most delightful specimen of our old Carolina gentlemen—a scholar worthy of the name—the mirror of all social virtues & accomplishments—Gen: Thomas Pinckney."[73] It was elegy drawn not only from Goldsmith's "The Deserted Village" but from Wordsworth's sonnet, "London, 1802":

> Milton! thou shouldst be living at this hour:
> England hath need of thee; she is a fen
> Of stagnant waters: altar, sword, and pen,
> Fireside, the heroic wealth of hall and bower,
> Have forfeited their ancient English dower
> Of inward happiness. We are selfish men;

Oh! raise us up, return to us again;
And give us manners, virtue, freedom, power.

It was the cry of the Romantic conservative.[74]

It is crucial to observe that whatever the standing of such elegy as prophecy or social criticism, it was unquestionably the product of the two themes, alienation and Romanticism, the occasion and the formative language. The city had, after all, been beautiful and vexed by politics and economics in the eighteenth century without producing such an image. But by the 1830s Charleston had an intoxicating chemistry: beauty, intimatable decline, rancorous dispute, and a generation literate in the new language of alienation. Charleston became an education in moral awareness, the occasion for and example of the *Bildungs- roman,* the embodiment of graced childhood evolving into pained self-consciousness and migrant alienation. The city became the archetype of the Romantic spiral, though downwards not upwards.

That such an image was not idiosyncratic to Legaré is apparent from others of his generation. This is Preston, writing to Waddy Thompson in 1855, after the death of Preston's wife, in the same letter in which he had spoken of the decay of friendships and the price of politics: "Things have much changed here. Poor Carrington is in his grave. My sister is a widow. There is an old dead tree in the field near which does not seem to have changed since I saw the sun glinting on it last year. It is still naked and lifeless but does not seem nearer to falling. The wind does not shake it, the lightning does not strike it. There is no other limb to drop from it but near it is green grass and few flowers."[75] It is the Romantic language of organic change applied to society. And here is Legaré in a letter that, when published in 1846, the *Charleston Courier* found especially evocative, "impossible to read without emotion." It is in a letter written to Alfred Huger in 1834 after Legaré had heard of the death of Thomas Grimké and had paused to reflect, in his exile, upon the passing of Stephen Elliott and John Gadsden: "The worst of it is that, as such persons have never been produced any where else in America than in the low country of South-Carolina, so that soil is now worn out, and, instead of these oaks of the forest, its noble original growth, is sending up, like its old fields left to run to waste, thickets of stunted loblolly pine, half choked with broom grass and dog fennel. Take it all together, there are few spectacles so affecting as the decay of our poor parish country, which I often think of, even at this distance, with the fondness of disappointed love."[76]

CHAPTER 4

Italy and the Southern Romantics

IN THE Joseph Manigault House in Charleston there is a striking portrait of Charles Izard Manigault and his family, painted in Rome by Fernando Cavalleri in 1831. They are shown on a rough terrace near a scanty tree, while in the background can be seen the Tiber, the Castel San Angelo, and St. Peter's. Manigault holds a top hat and is enveloped in a Byronic cloak. His wife, Elizabeth Heyward, sits and gazes loyally, perhaps a touch skeptically, at him while one child nestles at her knee, also looking at the father, and another in mock heroism rides a small dog. This painting testifies to a tradition, consciously sustained. In the same year Charles Izard Manigault had been given a portrait of his grandparents, Ralph and Alice Izard, done by John Singleton Copley in Rome in 1775. In it the couple sit upon gilded furniture before a rich silk hanging, a classical urn, a column, a view of the Colosseum, and antique statues of Orestes and Electra embracing. The contrast of tone and theme between these paintings, done of South Carolinians fifty-six years apart, is instructive. In the earlier painting, set against a mingled eighteenth-century and classical background, there is an air of nonchalant self-assurance. In the later, though there is no doubt of the social standing of the Manigaults, the foreground is modern, naturalistic, even a little seedy, while the background is of medieval and Renaissance Rome.[1]

Izards and Manigaults were not the only Southerners with an interest in Italy. The Middletons had an especially strong connection. Arthur Middleton, signer of the Declaration of Independence, studied the fine arts in Rome in the early 1770s. His son, John Izard Middleton, was to marry in 1810 Eliza Falconet, the daughter of a Swiss banker from Naples. At Middleton Place, near Charleston, can be seen his delicate watercolor *View from My Window at the Hotel Si-*

Charles Izard Manigault and His Family in Rome,
by Fernando Cavalleri (1794–1865).

Courtesy of the Charleston Museum, Charleston, South Carolina.

Mr. and Mrs. Ralph Izard (Alice Delancey),
by John Singleton Copley (1738–1815).

Courtesy of the Museum of Fine Arts, Boston, Massachusetts.

Remains of the Temple of Hercules at Cora,
by John Izard Middleton.

Reprinted from Middleton, *Grecian Remains in Italy* (London, 1812).

Pausilippo, Near Naples,
by Charles Fraser (1782–1860).

Courtesy of the Carolina Art Association–Gibbes Art Gallery, Charleston, South Carolina.

bella, Tivoli, painted in 1808, while at the Gibbes Gallery is his painting of the Temple of Neptune at Paestum, done in 1819.[2]

John Izard Middleton was educated at the University of Cambridge and was, as Charles Eliot Norton was to testify, among the pioneers of American classical archaeology. In 1812 in London he published *Grecian Remains in Italy,* a book painstakingly illustrated with his watercolors of classical ruins. "I write, because I have drawn," its preface honestly confesses. The volume is a curious antiquarian discourse on the "Cyclopian" (Middleton's word for the pre-Roman colonizers of Italy) antiquities that litter the countryside around Rome, a book part walking tour, part topographical description, part commentary on classical texts. The author has the air of the randomly erudite philosophe, not least in his quiet confidence that in scholarship there might be progress, "that the spirit of the times has fitted both us and themselves [our contemporaries] to see more than our forefathers," even though in the Napoleonic era Middleton found it necessary to acknowledge the instability of a revolutionary time. It is a book that, in the manner of Herder, deprecates the Romans in order to celebrate the Greeks. "There is something," Middleton writes, "in the sight of Roman monuments of antiquity that inspires the philosophic beholder with a sensation of regret, as well as of admiration. We remember that they were raised at the expense of the freedom of the rest of the world. With the exception of some of the monuments of art constructed in the earlier days of the republic, they were all erected by enslaved nations; so that the means by which they were raised must be more or less revolting to mankind in general, and some particular monuments to particular nations; as, for example, the Colisseum to the Jews." The sentiment is early enough that its probable referent is the American Revolution, not the condition of black slaves. At least, for most of his adult life Middleton traveled and lived in Italy and France upon the earnings of his Ashley River plantation. But such ambiguities were the commonplace of Jefferson's time, and it is just possible that a distaste for slavery was a motive in Middleton's absence from South Carolina.[3]

Expatriation continued to distinguish the Middletons. A later Arthur Middleton lived in Paris, Madrid, and Rome. His second marriage, in 1841, was in Rome to Paulina, Countess Bentivoglio, daughter of the castellan of San Angelo. His heir, Henry Bentivoglio Van Ness Middleton, was born in Charleston in 1843, received his education in Paris and at the South Carolina Military Academy, and served in the Confederate army. In 1866 he went back to Rome, became a captain of the Papal Zouaves, then an officer at the court of Victor Emmanuel. In 1869 he was married in Rome to Beatrice, Countess Cini, a grandniece of Pope Leo XIII. They had three children, Costanza, Virginia, and Giulio Arturo. So was created a symbol for the link between the American South and Italy in the figure—mingling the blood of Popes with that of South Carolina planters—of Giulio Arturo Middleton.[4]

All these lie outside the familiar patterns of antebellum Southern culture, yet Italy saw a steady succession of Southerners in the early nineteenth century. William Campbell Preston and James Henry Hammond came on the Grand Tour. William Boulware in Naples and John M. Daniel in Turin came as diplomats. Washington Allston and James De Veaux came as students. Richard Henry Wilde came as an expatriate. They bought paintings and sculptures. They themselves painted, sculpted, and studied architecture. They patronized the art of Americans in Italy; for example, John S. Preston commissioned Hiram Powers in Florence. Even those who never went to Italy traveled there in imagination, as can be seen in Charles Fraser's landscape of Pausilippo, near Naples, painted around 1840, but in Charleston.[5]

These are mentioned, not because they are central, but because they offer opportunities of perspective.[6] That something can be learned from those who leave home is a truism of cultural criticism, the more so when one considers the early nineteenth century, because then Romanticism was redefining the meaning of home. Therefore to define the peculiar crosscurrents navigated by American Southerners when they were placed in contact with the definitive South of the European imagination, Italy, will be useful.

One must begin with what Europeans made of the issue, for this helped to form what Southerners thought and felt. The English and Germans especially invented the counterpoint between North and South. In the 1750s Johann Winckelmann went to Rome, there to publish his *History of Art among the Ancients* in 1764, to contribute to the discovery of Herculaneum and Pompeii, and to be the librarian of Cardinal Albani and custodian of the treasures of his villa. Goethe followed for a stay of two years from 1786 to 1788, a record of which can be found in his *Italian Journey*. By the time of August von Schlegel, who traveled with Madame de Staël in 1804, a trickle had become a stream, and there existed a permanent colony of Germans, following the example of Winckelmann the scholar or Wilhelm Tischbein the artist. This tradition is still alive, though a premature and personal elegy for it may be found in Thomas Mann's *Death in Venice*. Parallel, if later, came the English. In 1764 Gibbon sat amid the ruins of the Capitol, while barefooted friars did not sing in the Temple of Jupiter, and less than a year later came the Scot James Boswell in search of less decorous amusement. In the late eighteenth century Sir William Hamilton, the British consul in Naples, collected not only the pleasurable Emma but a formidable collection of antiquities. Again an artistic colony developed, into which Coleridge, Shelley, Byron, and Keats were to fit. This tradition, too, survived, to be gently satirized by E. M. Forster in *A Room With a View* and embodied by Max Beerbohm at Rapallo.[7]

The French, less beguiled travelers, came more reluctantly, except as Napoleonic conquerors, though we have later the more than slightly invented memories of Stendhal, in his *Roman Journal* of 1827–29. Like the plantation houses of the South, the country homes of northern Europe are still packed with the booty of such travel, with paintings of the Forum, views of Pompeii, imitations of Canaletto, prospects of Florence from Fiesole. Charles Eliot Norton, traveling in England in 1856, observed to Arthur Hugh Clough, "How much of Italy lies enclosed in these country-houses."[8] And Norton was fitted to notice and judge, being himself an Italian traveler in the tradition of the northern United States, whose novelists were James Fenimore Cooper and Nathaniel Hawthorne and whose sculptors were Hiram Powers and Horatio Greenough.

Many other nations played their part. The Danes gave up the sculptor Thorwaldsen, whom James De Veaux of South Carolina was to call "the master spirit" when he visited Thorwaldsen's Roman studio.[9] The Swiss were later to offer Jacob Burckhardt, but he was formidably preceded by Angelica Kaufman, the artist, and by Sismondi, the historian of the literature of southern Europe, both Italian and Spanish, and of the Italian republics. Both Sismondi and August von Schlegel were intimates of Madame de Staël and guided her intellectually and aesthetically. Indeed, various national traditions converge in Madame de Staël and her novel *Corinne, or Italy,* published in 1807. She herself was hybrid Swiss and French, she was influenced by German thought, she had traveled in England. And, it is relevant to note, she was a friend to John Izard Middleton, whom she had met in Rome and who migrated into her set in Paris and at Coppet, her Swiss retreat. Middleton's main interest was his pursuit of Juliette Récamier, a pursuit in which he, like so many, was only fleetingly successful: she was to give him, by way of a consolation prize, a copy of her portrait by Gérard, "le plus précieux des trophées," which he bore back to Charleston. Nonetheless, Middleton's contribution was more than merely amorous. He shared his troubles with Madame de Staél (and she with him), but also his thoughts. Partly at his suggestion, the hero of *Corinne* was made a north Briton.[10]

The plot of *Corinne* is worth a careful examination, both because it most precisely embodies the imagery of North and South and because the circumstances of its composition shed light on the instability of such imagery. It is a story of tragic courtship, its tragedy being the disappointment and death of an intellectual woman. Courtship is imbedded in a dialogue between North and South, England and Italy. Oswald Lord Nelvil is a melancholy wanderer seeking health and respite in the South. Corinne is the daughter of an Italian mother and an English father who has spurned the North to embrace a poetic vocation in the South. They meet when he attends her Petrarchan coronation on the Capitol. She shows him Rome while discoursing on the distinctions between North and South. They fall in love and travel to Naples, where each divulges a secret from the past. Nelvil confesses his guilt at having failed, through a Parisian dalliance, to reach the deathbed of his father. Corinne explains that her own father had been a close friend to Nelvil's father, that her mother had died when Corinne was an adolescent, and that she had then gone to Northumberland, only to find its society and her stepmother cold and suffocating, such that she had fled back to Italy. Dissatisfied, the two part. Nelvil returns to England and is attracted to Corinne's half-sister, still living in Northumberland. Corinne follows, is crushed to see his betrayal, and returns to Italy, there to die. It is a novel, therefore, about the cold rationality of the North killing the imaginative freedom of the South.

Corinne is intended to embody the Italian virtues of genius and spontaneity, without the vices of ignorance, envy, discord, and indolence. In her improvisation on the Capitol she praises Italy for her antique Roman glory, the gift to the world of the Renaissance, the balm of her climate, the moderation with which the ample gifts of nature are enjoyed. "Here sensations are confounded with ideas," she declaims, and life does justice to both earth and heaven. Genius is untrammeled, "because here reverie is sweet; its holy calm soothes the soul when perturbed, lavishes upon it a thousand illusions when it regrets a lost purpose, and when oppressed by man nature is ready to welcome it." Hence Italy is "a mystery which must be comprehended by the imagination" rather than by the cold judgment developed by an English education. History is the burden of the South, for its citizens are "much more remarkable for what they have been, and for what they might be than for what they actually are." This explains why the ruins of the past are stoically nourishing to the present: "the silence of the living is homage paid to the dead; they endure and we pass away." Hence the charm of Rome "is to reconcile the imagination with the sleep of death. Here we learn resignation, and suffer less pangs of regret for the objects of our love."[11]

Italians are described as greatly vehement, but indolent. In society they are unstudied, never letting themselves be "thwarted in their pleasures by vanity, nor turned aside from the object of their pursuit by applause." Italian women are strangers to coquetry, and romance is little known, because its nature is secrecy and Italian love is rapid and public, untouched by domestic felicity. Such openness and familiarity of manners has a double consequence: it militates against aristocratic privilege and distinctions of rank, but it also means that Italians are often tyrannized by government, though they compensate by cunning. Hence the country is Balkanized, both because the Italian can resist neither native nor foreign tyrants and because local character varies from polity to polity, from Piedmont to Naples. Nelvil and Corinne, amid their disquisitions, travel from Rome to Naples, to Florence, and to Venice, and in each distinctions are drawn. But religion is a unifying force, and in it, Corinne argues, antiquity lingers. Paganism was a religion that deified life, while Christianity deified death, but in the Catholicism of Italy the latter is mollified by the legacy of the ancients. The gloom of Northern Gothic is contrasted to the awe inspired by St. Peter's, "a monument . . . like continual and sustained music," "an image of the infinite."[12]

The Italian language is held to be musical, soft, pleasurable, fecund, better adapted to poetry than to prose. Italian literature in its decadence has focused on wit alone. In the drama, comedy is caricature, because society is not complex enough to sustain the nuances of plot and sensibility; tragedy is thin, because the profound is avoided; satire is impossible for a race devoid of morality.[13]

England, by contrast, stands for mourning and melancholy, the uniform and veiled. Nelvil is brave, dignified, apparently cold but actually emotional and reserved. Reason predominates over imagination in the North, where all is "subordination, regularity, silence, and serious deportment." The English are incorrigibly domestic, insensitive to the exotic, their thoughts bent always homeward. Their society has no interest in science, literature, painting, or music, and so there "the mind, stranger alike to activity or meditation, becomes narrowed, susceptible and restrained, making the relations of society at once painful and insipid." Nelvil is said to have the intelligence necessary to admire imagination and genius, but he had put a premium upon domesticity, believing that "the original destination of women and even men, was not the exercise of the intellectual faculties, but the fulfillment of private duties." He had "severe principles of morality," because "the manners of England, the customs and opinions of a country where men feel themselves so happy in a most scrupulous regard for duty, as well as for law, confined him, in many respects, within narrow limits." Such a constrained morality had been fashioned partly by religion, where the contrast between North and South is marked. The Protestantism of the North is "serious and rigid," while Catholicism is "cheerful and tender." The Reformation, though it stood for freedom, created puritanical constraint; Catholicism, though despotic, generated indulgence. By a similar logic, Northern literature is marked by "profound melancholy," by attention to the internal, the "knowledge of the human heart."[14]

Climate is thought to explain much. Corinne's reasoning, in all its attenuation, is worth giving in full. "When we contemplate a fine view in the north," she says to Nelvil in Naples, "the climate in some degree disturbs the pleasure which it inspires: those slight sensations of cold and humidity are like a false note in a concert, and more or less distract your attention from what you behold; but in approaching Naples you experience the friendly smiles of nature, so perfectly and without alloy, that nothing abates the agreeable sensations which they cause you. All the relations of man in our climate are with society. Nature, in hot countries, puts us in relation with external objects, and our sentiments sweetly expand. Not but that the south has also its melancholy. In what part of the earth does not human destiny produce this impression? But in this melancholy there is neither discontent, anxiety, nor regret. In other countries it is life, which, such as it is, does not suffice for the faculties of the soul; here the faculties of the soul do not suffice for life, and the superabundance of sensation inspires a dreamy indolence, which we can hardly account for when oppressed by it."[15]

A basic premise of the novel is the impermeability of cultures. The alien is viewed always with misgiving. Nelvil mistrusts Paris, especially because he had permitted himself to be caught up in its "intellectual vortex." He mistrusts the Italians. In turn Corinne dreads England, its taciturn people, its chilling weather, its tea parties, its hostility to intellect in women. Cultural barriers are impassable, even by love, for "love never entirely effaces character." An English friend of Nelvil's observes succinctly of Corinne: "Such a woman is not formed to live in Wales . . . believe me, my dear Oswald, only Englishwomen are fit for England."[16]

Hence *Corinne* is very much a novel about the fear of deracination, written by a woman in exile. "Exile, to characters of acute sensibility," Madame de Staël observes, "is at times a more cruel punishment than death itself; imagination is displeased at every surrounding object, the climate, the country, the language, the customs, life as a whole, and life in detail; every moment, and every situation has its concomitant pain; for our native country affords us a thousand habitual pleasures of which we are not conscious until we have lost them. . . . You feel a thousand interests in common with your own countrymen which foreigners do not understand; everything must be explained and commented upon, instead of that easy communication, that effusion of thought, which begins the moment we again meet our fellow-citizens." Cosmopolitanism is not entirely dismissed. Corinne, for example, brings back from England the advantage of having studied English literature, "the profounder manner of thinking and feeling which characterises your poets," which gives her the advantages of a double education.[17] But the more basic message of the plot is the wisdom of not transcending cultural boundaries. After all, Corinne's love for a Northerner, her second visit to England, bring death.

De Staël had changed her mind about this business of North and South. Her judgment of Italian literature in *The Influence of Literature upon Society* (1800), written before she had seen Italy, had been more severe, more conventional in its belief that Italy represented the inferior spontaneity of childhood, while the North stood for adult complexity. Though she still slights Italian literature in *Corinne*, the tone is more generous, embedded in an assessment of Italian society that gives more weight to its capacity to heal and soothe. The difference is the consequence of Madame de Staël's anguish after the death of her beloved father, Jacques Necker, and the burden of her enforced exile from Napoleon's France. Then, too, her decision to identify herself with Corinne, and Corinne with Italy, altered matters. The greater freedom, sexual and intellectual, that she felt Italy gave to women deepened respect.[18] Moreover, she was drawing a contrast, not between France and Italy, but between England and Italy. In her definition of the North in 1800 there had been, not France, but England, Germany, Denmark, and Sweden. And she had found on her travels that England, though politically admirable, was socially sterile. Lastly, the earlier work, closer to the *ancien régime,* had been more conventionally the perspective of an Enlightenment thinker, impressed with the value of cosmopolitanism, not yet touched by contact with German thought. August von Schlegel, the tutor to her children, was a companion on her Italian journey.[19]

The Influence of Literature upon Society, like Schlegel's later *Lectures on Dramatic Poetry*, had drawn a tidy progression in letters and culture from the classic to the Romantic, from the public to the private, from the external to the introspective, with the North as Romantic, the South as classical. *Corinne* badly scrambles this equation, because suddenly, the merits of Italy appreciated, Italy becomes Romantic, England neoclassical.[20] The linearity of the historical progression becomes confused. English literature, praised in *The Influence of Literature upon Society*, is devalued in *Corinne* by an assessment of the anti-intellectuality of English society. The value of the introspective and private is mitigated by stifling domesticity. The density of society is the enemy of individual freedom and genius. Protestantism, in conventional Romantic theory the perfector of Christianity, the spiritual enemy of the classical, is questioned. Moreover, the fluidity of history, so essential to the Romantic vision, is cast into doubt by the intractability of national character.

One implication of *Corinne* was important. The Enlightenment, stressing cosmopolitanism, had had no need for the figure of the expatriate. A citizen of the world cannot leave home except by stepping outside the republic of letters and mingling with the unphilosophical, whom he can find as readily in his own country as elsewhere.[21] Romantics, stressing the connectedness of character to history and society, had to find a place for the wanderer, whose unconnectedness might reflect back on the bonds of culture. Consideration of *Corinne* shows how unstable were these categories, because the value of the expatriate is his commentary upon what is left behind, and what he finds. And as any expatriate will testify, what is left behind is changed by what is found. This is why the analysis of *The Influence of Literature upon Society* had become the different analysis of *Corinne*, by the act of experiencing Italy.

So it is fitting that John Izard Middleton had been implicated in the genesis of *Corinne*, because he embodied the ambiguities of culture, having been born in South Carolina, educated in England, but resident in Italy and France. For though the novel stresses cultural rigidities, it sometimes undermines the premise. Corinne herself, like Madame de Staël, is a hybrid who chooses her culture. Nelvil is offered the option of becoming Southern, though he declines. It is unclear how self-consciously Madame de Staël was making this point, perhaps very little. For a student of nations, she could be vague about those not her intimates. In the novel, for example, Nelvil is supposed to be a Scot but is throughout used as a metaphor for the English.

IT WOULD be a matter of interest to trace how these images of North and South formed in Europe made their way into the parallel imagery of North and South formed in the United States. The transmission was by no means simple, the editing was complex, the additions extensive. But that is too large a question to explore here. Rather it will be useful to explore two collateral issues. What did Southerners traveling in the knowledge of such imagery make of Italy? What light does their experience of Italy throw back upon their self-awareness of American culture?

The first question is easier to answer. Southerners came with a conventional bundle of American attitudes, partly condescending, partly admiring. As Brantz Mayer put the matter in the *Southern Quarterly Review* in 1846, "As for Italy, she has, in turns, had the tourist's sigh, his love and his anger . . . we do not know whether to bestow our blind adoration or unmitigated contempt."[22]

They tended to like the scenery, but less often the people who inhabited it. As James De Veaux candidly put it: "The people enter not my calculations,—the climate, the scenery and the arts make the chief of [Italy's] charms." Passing through Lombardy in 1833, William B. Crawford of Alabama observed, "The people are a wretched looking set, and would hardly be suspected of being descended from the ancient inhabitants." Some dispensation was granted for urban dwellers, as opposed to peasants, for their gaiety and passion for amusement, if the traveler was inclined to judge leniently an amusement that might turn to "low vices and brutality." And still more was granted by Southern men to Italian women, in De Veaux's words, "Heaven's best gift to man,—the girls!" "Nothing can excel the loveliness and surpassing beauty of the female form develloped in all the loveliness and ellegance of most exquisite beauty," Crawford tumbled out, of the ladies he saw at the opera. Richard Haynesworth, a sailor, came ashore in 1857 to endorse this opinion in blunter terms: "There are many beautiful women here in this city of Genoa, and I pass no inconsiderable portion of my time admiring them. I generally carry my big whiskers and mustache to the opera in company with a six inch lorgnette, and stare around the house as impudently as any." Better yet were ballerinas in "exceedingly short petticoats."[23]

They complained of bad roads and expected to suffer from the harassment of bandits. Henry H. Cumming of Georgia was unusually sanguine and cheerful in writing to his father in 1819 that reports of banditti were much exaggerated: "Bad as they are they are a very civil sort of people *considering their profession:* they generally make prisoners of those they intend to rob and treat them very well as such except that they sometimes exact very large sums for their Ransoms, however as I shall not travel in much *style* I shall be able, by beating them down a little, to buy myself off on moderate terms."[24]

They despised both the government and the religion. William Crawford thought Milan had been improved by the modern rule of the French, and William Campbell Preston thought the same of Rome. It was a pity, the latter wrote to Washington Irving in 1818, that Napoleon had not continued his dominance of Italy: "He was curtailing the power of the clergy—he was suppressing the convents—he was introducing the useful arts, he was employing the poor in repairing the highways or rescuing the monuments of antiquity from the ruins under which they are buried—but under the spiritless and paralyzing dominion of priests everything languishes." Few had good words for the Roman Catholic church. Despotism, cruelty, superstition, parasitism, were its characteristics. Charles Pelham of South Carolina, entering St. Peter's in 1845, was being unusually mild merely to think the rites "prosaic & dull." "It is astonishing," William Crawford had more typically observed, "what numbers there are to be seen, parading the streets, of these holy loungers, these drones of society, that live on the labour of the industrious and are supported by ignorance and superstition."[25]

Preston explained the problem with his usual precision. Observers of Italy might be divided in spirit into Catholics and Protestants: "The one sees in every thing the consummation and perfection of a noble hierarchical system fraught with whatever is glorious in Religion and admirable in piety. The other, the Protestant, sees nothing but a degraded and creaking superstition depressing the human soul and body into vice and crime, and with so deep a degradation that men are transformed to such an extent as not to perceive their foul disfigurement, but boast themselves more comely than before and are content to roll with pleasure in a sensual sty." Protestants outnumbering Catholics among Southern travelers, the latter opinion predominated.[26]

Yet there were Southern Catholics. Indeed Catholicism could occasion incongruity for Southern sensibilities. De Veaux attended in 1843 a meeting of the Congregatio de Propaganda Fide, at which Jeremiah Cummings of Washington gave his brief student oration in Latin to general applause, to be succeeded by three or four "coal black" Ethiopians. John England, the bishop of Charleston, had had to expend much ink in explaining the relationship between the Church and slavery. And he had sent letters from Rome in 1834, much concerned to refute the charge of "monkish ignorance" and "superstition." His letters, written from within the citadel of the Roman Catholic hierarchy, show a detailed grasp of the workings of the Church and its place in Italian society that beggars the scanting prejudice of the tourist.[27]

Armed only with such prejudice, few Southerners would have come. But their heads were full of antiquity and the Renaissance. "Long had it been my most ardent and one of my earliest wishes, to visit Italy, so endeared by every school boy recollection," Crawford observed. De Veaux visited the Campidoglio with a friend, who "warmed into a classic fit," reinforced with notes from Oliver Goldsmith, and launched into pointed declamation upon Caesar's murder, the rape of Lucretia, and had barely reached the Sack of Rome before their old attendant called a halt so that he might go home to his dinner. Preston offered the formal reason for the taste for antiquity: "I was stupified with amazement at St Peters but my most frequent visits are to the Capitol the Forum and the Coliseum. I believe that Americans from their republican sympathies are more interested in the history of Rome between the two Brutus' than any other people, and therefore we would visit the remains of that period with deeper feelings." But this motive was overlaid with Romanticism. Crawford in 1833 punctuated his journal with long quotations from Byron's *Childe Harold* and recommended that the ruins of antiquity be viewed by moonlight, the better to let imagination recreate the remote past.[28]

The acute were aware that they were but the last in a stream of pilgrims that wandered across millennia. Preston summed up the difficulty of the traveler as a self-conscious heir to so many travelers: "In Rome more conspicuously than in any other place, one need not expect to find any thing that has not been thoroughly pried into nor to experience any emotions which have not been described in prose or poetry." Decades later, Henry James was to find the same difficulty in writing of Venice and bravely make the best of a bad job: "There is nothing new to be said about her certainly, but the old is better than any novelty. It would be a sad day indeed when there should be something new to say."[29]

I want to return to his question of the similarity of Southern responses in Italy to those of Hawthorne, Cooper, and Norton and to argue that it signifies the incompleteness with which antebellum Southerners had alienated themselves from American culture. But for the moment it will be useful to explore closely two less casual figures on the Italian scene, Washington Allston and Richard Henry Wilde. The case of Allston is chosen, not because he represented the South, but because he was someone formed before the category of South-erner became compelling and because he offers the instructive paradox of a cosmopolitan whose art became Romantic. Wilde is chosen for embodying the figure of the Romantic expatriate.

Allston was born into a low-country planter family near George-town, South Carolina, in 1779. His father died in 1781, and he was brought up by his mother Rachel and stepfather Henry Collins Flagg. His schooling was in Charleston, in Newport, then at Harvard, from which he graduated in 1800. There was a struggle between Allston and his stepfather over the choice of a career. Flagg, a doctor, preferred medicine, and without enthusiasm Allston dabbled in medical training after his graduation. But the attainment of his majority, the acquire-ment of his inheritance, and the death of Flagg in April 1801 settled the decision for painting. A month after his stepfather's death, Allston sailed for Europe, where alone an artistic education could be acquired. Apart from a brief return in 1809–11 to marry, he was to live in Lon-don, Bristol, and Rome until 1818. His inheritance exhausted, his in-come in England disappointing, he reluctantly opted to remake his fortunes in Massachusetts. The failure of that venture, the albatross of his great painting, *Belshazzar's Feast*, is well known.[30]

Though he was the son of a revolutionary and knew only an inde-pendent United States, Allston was remarkably indifferent to the claims of nationality. In 1822, when regretting the impossibility of be-coming a Royal Academician as long as he resided in the United States, he observed, "I cannot help thinking the law that excludes for-eigners or artists residing in a foreign country from the honor of membership a very narrow one. No other Academy has such a law. The art belongs to no country."[31] So there was simplicity in Allston's movements, a reflection of the intensity of his vocation as an artist. He moved when the development of his art required. He judged that he needed Europe, England, and Italy, and so he went there. Technique acquired, he judged that he might prosper better in the United States and moved back. There is very little attendant pother about home and abroad, none of the clouds of anxiety and hope that Henry James brought with him later in the century, which has so informed our sense of the transatlantic dialogue of Europe and America. It is true that Allston spoke of America as his native land, of homesickness, and of a wish to be its first painter, but he also spoke of himself "as one of the British school" of painters and once wrote a poem that speaks of Britain as "thou noble land, / Our Fathers' native soil," and as-serts that "Yet lives the blood of England in our veins." He seems to have slipped on these categories, according to his audience, being American in letters to Americans, being British in letters to Britons, and never carrying much conviction in either case.

Allston did have a sense of being a provincial, but that related more to his apprenticeship as an artist than to a theory of the condition of American culture. He had a stronger feeling that it was his natural right to inherit the great tradition of Western art. Just as an Italian provincial might travel to Rome to study the Old Masters, so he would travel. He was to write from London to his Charleston friend Charles Fraser in 1801, "Why, then, my friend, should you despair? You have talents; cultivate them—and it is not impossible that the name of Fraser may one day be as celebrated as those of Raphael and Michael Angelo." This ambitious ease looks spurious, but was not. An artist in 1800 could look back upon three centuries and more of steady cumulative achievement in Western art and feel that he had inherited an intact and dynamic tradition, whereas the modern artist is disconnected by choice and necessity and can only look back upon "a hundred and fifty years strewn like a battlefield with the wrecks of shattered schools and confused and conflicting purposes which broke down with the generation that produced them, to be trampled underfoot by the next." The perspective of continuity is confirmed by James De Veaux in Rome, writing to a friend in Columbia, South Carolina. "The gods be praised! that my *home* is here! . . . if I succeed in getting a start here, who knows but I will be here to receive and do the honors of the city to your boys, when they come upon their tour?—and should you come yourself, I may receive you as Raphael did Leo X!—io sono contento."[32]

Allston was in Rome between 1804 and 1808. He saw Madame de Staël at the illumination of St. Peter's. "She had a beautiful hand and arm," he remembered, "and displayed them to great advantage by waving a wreath which she held in her hand, but a face like a figurehead—coarse features and a vulgar mouth." As it did for her, the experience of Rome seems to have succored in him a taste, not for the neoclassical, but for the Romantic. England had been cold technique, necessary though that was, but Italy was imagination and life. Allston had had some glimpse of this in the Louvre: "Titian, Tintoret, and Paul Veronese absolutely enchanted me, for they took away all sense of subject. When I stood before the *Peter Martyr, The Miracle of the Slave,* and *The Marriage of Cana,* I thought of nothing but the gorgeous concert of colors, or rather of the indefinite forms (I cannot call them sensations) of pleasure with which they filled the imagination."

We have the testimony of his friend Washington Irving that Allston moved through Rome in an ecstasy of admiration: "His eyes would dilate; his pale countenance would flush; he would breathe quick, and almost gasp in expressing his feelings when excited by any object of grandeur and sublimity." That invigoration was his strongest memory of the city. When John F. Cogdell of Charleston was planning an Italian journey in 1836, Allston wrote to him: "You will, no doubt, when there, become more than a mere traveller and spectator. Surrounded as you will be by the finest works of art, I dare say that you will not be in Rome a month before you are hard at work, up to your eyes in clay. With the excitement that must there meet you at every step, you, I am sure, will not be content with simply looking. You will find yourself growing younger in body and more elastic in mind."[33]

Allston was attracted to the art of the High Renaissance. Despite Coleridge's advocacy, he had little taste for the Gothic, except for a predilection for portraying terror and a gift for telling ghost stories.[34] His novel *Monaldi* is a conventional early Romantic tale of love, revenge, jealousy, reconcilation, and death. Like many Americans, including some Southerners, who were to visit Rome later, Allston was largely blind to the Baroque, except in the form of the late Venetian school.[35] His Rome was not Bernini's, certainly not a Rome of living Romans, but the legacy of an earlier past and the society of other foreigners. Coleridge called Rome "the Silent City." Allston dissented from the justice of the title, not because he listened to Italians, but because he listened to Coleridge's torrent of talk in the Caffé Greco and the gardens of the Villa Borghese. What was Rome? Allston was later to ask. It is "the great University of Art, where all this accumulated learning was treasured."[36] This was a sentiment that Goethe before him had cited from a letter of Winckelmann: "I believe that Rome is the school for the whole world and I, too, have been purged and tested here." It was a university that many were attending at the same time at Allston: Coleridge, Irving, de Staël, Sismondi, Schlegel.[37]

It is not fanciful to stress that by being a student Allston helped to form the character of the university. German émigré painters in Rome were markedly influenced in technique by Allston. Coleridge himself placed him only behind the Wordsworths in esteem and love, and there are marked resemblances between the metaphysics of Coleridge and that of Allston. It is doubtful that the influence was all one-way, though the loss of Coleridge's Roman notebooks makes it hard to document. As noted, Allston was in the midst of a tradition of residence in Italy by Southerners such as Arthur and John Izard Middleton.

James De Veaux was to enter Florence in 1842 with Allston, "our *wonder*," firmly in his mind. But Allston also helped, as a later presence in New England, to found the American literary and aesthetic tradition of Italian experience that was to lead through Nathaniel Hawthorne to Henry James and is now carried on by Gore Vidal.[38]

The school of English art, that of Joshua Reynolds, had proclaimed the primacy of form. Allston's experience of Rome, though it affirmed the necessity of form, impelled also a belief in the mystic usages of imagination and genius. Raphael and Michelangelo pointed the moral. Allston was to write that Raphael was "the greatest master of the affections in our art. . . . What particularly struck me in his works, was the genuine life (if I may so call it) that seemed, without impairing the distinctive character, to pervade them all. . . . This power of infusing one's own life, as it were, into that which is feigned, appears to me the sole prerogative of genius." Michelangelo was still greater, the bringer of "messengers from the other world." So he was to advise Henry Greenough, "Be industrious and trust to your own genius; *listen to the voice within you,* and sooner or later she will make herself understood, not only to you, but she will enable you to translate her language to the world, and this it is which forms *the only real merit of any work of art.*"[39]

Rome helped to confirm Allston's taste for landscape, and for classical and Biblical subject matter. This, in turn, helped to cut him off from the developing school of American national art and was to be largely responsible for the abrupt decline of his reputation in the late nineteenth century.[40] His landscapes were not American but either after Claude or before Turner. He declined to paint patriotic murals for the Rotunda of the U.S. Capitol, suggesting instead Christian allegory, because "the Scriptures belong to no country, but to man."[41] He was uninterested in portraiture, the chronicle of American faces.[42]

The South as Italy features abundantly in these equations, the Southern United States almost nowhere. After his departure in 1801, Allston never went back to South Carolina. He saw his mother but once more, in 1809, though she lived until 1840. Living in Cambridgeport, he talked occasionally of revisiting his birthplace, but nothing ever came of it, though he corresponded in a friendly manner with the likes of Charles Fraser and John F. Cogdell and seems to have been a friend of Hugh Legaré's. A South Carolinian was among the patrons of the ill-fated *Belshazzar's Feast.* South Carolina Unionists, through the intermediary of Edward Everett, entreated him in 1833 to paint a scene of "the circumstances under which our national flag was

Italian Landscape,
by Washington Allston (1779–1843).

Courtesy of the Addison Gallery of American Art, Phillips Academy, Andover,
Massachusetts.

unfurled by the American Ambassador at Mexico," the object being "to spread before the eyes of our countrymen, and particularly of the rising generation, the unseen but highly moral protection afforded by a great, because united people." Allston declined in a letter to William Drayton, while lauding the purposes of Unionism. He added, doubtless with sincerity but certainly with formality: "Though my lot in life has been cast in other lands, I have never forgotten that of my birth. I cannot therefore but attach a peculiar value to any mark of regard from that portion of my country."[43]

A birthplace that is merely a "portion of my country" is scarcely a home and cannot occasion expatriation. It can be objected that Allston, fatherless, the stepson of a New Englander, educated largely outside of South Carolina, had little occasion for being a Southerner. The point is well taken, yet not central. Allston's indifference to the South was of a piece with his indifference to nationality *in toto*. He did not fail to be a Southerner in order to become a New Englander any more than he failed to be an American in order to become a European.[44] Such categories were unimportant to him. The Romanticism of his art mattered, but the political imagination of Romanticism that informs *Corinne* did not.

The case of Richard Henry Wilde is very different, partly because it is much later. Wilde was born in Dublin in 1789, and his parents moved to Baltimore in 1797. On the death of his father in 1802, Wilde went to Augusta, there to become lawyer, politician, widower, and poet. Wilde seems to have been a fairly conventional Georgian slaveholder and politician. He supported William H. Crawford for the presidency, followed the faction of George M. Troup, became a candidate for the States' Rights party, and was later a Whig. On and off he served in Congress. He tacked between Nullifiers and Unionists in the early 1830s, but he drifted on to the States' Rights ticket by dint of skepticism of Jackson, and this led to his defeat in 1834.[45]

Like Hugh Legaré leaving South Carolina for Brussels, Wilde was driven away by the tangled bitterness of politics, in his case to Florence. As the classic prescription of expatriation requires, he not only wished to be somewhere else, he wanted to leave a dissatisfying home. Experience had indicated to him that he was "not at all fitted" for the life of a politician, and he was irked by the unreality of both public praise and public vilification. As he was to put it later in verse: "Spurning restraint, disdainful of the crowd, / Statesman I am not, and never will be, / For rule too indolent, for strife too proud. . . ."[46] Italy, by contrast, offered a people to whom he did not belong, to whom he owed nothing, and to whom he was not accountable. Italy offered too the chance of "travel—study—science—literary occupation—the arts— the untroubled enjoyment of Nature." In short, it offered a life "uselessly delightful." Like Keats before him, he thought that his poor health might be redeemed by a gentler Italian climate.

As a poet, Wilde was more than primed for an Italian venture. The tradition of Byron, Keats, and Shelley was now well established, and for years Wilde's verse had conformed to their themes. His mind ran on Byron as he traveled south from Paris through Switzerland. Just as Corinne had spoken of Rome as offering the reconciliation of imagination with the sleep of death, so Wilde wrote in September 1835 from Florence, "My eyes filled with tears, as I thought this would be the appropriate end of my wanderings—a place where it would be sweet to die!"[47]

Wilde found in Florence an established, if small, American colony. There were the sculptors Hiram Powers and Horatio Greenough. There was George Washington Greene, the grandson of Nathanael Greene, who was married to an Italian and was later American consul in Rome, where he helped the career of Thomas Crawford. There was the artist Francis Kinloch, of South Carolina, who shared lodgings with Greenough. Charles Sumner, William Ellery Channing, and Edward Everett passed through. But Wilde did not confine himself to Americans. Knowing Italian, he mingled with Italians, not only by having a bastard, Niziero Novelli, who was born just after Wilde's abrupt departure for America in 1840, was consigned to the Ospedale degli Innocenti, and was handed over to a local peasant.[48]

It was through an invitation to the house of Count Mariano Alberti, where some newly discovered and controversial manuscripts of Tasso were read, that Wilde began his literary researches. In 1842 he was to publish in New York his *Conjectures and Researches Concerning the Love, Madness, and Imprisonment of Torquato Tasso,* though the manuscript had been completed in 1837: a book consisting chiefly of excerpts from and translations of Tasso's verse and letters, culled to demonstrate Tasso's sanity, that shows great awareness of the historical problem of evidence. Unpublished, and now in the Library of Congress, were an anthology of Italian lyric poets, translated by Wilde himself, and a biography of Dante. Wilde went much further than most American visitors in the depth of his acquaintance with Italian culture, perhaps because he had expected to live out some twenty years in Italy. He did not content himself with picturesque descriptions in letters to American magazines nor even, as Madame de Staël

had, rapid judgments of Italian literature or society. He undertook serious research in the grand-ducal archives of Florence, consulted manuscripts in the Riccardi Library and in Ferrara, searched the papers once
assembled by the Florentine antiquarian Antonio Magliabechi, vainly
solicited access to the depositories of Vienna, pined for access to the
Vatican, checked published correspondence against extant originals,
carefully footnoted his sources, corrected the bias of older biographies. Such Rankean energy carried him through some five hundred
pages on *Tasso* and a thousand in draft on Dante before flagging. But
his zeal had earlier been sufficient to uncover a lost fresco portrait of
Dante, concealed with whitewash in the chapel of the Bargello. This
was modestly to participate in a tradition of American involvement in
Italian art that was to reach a consummation of baronial discrimination with Bernard Berenson.[49]

Wilde wrote much poetry in Italy, most of it lyrics, about women,
death, loss, melancholy, parting. He continued to write his epic poem
Hesperia, which is in the manner of *Childe Harold,* with echoes of
Wordsworth and Thomas Moore. It interestingly scrambles the equation of Italy and America. The dedication is ostensibly to "La Signora
Marchesa Manfredina di Cosenza," a mask for Mrs. Ellen Adair
White-Beatty of Kentucky, with whom Wilde seems to have had a flirtation. Hesperia is the name the ancient Greeks gave to Italy, but
Wilde applies it to America, "as, since that time, the West has moved
westward." It has four books, focusing on Florida, Virginia, Acadia,
and Louisiana. Much is pastoral, reverie on nature, and the remem-
brance of nature's power. Interlarded are Wilde's memories of places
and people. There are modest passages of celebration of America's
revolutionary history but still more assertion that America is the land
of the future, a historyless land, inhospitable to poetry. In testimony
of his awareness of the European tradition, *Corinne* is twice alluded
to, the first time to explain that, apropos of the United States, "the
most beautiful countries in the world, when they bring to mind no
recollection, when they bear the stamp of no remarkable event, are
stripped of interest when compared with historical countries."[50]

A slice of the epic is a Romantic dissertation on the rise and fall of
cultures, "the changing fortune of each various race." Like Corinne,
Wilde seems to have learned the grim lesson of Italy's past: "The soil
we reap is of our ashes made, / Ruins on ruins rise, and tomb on
tomb." There is no escape from history: "Nature's sublime and most
incessant care / Is to create, destroy, and reproduce; / Love, Death, her
ministering angels are. / Time measures ceaseless change. . . ." Fleet-

ingly Wilde mentions that in America "man may yet his vices spurn," but he immediately and unconvincingly adds that this is but a "cheerful probability of Hope, / For man's despair a palliative or cure."[51]

Hesperia has, in its fourth canto, passages on Italy. They Byronically catalog a land of literature, history, and pastoral beauty, "the land where Tasso loved and raved . . . Petrarch sighed and sung. . . . Where in their second birth arts, letters sprung." The memory of home, of America, is not banished by this: "I bear my theme, / To Venice— Florence—wheresoe'r I roam, / Mingling the past and present like a dream, / To find in all the thought of thee and home." Yet Italy, too, is home, "My Italy! although of thine not born, / Nor worthy mine own land's maternal breast, / Thy child in heart I am. . . . Mother of my Soul! at whose behest / My life's high enterprise was first begun. . . ." Yet Italy is fallen on hard days, "Wronged and despised, and chained and scourged," beset by tyrants both foreign and domestic. She must rise up, do more more than talk of liberty, manage more than "plots and curses." Britain and France will help in this Risorgimento, he prophesied, accurately; America, alas, will not. Here, too, Wilde drew a melancholy conclusion. Italy was not free, but then neither was America, for "all the earth are slaves! whom call we free? / Each bends before some favorite idol's shrine: / Misers make gold their only deity, / And in the midst of riches trembling pine." Caprice, envy, greed, faction, deceit, are everywhere. The knowledge of this occasions pastoralism. Freedom can only be sought "on the wave, / or mountain-peaks that seem the Heavens to kiss, / In the dark forest, or the hermit's cave."[52]

Wilde was a true expatriate. While Allston had slighted the matter of home, Wilde cared for it with enough ambivalence to embrace exile. Only financial necessity forced him to leave Florence in 1840, and he expected and wanted urgently to return. He was driven back on the law and politics with the utmost distaste, for he felt that America would kill his intellectual and literary endeavor, his "high enterprise." In New Orleans in 1846, a year before his death by yellow fever, he met and liked Sir Charles Lyell, visiting the Delta on a geological tour. Lyell presented him with a copy of Dante Gabriele Rossetti's *La Beatrice di Dante* and two other works on Dante, in one of which was reproduced the Bargello fresco that Wilde himself had uncovered. "This roused for a little while my 'passione Dantesca,' but it has all died away again," he wrote to Hiram Powers, still in Florence. "Such things can't live in the atmosphere of Law and Commerce. It is like putting some innocent warm-blooded animal into carbonic gas."[53]

This sentiment, the usage of Italy as a refuge from a vulgar America, was to be echoed by Paul Hamilton Hayne in 1855, writing from Marietta. "I hear nothing about me now but politics, slavery, & antislavery ad nauseam. Fat old gentlemen catch me by the button, & want to know with a fierce look what I think about Nebraska. My days are rendered wretched by such persecution. Thank God! I shall have a prospect in time of living in Florence under a quiet despotism." Earlier James De Veaux had commiserated from that same Florence with a friend, a candidate for political office in South Carolina, obliged to endure "paper puffs, retorts, sly squibs, foul inuendoes, barbecues, stump speeches, whoops, hurras, a few stiff 'brandy and waters,' then a fight, with a knock down and drag out, to finish the first flushing of a maiden speech!"[54] These sentiments, of Wilde, Hayne, and De Veaux, presage Henry James, who was to abandon the political imagination of New England to find solace in a purely aesthetic Italy. But this willingness to neglect the political achievement of America, to make light of the Founding Fathers and the beacon of commercial progress, to embrace the apolitical imagination, was, as has been seen, rare among antebellum Southerners in Italy. And this rarity meant a delicate irony. If the principles of American republicanism were the heirs of a Machiavellian moment, those same principles most inhibited the American from sympathizing with Italy, awash in Grand Dukes and Papal States. An indifference to the American political imagination, including its half-buried religiosity, helped greatly in impelling some Americans towards Italy. For Italy offered a relief not only from politics but also from commerce, and it was a truism that republicanism created the conditions for a burgeoning commerce.

This helps to explain a silence among Southern travelers, which makes an oblique commentary upon the nature of cultural nationalism in the Old South. Almost absent are reflections upon the meaning of the American South, occasioned by Italian travel. Reflections upon the United States, of which the South forms a part, are common enough. But there is little on the South itself, although those travelers were soaked in the tradition of Byron and Madame de Staël, with all their imagery of North and South.

It is hazardous to interpret silence, but it may be suggested that such imagery, though used within the cultural dialogues of the United States, was not yet robust enough to bear expatriation. The South as a spiritual home, alienated from American culture and so available to be linked to non-American cultures such as Italy, had yet far to go. In the twentieth century such linkages were to become common. There were to be the letters of Allen Tate from Paris in 1929, which ponder the relationship between the South and Europe, especially France. There was to be Robert Penn Warren's *All the King's Men,* begun as a verse play when Warren was in Italy. There were to be C. Vann Woodward's essays on the irony of Southern history.

This explains what might otherwise seem a paradox. It might seem logical that Southerners would be the first to see a parallel between the South and Italy. Yet Allston did not see it, nor did Wilde. In fact, it is antebellum New Englanders who first systematically draw the analogy between the South and Italy. This, for example, is Charles Eliot Norton, the translator of Dante, writing from Charleston in 1855: "The climate, the southern habits, the social arrangements, all give a picturesqueness in their separate ways, and there is a fine air of age, and dusty decay which invests whole streets with the venerableness of the past.—It is like Italy in the feeling that belongs to it,—and ought to have painters and poets. The air is full of indolence, and the sense of repose finds everywhere a gratification to which it is unused in our sharp driving, restless North." [55] This intimates the logic by which, after the Civil War, the South became an iron lung for industrial America, just as Italy had offered sensual release for the chilled northern European. Today Charleston has become Spoleto.

This was a measure of the mingled contempt and apprehension with which the antebellum New Englander regarded the South. Just as the American critique of Italy had emphasized the dissipation of the achievements of antiquity and the Renaissance, on account of the crippling intellectual and social despotism of the Roman Catholic church, and in turn emphasized the contrary fate of a free republican America, so the antislavery advocate saw the Slave Power as threatening a similar decline. It was a powerful analysis, in which the steamy vices of monastery and convent were displaced upon plantation seraglios. [56]

There were, it is true, a very few antebellum Southerners who drew the parallel between Italy and the South. As has been seen, Henry Cruger spoke in 1832 of Charleston as a Venice, moldering, sinking. But Cruger wrote just before abandoning Charleston for New York, because he felt that Charleston was failing to match the insistent demands of American progress and vitality. That is, he was alienated, persuaded that the South was drifting into failure. This made it possible for him to see a parallel in Venetian decline. Brantz Mayer of Baltimore was more typical in remarking of Venice, "In the spring of 1833, we passed a fortnight in this curious city of palaces, prisons, shrines, art, despotism and degradation. Amidst the solitude of her abandoned dwellings, against which the gondolas rested, unoccupied and motionless, our feelings came back with a rebound, from the grave of the old Republic to the active life and energy of our new one!"[57] Madame de Staël had been more generous to the fact of decline, in arguing that the merit of Italy was the grace with which failure was understood, history was borne, resignation was learned, death was embraced. But for most Southerners these were lessons of limited resonance before 1865. The lessons of resignation are, after all, those of the Southern Renaissance, which was to abjure the political imagination. Richard Henry Wilde was rare in his willingness to declare the United States, including the South, futilely optimistic about the human condition. His fellow Americans, his fellow Southerners, came to Rome and, though they stood in awe of the past, were more in awe of their own share in American exceptionalism. This is why American Southerners before the Civil War could not see that they shared any complicity in the imagery of a European South.

CHAPTER 5

Modernization and the Nineteenth-Century South

STUDENTS OF the South have not infrequently arrived late to historical theory about to go, or just gone, into disrepute. Modernization
theory is no exception. Southern historians have begun to flirt with it
just when it has come to seem little more than the natural successor to
Social Darwinism as a beguilingly comprehensive explanation of historical change. The "Third World" has been treated (and still is by
some) as out in the jungle of economic and social history, there await-
ing the opportunity of Lamarckian will power to join that happy few
who bellowed instructions from well-defended clearings about the
appropriate techniques for accelerating evolution. William Graham
Sumner did not doubt that the apex of evolution had been reached in
his Yale classroom and local church. We did not question that modernity was us: our kind of class structures, nation-states, democratization,
standing armies, educational systems, replacement of kinship networks with bureaucracies, our complicities of formal and informal im-
perialisms. While many of the most energetic proponents of modernization theory, such as Walt Rostow, were Americans, most of the basic
theoretical work was European. Indeed, Americans applied the theory
earlier and with more zest to societies such as Japan and Korea than
they did to themselves: it was only in 1976 that Richard D. Brown, in
Modernization: The Transformation of American Life, 1600–1865, applied
the concept systematically, and briefly, to the American historical experience. Yet the fount, European theory, never quite took account of

This essay was first published as a review essay, "The Nineteenth-Century American
South," *Historical Journal* 24 (September 1981): 751–63. Although the literature on modernization in the late Old South and early New South has grown apace since 1981, I have
thought it best to leave this essay largely untouched. Here and there I have added footnotes in square brackets.

the eccentricities of America—its lack of a sufficiently traditional society from which the graph of modernization could be plotted, its lack of aristocracy, its diffuse religion, its migratory and broken kinship networks, its belated and ambiguous centralization. It tended to be considered as a footnote to European history or as the first of the new nations, a rough blueprint for the eager "Third World," by those historians who had a taste for fitting the United States into an international pattern.[1] Most American historians, of course, the workhorses of the profession, had no such taste and were inclined to cling to the notion of American exceptionalism. Conversely, those who dabbled in European theory were least likely to have an intimate acquaintance with the raw data of American history.

Of late this unsatisfactory schizophrenia has lessened. American historiography, once practiced with a complacent and denuded Rankeanism, has become awash with Annalistes, Russian formalists, structuralists, Hegelians, Marxists both Althusserian and Thompsonian cakes and ale. What Gramsci thought to learn in the factories of Turin and the prisons of Mussolini has been transferred to the slave quarters of Louisiana. American historical writing has become as cosmopolitan as the Metropolitan Museum of Art, fascinating and yet mostly borrowed, as international as the jet that carries Harvard and Stanford illuminati to the latest conference in Rome. This bibulous intellectual interchange might be an unmixed blessing were it not for a persistent fact of the relationship between Europe and the United States. Theory has not been an American strength. As David Potter once observed, "If Americans have failed effectively to interpret their experience to people in other societies, it is in part because they have not always been able to explain it to themselves."[2] European theory, worked out in and for European conditions, has still a disproportionate prestige for American intellectuals, while American history remains an exotic irrelevance for most European theorists. The circle of intellectual influences is not closed. Harvard brings back from Paris the latest insight and applies it to Massachusetts. Paris brings back from Harvard the comforting memory of men in agreement. La Vendée and Alabama are not created equal in the birth of theory.

If the United States has been the junior partner of European theory, its Southern region has been on the distaff side of American studies. Thus dispossessed, the South has been hard to locate in the curve or curves of modernization and made to do service in a number of theoretical categories—as incompetent American democratic capitalist, as extenuated European traditional, as Third World plantation colonial. One might agree that with the New South at last triumphant, the South has arrived as a modern society, but at a moment when we no longer agree on the definition, inevitability, or permanence of "modernity." It is little wonder that new books on the South, recently sensitive to the issue, are less than unanimous in their reflections.

John McCardell's *The Idea of a Southern Nation: Southern Nationalists and Southern Nationalism, 1830–1860* is a useful starting point, not because it breaks fresh ground, but as a handy and economically written synthesis of traditional approaches to Southern nationalism, that crucial element in any theory or fact of the region's modernization. McCardell, unusual for the young scholar, who is reared to believe that historiography is institutionalized parricide, seems content that tradition needs, not correction, but summary. "So valuable has been the work of . . . students of Southern history, so thorough their research," he writes, "that a comprehensive examination of the growth of an ideology of Southern nationalism is now possible." As befits a student of David Donald, he regards that nationalism as an aberration mercifully defeated, a misreading of the genuine social unity of North and South. "It is incorrect," McCardell observes, "to think of Northerners and Southerners in 1860 as two distinct peoples. Their intellectual, political, social, and economic beliefs were generally shared and were not determined solely on sectional grounds. But one issue—slavery—gave such an ideological charge to all other questions that by 1860 America was on the verge of civil strife."[3] So slavery became a distorting mirror, turning the sectionalism of the American Revolution into the nationalism of Yancey through the catalysts of the Missouri and Nullification crises. It created the proslavery argument, the demand for and birth of a "Southern" literature, the economic analysis that falteringly sired the Southern Commercial Conventions of the 1840s and 1850s, the defection of Southern religion from national organizations, the "Southernization" of Manifest Destiny, the role of Southern nationalists themselves in secession. All this is familiar, though previously scattered in books such as William Taylor's *Cavalier and Yankee,* Donald Mathews's *Slavery and Methodism,* William Jenkins's *Proslavery Thought in the Old South,* or William Freehling's *Prelude to Civil War.*[4] McCardell makes a brief bow in the direction of Clifford Geertz's definition of ideology as a response to social, cultural, or psychological strain, a bow that, as John Higham has suggested, has become almost mandatory for American intellectual historians.[5] But in McCardell's neutral pages, this definition only serves to reinforce the older view that slavery was the entering wedge of a misperception, that it grew beyond bounds, and that the intensity of Southern nationalism was the mark of that guilty unreality. So we get a narrative conceptually indistinguishable from one that could have been written thirty years ago. Doubtless the book's narrative ambition partly explains McCardell's unwillingness to arbitrate crucial disagreements among Southern historians. He is eager to keep prose smooth, and at each moment of reliance upon historians of divergent perspective he placates and tidies, and we arrive at Fort Sumter in a more benign temper than seems plausible or necessary. It is a progression that usually mollifies, but sometimes ignores, difficulties in the historiography. Not least among these is that the energy spent upon the South's social and political history has not been matched for its intellectual history, which may explain why McCardell tends to treat the region's mind as a simple deduction from its social life. And perhaps greatest among these is that, as with most books on the South, it wishes desperately to explain the Civil War, so the Old South itself, its dynamics and character, becomes obscured by the narrative fixation upon secession and Appomattox.

The possibility that the South was a modernizing society is not considered by McCardell, which is a function of his traditionalism. Thereby he deprives himself of a useful rationale for studying the region's cultural life and of making necessary connections with the "new" social history. Without such links, studies of that cultural life will be condemned to a certain sterility. Scholars of the Old South can usefully weigh Joyce Appleby's recommendation to students of seventeenth- and eighteenth-century England that modernization theory has unduly neglected the intellectual response to modernization and that the "particular conceptual bridges men and women build to carry them into the unfamiliar territory of a radically altered future must be examined as discrete developments because there is nothing in modernization theory to account for them as parts of a process."[6]

Curiously, a clearer lead is given, even for the intellectual historian, in Mills Thornton's *Politics and Power in a Slave Society: Alabama, 1800–1860*. Here the Civil War is regarded as accident rather than substance. The details of state politics are ruthlessly to the fore and considered, not as handy illustrations of Southern or national affairs, but for their own sake, a sake that happens to aid in understanding secession. "To comprehend why," Thornton writes, "when a stone is thrown into a pond, there is a splash, it is necessary to understand the nature of stone, but it is equally necessary to know something about water."[7] And what was the quality of Alabama water, ruffled by the stones of the Kansas-Nebraska Act and the election of Lincoln? Muddy and turbulent.

The contention that slavery was at the root of Alabama politics will surprise no one. The claim that those politics were thoroughly Jacksonian in rhetoric and practice will startle a few, reared on quasi-feudal theories of Southern political life, though it should not. Evidence has been abundant for several years that the Old South underwent the same democratization that marked Northern society, and has recently been reinforced by William Cooper's *The South and the Politics of Slavery, 1828–1856*.[8] Both Cooper and Thornton have helped to resolve a schizophrenia in which slavery and Jacksonianism have been kept discrete. Students of Jacksonianism and the "common man," such as Fletcher Green and Frank Owsley, have sloughed off the matter of slavery as a cuckoo in the nest of a yeoman Southern society, a bird destined to tumble out. Scholars of slavery, such as Eugene Genovese, have assumed without stooping to proof that the slaveholding elite (itself an extensive body, as Otto Olsen has shown) controlled Southern society. George Fredrickson has made a useful stab at resolving the contradiction by characterizing the Old South as a *Herrenvolk* democracy, but Thornton is the first historian to provide a satisfactory explanation of the vital connection where it most matters, by documenting the day-by-day, election-by-election pressure of a functioning democracy in a slave society.[9]

Thornton argues that Alabama politics, popular and Jacksonian, were imbued with the republican ideology of fearing enslavement by a centralizing tyranny. If here Thornton sounds like the Bernard Bailyn of the Black Belt, the implication is not unjust and would not be resisted. Much interesting work upon early nineteenth-century America has of late been mining Bailyn's insight into the Revolution.[10] That Alabamians should have seen an embodiment of tyranny in the Republican party and the free-soil movement, which challenged their right to export their slave version of American republican democracy to the West, or that the North posed the challenge of a modernization that agitated the quintessential Jacksonian fear, the extinction of individual social autonomy, are not entirely novel insights. What is novel and striking is Thornton's suggestion that the pressure of modernization came not only from the North but from within Alabamian society, was posed not merely by Northerner upon Southerner but by Alabamian. "The boom in cotton prices during this decade [the 1850s]," Thornton explains, "generated investment capital, permitting the construction of a rail network. Areas of the State previously isolated began to move into the market economy. The banking system, essentially abolished during the depression [of the late 1830s], was re-created. Cities grew rapidly, and a portion of the electorate, dazzled by the new prosperity, began to vote for candidates who advocated aggressive governmental programs to develop the economy and to assist the citizenry. Government at all levels became much more active; its expenditures increased enormously. A statewide public school system was created. Control of the political mechanism began slipping away from the hands of poorer citizens, as the influence of great planters in the state's political life assumed significance for the first time. These events, refracted through the remaining elements of the state's political ideology, assumed a profoundly menacing appearance and this intensified the fears which had been the raw material of Alabama politics from the earliest days."[11] These fears the Southern Rights movement, led by William Yancey, exploited. Secession became a flight not merely from ominously modernizing Notherners but from the confusions of a changing Alabama as well.

This is an ingenious and satisfying argument, rich in implications not only for antebellum and Civil War historiography but also for Reconstruction, for it helps to locate some of the roots of Reconstruction legislation in the 1850s.[12] The ingenuity can be gauged from its reconciliation of historiographical viewpoints previously deemed defiantly at odds: Owsley's common man, Bailyn's revolutionary ideology, and, not least, David Donald's contention that the pell-mell growth of American society combined with an "excess of democracy" to create the conditions for civil strife.[13] Equally it gives flesh to the bare hint in Richard Brown's book that the "growing tension between the eager modernization of the North and the incomplete, reluctant modernization of the South was influential both in bringing on the war and in determining its outcome" and makes less puzzling the clear evidence, adduced by Raimondo Luraghi and Emory Thomas, that the Confederacy managed a modern war with remarkable thoroughness and little ideological discomfort.[14]

The main difficulty with Thornton's case lies not with Alabama. Here he has been thorough to the point of redundancy, as though conscious that only by bludgeoning his reader into submission can he make so unorthodox an interpretation successful. But he suggests that Alabama may be said to stand for the South, thus yielding to that old and almost honorable weakness of the state historian, the guilty feeling that state politics are not quite enough. It almost always comes in the dying paragraphs of such histories, and one would have hoped that Thornton, usually sensible and properly aggressive at the volume's opening about the greater significance of state over national politics in the early nineteenth century, would have resisted temptation. Here one is skeptical. Not all Southern states participated so richly in the boom of the 1850s to generate the investment capital, whose use was so beguilingly menacing to Alabamians. Not all Southern states, least of all South Carolina, secession's catalyst, participated so thoroughly in the Jacksonian revolution, though all were heirs of the Revolution's republican ideology. Not all Southern Rights leaders were young men seeking a place in the political sun. In short, not all Southern states made so abrupt a transition from a decentralized Jacksonian political economy to a modernizing one, nor were all so unused to having great planters, booted and spurred in the manner of George Fitzhugh's daydream, in the saddle. And the tension of that abruptness is so crucial to Thornton's case, so lovingly demonstrated by statistics of suicides, murders, and divorces, that its softening elsewhere in the region casts serious doubt upon the extendability of his thesis.[15] Nonetheless, the synthesis he suggests has profound implications for the study of antebellum Southern society; not the least of its virtues is that it allows social, political, and intellectual historians common ground on which to jostle.

To turn from Thornton's book to Kenneth Stampp's essays in *The Imperiled Union* is to move into a different moral world. Thornton is a Southern conservative of the younger generation, Stampp a Northern liberal of the older, though both, even as they might disagree about the merits of democracy, are proponents of the republican tradition. Now that David Potter is dead (and the posthumous publication in 1976 of Potter's *The Impending Crisis* is a reminder of the depth of that loss), Stampp is the senior student of the Civil War: soundly in the tradition of American liberal nationalists, unwilling to enter into full sympathy with the dilemmas of the South and its peculiar institution (and nothing has marked recent historiography more than the willingness to take seriously evidence from Southern sources, previously deemed irremediably tainted), sanguine about the merits of the Union and its preservers, possessed of a vision that still radiates from the Whiggery of Abraham Lincoln, conscious of detractions from that position but robustly capable of response. Only such a figure could have written the first and most useful essay in this collection, "The Concept of a Perpetual Union," to outline the notion's tentativeness in 1787 and ambiguity in the controversies of the early nineteenth century, the early strength of the secession argument, the lateness of an adequate defense of the federation's perpetuity. One says only such a figure because this essay is haunted by the moral responsibility of the war and the old question whether the Union had the right to insist upon survival at the price of such havoc, and recent scholarship has shown itself uninterested in the moral rationale of the Union, even as it has been engrossed by the reprehensibility of aspects of American society. Such an engrossment, exemplified in works like Eugene Berwanger's *Frontier Against Slavery,* Leon Litwack's *North of Slavery,* and George Fredrickson's *Black Image in the White Mind,* has, as Stampp admits, destroyed the Republican party's "pristine image as the political arm of the northern crusade against slavery and racial injustice." But one cannot but be impressed by Stampp's essay "Race, Slavery and the Republican Party," which insists with cogency that northern Republicanism, from whatever motives, was more moderate in its racism than the Democratic party of Stephen Douglas, a small comfort for blacks but crucial in the context of mid-nineteenth-century politics. Equally useful are Stampp's reflections upon that econometric dodo, *Time on the Cross.* Less interesting, almost a curiosity, is his attempt to enter that most ancient of Civil War controversies, the repressibility or irrepressibility of the conflict, which had mercifully faded from view as a teleological circumlocution. The essay hazards a first-rate discussion of the historiography of Civil War causation, no mean feat, since so many others have done it, before it launches into a variant of what Stampp has dubbed the "slavery-cultural interpretation," deployed to demonstrate irrepressibility. To reach that dull conclusion, Stampp does contrive an interesting and novel gambit. It was crucial to the argument of historians such as Charles W. Ramsdell that the "excesses" of abolitionism unnecessarily created the sectional conflict. Stampp neatly turns the argument around by asking, not that abolitionism should have been softened, but what Southerners would have had to do about slavery to ensure an atmosphere of sufficient political tranquillity within the Union. They would, in his opinion, have had to avoid aggressive proslavery positions, adopt reforms of slavery, accept a federal policy of excluding slavery from the territories, and open the peculiar institution to criticism and proposals of gradual manumission. Since none of this happened, or logically could have happened, Stampp concludes upon the irrepressibility of the war. In so doing, for reasons (I hope) of rhetorical symmetry, he uses language about Southerners as intemperate as that of a Ramsdell or an Owsley upon abolitionists. He writes of the "reckless Southern agitation of the slavery expansion issue," speaks with horror of their encroachments upon freedom of speech, the right of petition to Congress, and, almost most heinous, their violations of the U.S. mails.[16]

Stampp's essays imply that there are certain problems a historian is condemned to explain, that no American historian may be said to have earned his laurels until he has hazarded the Civil War, just as the French historian has the French Revolution, and the classical actor, *Hamlet*. Perhaps the reader may be forgiven for chanting the familiar lines of standard historiographical soliloquies as the historian declaims them and be content that the occasional word has a different emphasis. What is implicit for Stampp is explicit in the collected essays of Eric Foner, *Politics and Ideology in the Age of the Civil War*. Foner's work is distinguished by an attempt to keep in balance the new findings of social historians, both European and American, with the older questions of sectional conflict. He seems dissatisfied with the older historiography of the Civil War, yet he is discontented with a new social history that deals in units of historical analysis—the family, ethnic groups, childhood—that are difficult to mobilize in the service of questions like Why was there a Civil War? In modernization Foner finds a useful analytical link, while being aware of the term's imprecision. The Democratic party, he suggests, might be viewed as the representative of two premodern groups, the immigrant Irish and the white South. But among those groups associated with the Republican party that came closest to an ideology of modernity Foner finds great ambiguity. Indeed, it appears easier to locate modernization than to pinpoint modernizers. The abolitionists, although promoting models of internalized self-discipline fit for an industrial society, also obscured the necessity for industrial reform by concentrating upon slavery, not as a social crime, but as the aggregate of individual slaveholders' transgressions against morality. And Northern labor leaders, initially opposed to abolitionism as a distraction, latterly supported the free-soil movement as the reservator of the frontier's safety valve, as, indeed, an escape route from modernization. Foner shrewdly observes, "Lincoln's Union was one of self-made men. . . . If modernization means the growth of large-scale industry, large cities, and the leviathan state, northerners were no more fighting to create it than were southerners." Thus the Civil War becomes an irony, because each side "fought to defend a distinct vision of the good society, but each vision was destroyed by the very struggle to preserve it."[17] For, as Foner sees it, modernization, though implicit in antebellum Northern development, was immensely accelerated by the war itself.

But Foner and Stampp tend to accept Genovese's characterization of the Old South as premodern, ruled by a planting elite opposed to and appalled by the evident modernization of the North and needing secession to evade a modernity that would crush them. But Thornton's analysis, if it proves true not only of Alabama but also of the South, demonstrates that modernization was not something that started north of the Potomac and was only permitted South by the failure of the Confederacy and the abolition of slavery. It was present in the Old South and generated the same tense ambivalence that Foner has documented in the North. If so, we glimpse an irony even more savage. It may be that if modernization was a fear of both sections, the origins of the war lie partly in each projecting the dark ground of their trepidations about themselves on to the other, and fighting at Gettysburg private demons in the reassuringly tangible form of a palpable enemy.

Such a suggestion has, of course, formidable difficulties. The potential of the slave economy to evolve into an industrial society has usually been denied, dogmatically by Genovese on the ground that slavery is inherently premodern, more persuasively by Gavin Wright with the contention that the cotton economy did not in the long run generate enough investment capital to make "takeoff" possible.[18] Yet evidence has long been abundant that planters often invested in factories and that slavery did not seem incompatible with manufacturing. Urban life did loosen the shackles of the institution, but many seemed willing to pay that price to reap profits. Immanuel Wallerstein has argued that slavery cannot be regarded as an anomaly in a capitalist system, a point that the Southern planter Frederick Porcher asserted before the Civil War: "When the labouring class is a body of slaves, and only so much capital, its destiny depends upon the decision of the Capitalist."[19] But the suggestion does not, strictly speaking, require that full modernization (whatever that may be) was possible within a slave society, merely that there should have been enough evidence to persuade contemporaries that it might be. It is well to remember that, outside the North and Britain, the South had the fastest rate of urbanization and industrialization of any "Western" society.

The best answer to the question, What might have happened to the Old South? is, after all, what did happen. It is an answer too often neglected in the eagerness to keep Old South and New discontinuous. War is usually regarded as an aberration by American historians, the fratricidal war especially. Yet if we accept the irrepressibility of the Civil War, there is small reason for regarding the social changes created by the conflict as bearing other than an organic relationship to the society that entered the struggle. If secession was a desperate gamble not merely to keep the North at bay but to hold off change within the South itself, we should not be surprised that change came anyway. The Old South was truly a parent of the New, however unwillingly, the more so for begetting from need and not desire. The Civil War is intrinsic to Southern social development, not extrinsic.

Reconstruction, of course, played a vital part in Charles Beard's case for the Civil War era as a modernizing Second American Revolution, a contention long since abandoned. It is ironic that, with the issue of modernization reemergent in recent writing, Reconstruction should have come to seem weak and ineffective. Black history, for one thing, once intoxicated by the commitment to equality in what C. Vann Woodward called the Second Reconstruction, has taken on a Burger Court gloom. The civil-rights movement has come to seem, not blacks' definitive leap to parity, but only another useful but limited move in their old search for a place in the American sun. One is startled by a sense of déjà vu. Did not Ralph Abernethy, endorsing Ronald Reagan in Detroit in 1980, sound like Booker T. Washington treating circumspectly with the triumphant white South in Atlanta in 1895? Has not the cadaverous Strom Thurmond, restored to power as chairman of the Senate Judiciary Committee, talked of repealing the 1965 Voting Rights Act?[20] In such a context, Reconstruction historiography has become, in William Gillette's unimaginative phrase, "post-revisionist." "Post-revisionism does not reject revisionism," he explains in his *Retreat from Reconstruction*, "it is certainly not reactionary in the sense of returning to the undeserved abuse and prejudicial condemnation that characterized the views of the Dunningite historians. However, post-revisionism does seek to replace the tendency of certain neo-revisionist historians to overestimate the accomplishments of Reconstruction and provide apologies for its shortcomings; thus the post-revisionist approach attempts to provide a fresh view with which to analyse the limits of legislation and the manifest failure of Reconstruction."[21] Bagehot, I think, said it better in 1857: "It is the day after the feast. We do not care for its delicacies; we are rather angry at its profusion; we are cross to hear it praised."[22] The new historians of Reconstruction are very cross.

It is symptomatic that attention has switched from the fleeting egalitarian moments of the late 1860s, and we now have, for the first time, a systematic account of the Grant administration's Reconstruction policy, to repair an omission scandalous but significant when one remembers that Grant presided over two-thirds of that episode's course. Gillette presents, with mournful enthusiasm, a sorry tale of broken promises, petty cronyism, indifference, abrupt lurches of policy. Most clear is that Grant, whatever tactics he adopted, was doomed to preside over the liquidation of Reconstruction. Most striking is the level of political violence in the Reconstruction South, of government upon government, of citizen upon citizen, of white upon black.[23] If there is merit in seeing the South as a colonial regime, this is when its politics were most those of a banana republic. If ever the coup d'état flourished in the United States, it was during Reconstruction.

In Alabama in 1872, for example, the Democrats lost the governorship, while retaining both houses of the legislature. Republicans charged fraud and, with the connivance of federal judges, jailed several Democratic congressmen, whom Washington released reluctantly. So the Republicans organized their own legislature in the federal courthouse, while the Democrats held the statehouse, and federal troops were stationed warily between them. The new Republican governor, David P. Lewis, ungratefully repudiated the Democratic legislature that had ratified his election and recognized the rival Republican assembly. Grant, having troops, dictated that the Republican legislature would be accepted by Washington unless the Democrats expelled enough of their own party to ensure Republican control of the lower house. To add insult to injury, the Republicans even managed to wrest control of the state senate, a coup that preserved Republican control of Alabama for an extra two years.

In Louisiana in 1872 violence was used to decide the rivalry of Republican factions, when Grant deployed the advantage of 150 soldiers and two Gatling guns. In the same year the president generously provided a federal cutter, amply supplied with cigars and champagne, to detain fourteen senators upon the Mississippi River and prevent a quorum favorable to Grant's Republican opponents. Again rival legislatures appeared, one encamped in the agreeable surroundings of the bar of the Gem Saloon, and throughout 1873 rival Republicans fought each other violently throughout the state. In 1874 the struggle shifted to that between Republicans and Democrats. In September the White Leaguers, a paramilitary cadre of Democratic persuasion, attacked New Orleans with eight thousand men; seized the city hall, the statehouse, the arsenals, and the police stations; cut the telegraph wires; and barricaded the streets, at the loss of thirty-two lives and seventy-nine wounded. Grant sent five thousand troops and three gunboats to crush the rebellion.

In Arkansas in 1874 the Democratic and Liberal Republican claimant of the governorship, Joseph Brooks, seized the armory, the state-house, and the governor's office in Little Rock. The state saw a minor civil war between rival militia before the coup proved successful, with Grant's acquiescence. Reconstruction was the continuation of Civil War by other means; it was also, it seems, the continuation by the same means. In this context, the settlement of the disputed presidential election of 1876 by peaceful, if disreputable, negotiation was the ending of Reconstruction with a whimper and not a bang.

It cannot be said that Gillette's study, though it is detailed, useful, and truculent, helps much in assessing the social purpose and consequences of Reconstruction. Save in some recent writing upon the history of blacks, society has taken a second place to the chronicle of political shenanigans, which are the burden of the essays in *Reconstruction and Redemption in the South,* a recent and convenient symposium about events in Florida, Alabama, Mississippi, Virginia, North Carolina, and Louisiana. Much more helpful are Jonathan Wiener's *Social Origins of the New South: Alabama, 1860–1885* and Dwight Billings's *Planters and the Making of a "New South": Class, Politics, and Development in North Carolina, 1865–1900.*

If recent historical literature has slighted the matter of racial and social equality, that is not a tendency in which Weiner acquiesces. His book, whose title echoes that of C. Vann Woodward's *Origins of the New South* with a conscious challenge, makes social oppression central to Southern history. Wiener's Alabama is launched upon a "Prussian Road" to industrial modernity, a road sponsored by a conservative agrarian elite, in the interests of their survival at the price of repression. "Reconstruction," Wiener writes, "was the culmination of a bourgeois revolution, a life-or-death struggle over the nature and extent of the nation's transition to modern society. In this conflict, northeastern businessmen formed an alliance with urban workers and small farmers in the Northwest, against southern planters; the victory of this bourgeois coalition destroyed the national power of the planter class and thereby abolished the principal obstacle to democratic capitalist development. In so doing they ruled out the possibility that the nation would take what Barrington Moore has called the 'Prussian Road' to modern society, based on a coalition of northern industrialists with southern planters, against small farmers, urban workers and slaves, in a society which developed by preserving and intensifying the authoritarian and repressive elements of traditional social relations."[24] As for the South, things were, it seems, Teutonically otherwise. At least they might have been. In fact, Wiener's book is not about the South at all, not even about Alabama, but mostly about the Black Belt of Alabama. In this he is using synecdoche in a way as traditional in Southern historiography as it is absurd.

Several propositions are crucial to Wiener's case. The planter elite, he claims, survived the war diminished but intact, still in control of Alabama society and politics, but with a new relationship to the "social relations of production." The abolition of slavery posed a new problem of the social control of labor, both black and white. For whites, the solution was sharecropping. With the rise of tenancy, however, came the economic challenge of the merchant, "who tried to use the crop lien to gain control of plantation agriculture." By discriminatory legislation, planters succeeded in confining merchants to the hill country, away from the Black Belt. So planters necessarily became planter-merchants, and merchants became merchant-landlords. The greatest challenge, however, was the iron, steel, and coal city of Birmingham, the New South's most conspicuous industrial achievement. According to Wiener, this innovation was moderated and disciplined by the planter regime to make Birmingham not a challenge but an adjunct. Squeezed between planters who restricted corporation law, hindered local aid to industry, and reduced the social mobility of black and white labor and Northern steel manufacturers who feared competition, Birmingham behaved itself, especially when populism made a planter-industrialist coalition necessary. There was, Wiener concedes, a genuine ideological challenge in the New South creed, but the mythological Old South, so integral a part of that creed, was a sign of weakness on the part of the new bourgeoisie, a necessary concession to the still powerful planter regime. "By accommodating their position to the Old South myth," Wiener writes, "the New South ideologists lost a crucial battle in their attempt to win hegemony for their view of society, and betrayed their own class interests." [25]

This could be viewed as a healthy step towards placing Southern history into comparative perspective. As a piece of comparative history, however, it is most disappointing. For a book whose avowed contribution is the South's presence upon a "Prussian Road," it is startling that not a single reference to Prussian or German history can be found in its pages. Wiener relies upon Barrington Moore's *Social Origins of Dictatorship and Democracy* with touching fidelity, yet Moore makes only passing reference to Prussia and is there, by his own admission, most derivative from (though Wiener says nothing of this) Max Weber's early essays upon German social structure. It was perhaps a prudent omission on Wiener's part. The real Prussian road looks rather different from Alabama: the state inherited from pre-industrial times a tradition of intervention in the economy and continued that tradition at the moment of industrialization; the banks, as well as the state, were crucial sponsors of social and economic change, in distinction to the English experience of individual entrepreneurship; the Junkers were an aristocracy, demanding and receiving class deference and heirs to a military tradition, itself hierarchical; Prussia retained an explicitly undemocratic political structure; the bourgeoisie were slow to make political claims upon the state, in exchange for the material benefits of industrial profits; Bismarck, to preserve real power, made provision for a system of social welfare to retain the loyalty of the new working classes. None of these conditions is true of Alabama, and none can be deducted from the Prussian analogy without rendering it absurd. Alabama inherited an essentially laissez-faire political economy; the banks played no special role in its industrialization; the planters were no aristocracy, nor did they receive much deference beyond the prerogatives of wealth; Alabama had a democratic political system, notably in theory if less perfectly in practice; the bourgeoisie had no reluctance about making their political presence felt; the "Bourbon" regime developed no system of social welfare, and indeed, it reduced the scale of government activity. As Prussians, Alabamians cut a sorry figure.

Wiener takes no account of Thornton's book on antebellum Alabama, which must now stand as the most significant account of that entity. He does note that *Politics and Power in a Slave Society* "appeared too late to be included in this study," which is curious. Thornton's book has been available as a Yale dissertation since 1974, and other scholars, notably Michael Holt and William Cooper, have used it. Certainly the two books bear almost no relationship to one another: Thornton's Jacksonian Alabama, whose politics were "swept constantly by gales of extraordinary fury,"[26] abruptly disappears in Wiener's tidily dialectical Alabama, and the distinction is more than chronological. It is Wiener's estimate of the power of state government that most marks him from Thornton. While there is little reason to doubt the social repression of Black Belt planters, it is improbable that they or the state government, through which they exercised their power, had the ability to arrange matters with such precision. Wiener's book is an excellent example of that recent American historiography that borrows European theory without sensitivity to either the origins of the theory or the context into which it must be applied. It is clothing with the label ripped out, picked up at a garage sale.

Dwight Billings's volume on North Carolina is otherwise, written in a spirit less dogmatic and with a range of reference wider and more persuasive, although he, too, poses a challenge to Woodward's interpretation of the New South as a discontinuity from the Old, a society industrially transformed by a new middle class. Billings argues that antebellum North Carolina had begun a serious movement towards industrialization, that there seemed no contradiction between a slave society and modest industry, that postbellum development of cotton mills was an extrapolation from that prewar experience and was chiefly sponsored by planter families who fashioned a conservative modernization in which traditional social controls of both black and white labor were maintained. The only industry significantly created by a new bourgeoisie was that of tobacco, a by no means small exception. Partly, Billings draws upon theorists such as Immanuel Wallerstein and Barrington Moore, though he has bothered to read German history, so that he can highlight the dissimilarities of Prussian and North Carolinian experience. By this admixture, Billings defines North Carolina, not as simply a colonial economy (which was Woodward's tendency), but as "an economically peripheral region within the American economy"—like the colonial economies of the "Third World" but with considerably greater financial resources and options.[27] Most of the cotton mills, he establishes, were financed by Southern, and not Northern, capital. Unlike Wiener, Billings extends his analysis substantially to include the Populist revolt of the 1890s, an extension indispensable if Woodward is to be systematically refuted. Populism in North Carolina, as Billings sees it, was a revolt not of the poor and illiterate but of the lesser landed in disagreement with the conservative modernization of those whose power rested doubly upon land and factory. Thus the Republican-Populist fusion of the 1890s was a serious challenge to the conservatives, but the "progressive" triumph of Charles B. Aycock in 1900 was not so much a middle-class assertion as a reestablishment of conservative power, with a weak middle class striking a Prussian deal. The reforms of that progressive regime, in education, in social welfare, in the construction of a highway system, were a genuinely Bismarckian bargain, reforms that modified the techniques of social control, while not surrendering the substance of economic and political power. If this thesis sounds familiar to readers of Wilbur Cash, that is not a coincidence. Cash based his thesis solidly upon knowledge of Piedmont North Carolina, even as he grotesquely overgeneralized from that experience to the rest of the South. Moreover, those who would refute Woodward, the most important proponent of discontinuity in Southern history, have often been obliged to speak kindly of Cash, the advocate of continuity. Here Billings is modestly persuasive, mostly by the quantitative evidence that demonstrates planter involvement in industry, partly by politely indicating that much of Woodward's case rested on shaky and impressionistic evidence.

Billings offers a sensible, literate, and fruitful approach to the social problem of continuity. His modesty of tone is refreshing after Wiener's aggressive and complacent dogmatism, which leads the reader to feel that dissent might be construed as moral turpitude.[28] Billings has perhaps the lesser talents, but his tidiness and economy of line have the greater effect. Yet both usefully intimate the same strategic decision that informs the essays of Eric Foner: we have taken the Civil War too seriously as a divide, and the bridge across the psychological chasm of Appomattox may rest upon the uncertain timbers of modernization theory. Much remains undone, not only for Southern history in the nineteenth century but for modernization theory itself, which is best used, not as a way to document how societies approximate to or deviate from a Platonic form laid up in the file cabinets of the Rand Corporation, but as an approach to the varieties of modernity, of which none are conceptually definitive. It would be appropriate that the American South, one of the Industrial Revolution's most important stepchildren, should make a contribution to the latter task through its historians. Too often we have been content to provide—using appropriately for a Southern theme the slogan of a lost cause—an echo, not a choice.

PART II · NEW SOUTH

CHAPTER 6

The Middle Years: Edwin Mims

THERE IS A large hole in the middle of Southern intellectual history. The span between Appomattox and the Southern Renaissance is the most uninviting of Southern moments, drab, impoverished, obscure, unprescient. What is to be done with these years? The convinced aesthete has an easy answer. These Southern intellectuals and writers must be ignored as beneath notice, as miserable specimens of thinking men. This culture affords no poetry, no novels, no criticism, no historical narrative, nothing that a cultured man need have upon his shelves, unless he is eccentric or chauvinist. If you define Mark Twain as outside Southern literature proper (a matter disputed), little is left but a novel or two of George Washington Cable, the occasional short story if you have the stomach for dialect. No one is taken aside anymore by enthusiasts and told to read Thomas Nelson Page, populist polemic, local-color sentiment, and patriotic verse.

The historian is supposed to be above (or below) such considerations, being mandated to scrutinize reality, not judge worth. Yet the intellectual historian is a bastard kind of historian, with some stake in canons of literary criticism that cling quaintly to the issue of standards. With the Old South, he can investigate with the feeling that with so little known, much is to be discovered. With the Southern Renaissance, much has already been encouragingly defined. But these middle years are a problem. They can be studied as years of persistence, wherein the mind of the Old South staggered past 1865, mutated, and dwindled into nostalgia. They can be viewed as years of incipience, wherein foundations were laid for the coming glory of William Faulk-

Some of this essay was published as "Edwin Mims: An Aspect of the Mind of the New South Considered," *South Atlantic Quarterly* 73 (Spring 1974):199–212; ibid. 73 (Summer 1974):324–34. But it has been entirely rewritten and expanded.

ner, not the light, but bearing witness to the light. Few are interested
in these years for their own sake. Even when they are so studied, a
tone of reproach is usually audible. The New South is dismissed for a
mythic gerrymander, the Lost Cause is deprecated as a misguided civil
religion, the vitality of Populism is mourned, the grim narrative of racism is given.[1] It is all profoundly uninviting.

Part of the difficulty is that these were peculiarly the ascendant
years of the Southern bourgeoisie. That middle class saw itself as the
solution to the problem of Southern history, whereas it is now more
often viewed as part of the problem. As crucially, that bourgeoisie
offered "non-Southern" solutions, spoke in "non-Southern" accents,
retailed "non-Southern" models. It is testament to the strength of the
Romantic tradition of cultural nationalism, which was to be powerfully restated by the Southern Agrarians in 1930, that many have been
inclined to dismiss the New South intelligentsia as inherently weaker,
because apparently less indigenous.

There are great disputes among Southern historians about the issue
of social continuity or discontinuity across the gulf of the Civil War.
The intellectual historian is interested in the outcome of this debate,
but not as interested as the social or political historian. It has been a
rational venture to study the persistence of the planter class, but no
one would as rationally study the persistence of antebellum intellectuals as a class, however instructive the individual postwar careers of
men such as Robert L. Dabney. An intelligentsia stands a little aside
from the ordinary processes of social change. It is not quite a social
class, not even an interest group. Its members are self-nominated.
They inherit no property and transmit none. They are not obliged to
agree, are (if anything) obliged to disagree. Though we speak, and
with justice, of the inheritance of ideas and of intellectual networks,
these are metaphors, compared to the "hard" facts of economic life.
Intelligentsias are always newborn, just as they always have to define
their relationship to their predecessors. It is no accident that intellectual historians have found resonant the concept of generations, for its
delicate compounding of continuity and discontinuity.[2] Hence the intellectual wing of the Southern bourgeoisie, though often consisting
of the new men portrayed in C. Vann Woodward's analysis, was compelled into a sense of continuity that both embraced a redefined version of the Old South and articulated a vision of continuity with industrial society outside the region.

Edwin Mims is a useful case study, though it is a measure of the
neglect of his generation that he is forgotten, yet one of the leading

intellectuals of his time in the South. He offers an unusually sharp metaphor of the problem of continuity and change in Southern thought. Born when Grant was in the White House, he died worrying whether John Kennedy was too young to run for the presidency.[3] He survived to tell how the Victorian South felt in its heyday and how it felt when gone and a Victorian was obliged to live with the social change he had spent his youth demanding. He was present at many significant moments: the educational movement, the creation of a distinctive tradition of Southern literary criticism, the Bassett affair over academic freedom at Trinity College, the discussion over Southern culture both before and after the First World War, the development of the Fugitives and Agrarians, the evolution of a liberal theology in the Methodist church.

He is not the most attractive of figures, despised by men (such as Allen Tate and Robert Penn Warren) whose opinions one should not take lightly. His was a shrill voice, snobbish, naïve, sometimes lazy, racist, intensely moral and tending to priggishness, vain, never quite incisive but sometimes shrewd: a voice eager to please his audience, always looking over his shoulder to see what the world was thinking of him; but a voice, for all that, humane, anxious to understand and develop, tolerant by the lights of his time, place, and class. It was a voice strongest and most attractive when he was young and finding his way in the world, weakest and most complacent in late middle and old age.

He was born in 1872 in the small Arkansas village of Richmond, near Texarkana. It has since vanished from the map. His father, Andrew Jackson Mims, was a traveling salesman, moderately comfortable by the impoverished standards of the Reconstruction South. He sent his eldest son to a small but good preparatory school in Tennessee, the Webb School at Bell Buckle, and then at heavier financial sacrifice to Vanderbilt University in 1888. Mims worked hard and decided, after a little confusion at graduation, upon an academic career. He spent two years of graduate work on English history and literature at Vanderbilt before accepting the professorship of English literature at Trinity College, another small Methodist institution, in Durham, North Carolina. After his hurried arrival there in the spring of 1894, he was to stay for fifteen years, with only a brief sabbatical to do graduate work at Cornell University in 1896 and 1897, at a time when Trinity was in the forefront of educational change in the region. With John Spencer Bassett he helped to found the *South Atlantic Quarterly* and succeeded the historian as its editor in 1905. During these years he began to write extensively, for the *Quarterly* chiefly, on Southern culture and literature. In 1905 he published a biography of Sidney Lanier for the American Men of Letters series, published under the Boston imprint of Houghton, Mifflin, a series little given to recognition of Southern writers. Well received, this helped to establish Mims as one of the leading literary critics in the region, second only to William P. Trent. He was asked to edit the eighth volume, that on fiction, for *The South in the Building of the Nation,* as well as to write for other volumes in the set. Agreeable temptations came his way. He was discreetly offered the editorship of the *Sewanee Review* in 1908, and the University of North Carolina wooed him away from Trinity in 1909. He assented, on condition that first he be allowed to travel for a year in Europe. This served as prelude to a persistent request from his old university, Vanderbilt, that he return. In 1912 he did go back to Nashville, there to remain the permanent head of the English department, a benign dictator to some, an incubus to others.

For more than a decade he was absorbed in university affairs, until the excitement of the Scopes Trial led him to publish *The Advancing South: Stories of Progress and Reaction* in 1926. This brought an unexpected national celebrity, calls for lectures, visiting professorships, and the impulse to write a wider study, *Adventurous America: A Study of Contemporary Life and Thought.* This book was, moreover, a response to the younger men of his own department, the Fugitive poets, latterly evolving into the Southern Agrarians, men whom he had brought into the Vanderbilt department and with whom he had a complicated and tense relationship. In 1935 he traveled to Great Britain as a Carnegie Exchange Professor, and in the summer of 1936 he went on to visit Hitler's Germany and Stalin's Soviet Union. He retired in 1942 but continued his peripatetic lecturing, put together volumes of criticism on poetry and literature, and became his university's historian. In 1959 he died, aged eighty-seven.[4]

It will be useful to examine various phases of Mims's life and thought: his basic beliefs and assessment of the culture he had inherited and wished to change; his engagement in social reform; his reaction to his successors, especially the Fugitives and Agrarians.

His religion is an appropriate starting point. As a child, he was reared in a resolutely orthodox Methodist home. The Webb School, Vanderbilt, and Trinity College were all Methodist, places where ecclesiastics taught and administered, and the chapel bell was the most characteristic sound of the campus.[5] At Trinity, revival meetings were sponsored and encouraged by the president, just as later Mims was to organize revivals at Vanderbilt and superintend undergraduates who had signed cards denoting their salvation.[6] He was an occasional lay preacher and Sunday school teacher. His faith was deep, though not fundamentalist, when the Fundamentals had been defined. Such faith was supposed to be puritanical, in that he adhered to the old teaching not to drink, smoke, play cards, or dance. His public image was of frock-coated severity, and he belonged to that more restrained urban elite of the Methodist Episcopal church, South, who sought God in books as much as in the communal emotion of the country revival.[7] This was a style, mediating between private puritanism and public tolerance, that the moderate literati of the Scottish Enlightenment had long since established, though now the mediation lay, not between Knox's Presbyterianism and Hume's skepticism, but between evangelicalism and a Darwinist America.[8] Mims self-consciously associated himself with the new liberal theology of Northerners such as Phillips Brooks and Lyman Abbott. The Higher Criticism of the Bible was acceptable, religion was required to accommodate itself to a more complex and irreligious America, and evolution was countenanced. Mims was given to asserting that the Bible was, after all, only a book among books, albeit the most sublime. This liberalism, comparatively unusual in the South of the 1890s, had been encouraged in the young Mims by John Maurice Webb, the main influence upon him at preparatory school. Webb was, by all accounts including Mims's own, a gentle, tolerant, and literate man who was interested in the problems of evolution and theology at a time, the 1880s, when the issue still slumbered in Southern churches.[9]

When Mims left Vanderbilt in the spring of 1894, there was no intensity in his religious belief. Though it was part of his intellectual baggage, he paid little attention. Bored by illiterate preaching and Little Rock church members who upbraided him on the scandalous influence of Shakespeare, he noted, "I don't expect to go to church much this year."[10] Trinity College changed this decisively. The immediate influence was John Carlisle Kilgo, a former colporteur, who became the college's new president soon after Mims's own arrival. His preaching galvanized the rather sleepy faculty and students. "He has won all our hearts and will make Trinity a great institution," Mims observed.[11]

Kilgo's particular crusade was "Christian education," an evangelical attempt to preserve and increase the role of religious establishments in education. Abominating secular institutions, such as the nearby University of North Carolina, he mounted a campaign to deny funds to

Chapel Hill. By adroit politics, he contrived to hold down appropriations to state colleges. In the turmoil of North Carolina's Populist-
Republican revolt, he promised to support white supremacy and
Democratic candidates in exchange for his influence as a Republican
and a curtailing of Chapel Hill's expansion. Thus the years of Mims's
academic apprenticeship were spent among the loud clamor of religious polemic, exchanged in lecture, sermon, and pamphlet between
Durham and the University of North Carolina. In this he joined, with
the occasional twinge of doubt when he recalled John Webb's more
tolerant philosophy. But he joined, and the enthusiasm of the moment
was captivating. He concluded at the end of Kilgo's first year that it
had been "the greatest year of my life" for spirituality. "I have learned
to revel in the great spiritual thought of the poets, and then I have
paid more than usual attention to the Bible and Phillips Brooks, Far-
rar, etc., especially the life and character of Christ." [12]

Kilgo added little to the intellectual structure of Mims's religion,
but he contributed decisively to its emotional impetus. When Mims
went north to Cornell University and an atmosphere more secular, he
instinctively used morality as a standard of judgment in literature. At
the end of his year in Ithaca, he wrote of Kilgo: "Oh, but he's had a
great influence over me. I am profoundly grateful that I was under his
influence before I came to a place like this. I wouldn't have loved the
Church as I do now." By this idiosyncratic route, Mims found himself
squarely in the midst of the genteel tradition of American literary criticism. William P. Trent took up a similar position: "To pursue an art
primarily for the purpose of preaching through the medium of communication it offers between soul and soul, is to degrade two noble
functions of human genius; but to pursue an art in total oblivion of its
relations with thought and morals is always to hamper and often to
degrade art alone, since thought and morals will under all circumstances retain their dignity. . . . Perhaps we may express these truths
epigrammatically by saying that the modern artist ought never to be
an ascetic recluse, and ought always to be a thorough gentleman." [13]
This tradition inclined to make emotional appreciation more central
than technical criticism, the reader more significant than the author,
the amateur as important as the professional. At its best, such a doctrine dispersed an affection for literature widely through society. At its
worst, it degenerated into a Rotarian picnic. Mims was to touch both
extremes.

Thus Mims was to settle on Robert Browning as the preeminent
poet of his age, with Tennyson a close second. Thomas Carlyle was

relished for a vigorous belief in the greatness of individualism, *Sartor Resartus* being a central text in the Victorian struggle against agnosticism and worse, though the side of Carlyle that hated industrialism and excoriated the "nigger problem" was little explored.[14] Mims saw his poets as allies of Christianity against doubt. *In Memoriam* he thought was "the masterpiece of the nineteenth century," because it was "such a great poem for those who have doubts."[15] And Browning served a less obvious purpose, conventionality of sentiment, combined with obscurity of expression, which gave the expert some room for exegesis. Mims had no patience with art for art's sake, since literature must have a social relevance. If society depended for its survival upon right morality, it followed that literature should succor such values.

To speak of gentlemen, as did Trent, was to speak in class terms. The rareness of Mims's university education, in a South where a rudimentary secondary education was not yet usual, made him one of an elite. He embraced the fact with enthusiasm, perhaps with the emphasis of the parvenu. Populism appalled him, and he applauded when McKinley defeated Bryan in 1896. He could be patronizing towards the "common people." On the way to his own wedding in 1898, he observed of a newly married couple on the train: "It is interesting to watch them. They are ignorant, uncultured looking people, and marriage can mean but little to them. What a low conception of life they have! And so it is with marriage as with all other good things in the world." He liked to cite Matthew Arnold's idea that a cultured remnant would save the world. "After all, haven't we gone too far in our ideas of the people ruling—are they fit to rule, and can the future of the race be intrusted to their hands?"[16] Always the clue to this hierarchy, the admission ticket to this elite, was education and "culture," the bourgeois standard. It is significant that Mims appears to have had small contact with the remnants of the Old South's plantation culture.[17] He was inclined to take the myth of the Old South on trust, being ignorant of the reality, though he knew enough to remark that Thomas Nelson Page's Virginia was no norm and wary enough to point to the dark side of slavery.[18]

This elitism was offensive to many but not complacent. If the people were uncultured and their ignorance blighted the fortunes of the South, they must be educated. Even as an undergraduate, Mims had written approvingly of the university-extension movement in England. His mentor at Vanderbilt, William Baskervill, had helped to set up a summer Chautauqua at Monteagle, in southern Tennessee.[19] In the summer of 1895, Mims traveled to Lake Chautauqua itself and reveled in the public lectures and classes. Even during his honeymoon he went to a Chautauqua in Boulder, Colorado, where he interspersed love and Robert Browning. From 1919 to 1942 he regularly gave summer lectures at the Lake Chautauqua meetings.

Established at Trinity, he took with energy to the lecture circuit and joined in the formation of literary clubs, such as the Epworth League and the Canterbury Club. He proposed and secured the foundation of a public library in Durham, one of the first in the South. "I am anxious," he wrote, "to become well identified with the state and all its interests. . . . When I see how little people read, and that into their lives there never comes the light of the culture that comes from the world's best literature, I am only too anxious to do what I can to increase their interest in things that are so dear to me."[20] In 1902 he founded the North Carolina Teacher's Assembly, modeled on James H. Kirkland's Tennessee organization. He attended the meeting in Raleigh that launched Charles Aycock's public-schools campaign and helped to draw up the opening statement. By his own lectures and those by others, arranged by him, he acted as a publicist for the "crusade." Similarly, he used the *Quarterly* "as a sort of unofficial organ for the Southern Conference for Education," the coalition formed in 1901 of Northern philanthropists and Southern educational leaders.[21] Even as a pedagogue, he was a missionary, not only reading to freshmen Tennyson with "a good deal of *steam*" but obliging them to read Walter Hines Page's *The World's Work* and Clarence Poe's *Progressive Farmer*.[22]

It was conventional wisdom that the South needed men who could usher in the new industrial era. Henry Grady had taught that, and Buck Duke was producing cigarettes in his Durham factories that provided jobs and money, some of which went to keep Trinity College financially alive. But did the South need poets, much less professors who only studied poets? Mims replied by stressing the social utility of literature and addressing himself to the quality of Southern life, rather than to the bricks and mortar of its development. "Culture" widely dispersed among the people, guided by an elite of superior insight, would allow the South to define a civilization where the poet could share the status of the mill owner, where, indeed, the two need not be mutually exclusive. It was a tenuous position in a South not noted for its enthusiasm for the intellectual.

Mims's most succinct statement of a credo was his essay "The Function of Criticism in the South," published for the new *South Atlantic Quarterly* in 1903. In its way, it can be taken as the position of the new intellectual community. Mims drew upon Matthew Arnold's thought to present the critic as the honest propagator of "the best that has been, and is being, thought and said in the world." He was the expositor of a socially didactic cosmopolitanism, which would slice away the vain bombast that plagued Southern provincial culture. Mims was deeply optimistic about the venture and felt himself on the brink of a great age. A visit in 1893 to the Chicago World's Fair, with its vision of technological progress, had left him dazzled. While religion told him to frown upon the connection between science and materialism, he was sure that the demon could be mastered and made the servant of man's aspirations: "When we have absorbed all the good results from material advancement, when science has done its work, then the old world will seek a new and larger life in some things that science and materialism have kept down in this age." He was not very well informed about the exact mechanisms of industrial technology, but he accepted the ameliorative mystique of science's potentiality. "My! how I hope we'll live in a great age!" he wrote. And it was natural to add, "I wonder if we'll have a part to play, even though it may be a minor part."[23] The Agrarians were later to be as ignorant of science, while drawing the opposite conclusion.

Considering the plight of the South in the 1890s, such buoyancy was curious. Mims had some grasp of the poverty, the race problem, the economic backwardness. He did not live shut away from these things. "Few people have ever had to suffer more from war, and poverty and mistaken policies of government," he confessed. But plight bred optimism. One might erect on the tabula rasa of the South's inadequacy new and splendid institutions that would mold its life for generations. "We shall have the joy of constructive activity," his friend Walter Hines Page exclaimed. "We look forward to a golden age that we may surely help to bring, not back to one that never was." John Spencer Bassett reminisced to Mims in later years of this mood: "How gaily we rode out to cure the evils of the dear old land; we knew just where we were, just how far they had progressed and just how to apply the remedy. And you and I were equally young, equally fervent, and equally certain of ourselves."[24]

The missionary had models. In impressing upon the young Mims the virtues of non-Southern society, his year at Cornell University had been decisive. He had felt on the defensive in the midst of a literate and affluent society. The North seemed the source of most American "culture." And behind Boston lurked the image of Europe, the ultimate source, it seemed to him, of intellectual insight. Much of his life was spent in trying to bring these three—South, North, and Europe—into harmony.

The strategic heart of this position was the concept of the "belated section." "It may turn out that backwardness is an advantage as well as a disadvantage," Mims wrote as late as 1926.[25] The Arnoldian social critic would learn from other countries and regions, apply the lessons to the South, and improve upon the models. As a theory, it had crippling difficulties. Arnold's critic had been merely literary, emulating Saint-Beuve, admiring the Académie Française, urging the merit of Heine, at most pointing the moral of Prussian education. Southern industrial transformation was a larger mandate. The bourgeois intellectual did not have a profound grasp of industrial and social change elsewhere, he was not conversant with the whole of a complex Southern society, and he had very little political power. Moreover, the South was not always keen to be doodled on as a tabula rasa: it rather liked some of its old markings.

European travel in 1909 and 1910 pointed the moral. Paris for six months, spring in Italy, and summer in Germany were the fulfillment of an old ambition. Mims had made a short trip to England in 1900, but now lingered over the culture he had worshipped from afar. He plunged into French literature with daily visits to the Bibliothèque Nationale. He went, guidebook in hand, through the cathedrals and art galleries of Italy. He attended the passion play at Oberammergau. Yet he went as a tourist, an obscure professor with no access to specialist knowledge, traveling third class on the Italian railways. His range of anecdote in lectures was increased, he could now tell the difference between a Raphael and a Giotto, but his experience was naturally concentrated upon the vestiges of the Continent's past, not the lessons of its present. The only tangible result of the trip was a paper on French literature delivered to the Modern Language Association.[26] Likewise Mims flitted in and out of the offices of Northern publishers and universities, not its factories.

It is a comment on the vitality of his indigenous cultural tradition—the ideological death of the Old South, the confusions of the New South—that when Edwin Mims sought to systematize his ideas, he looked outside the region. It was not that he was ignorant of the Southern intellectual tradition. That he should have written on Sidney Lanier and Thomas Nelson Page is not surprising. But as a contributor to *The South in the Building of the Nation,* he had occasion to write on antebellum thought, in essays that show with clinical precision how the mind of the Old South was edited by the mind of the New South. On antebellum fiction, the essays betray some knowledge and insight. The familiar landmarks are there: Poe, Simms, Kennedy, Cooke, Longstreet, Hooper, Baldwin. Poe is praised, Simms regretted for indiscipline. Among Southern periodicals, the *Southern Literary Messenger* is stressed largely for Poe's sake, the *Southern Review* honored for having been the first of Southern journals, though its contributions are deemed "heavy and somewhat pedantic," and it is taken to task for slighting the prospects of American literature. Mims did have some sense that the mind of the Old South was not as closed as new convention had it, partly because he had been asked by Samuel C. Mitchell to write on European influences in the South. But his mind ran only to the exploration of belles-lettres, as befitted one of the new intellectual professionals. The rest of the intellectual landscape is glimpsed only through names. The verdict is decisive: "None of them, except Poe, and perhaps Simms, were professional men of letters; their literary work was incidental to what seemed to them more important. Most of them wrote carelessly, even slovenly. Furthermore, the absence of anything like a literary centre was a hindrance; there was little of the influence of one writer on another. Slavery, and the feudal system perpetuated thereby, militated against purely literary work."[27]

The importance of William P. Trent can be gleaned here. As a literary critic Trent was the cleverest and most successful of Mims's Southern contemporaries, and his influence was great. The distortions of his Simms biography have often been noted. But an accuracy in that work also needs stressing. Trent faithfully reproduced Simms's own sense of discontent with the cultural life of the Old South, indeed transcribed Simms's critique. Hence Mims was to write that Simms's essay "The Literary Prospects of the South," in *Russell's Magazine* in June 1858, was "the best discussion that we have of literary conditions in the South before the war. . . . brilliantly written, and . . . a manly, straightforward discussion of the place of literature in the life of a people and of the defects of the Southern people." That essay shows Simms arguing that Southern intellectual life was stunted because it lacked an urban center, an adequate manufacturing sector, a publishing industry, an educated elite, but that there were modest signs of improvement.[28] For those who know the essayists of the Old South, this is a familiar indictment, common in the 1840s and 1850s.[29] It is evidence for the contention that the indictment of the Old South by the New South began as the indictment of the Old South by itself, with the important distinction that postbellum critics had the luxury of condemning slavery and were converting a minority dissent into a majority opinion.

So this was an unnourishing tradition. The indigenous best offered to Mims religion and a respect for the legend of the Old South, expressed preeminently in the novels of Thomas Nelson Page. But the more coherent Mims's thought became, the more it rested on non-Southern sources. From the South came his religion, but the liberal cast he gave it owed most to Northern theologians such as Phillips Brooks and Lyman Abbott. From the South came his problem of relating culture and society, but he derived the definitive means of resolving the tension from Arnold and England. He wanted desperately to promote "culture" in the South, but his sense of its meaning relied heavily upon the precedents of New England and Victorian Britain.

His letters show the widening net of an acquaintanceship with influential Northerners and Southern reformers. Thus Mims acted out in social reform the alliance with the North that was the basis of his intellectual position. He tried, in his modest way, to act as a mediator between the sections. On the one hand, he strove to convince Northerners of a valid liberal sentiment in the South and to guide their interventions. On the other, he tried to prepare Southern sensibilities and perspectives, thus creating the mood that would be amenable to the efforts of Northern philanthropists. It was a delicate balancing act.

It all but came unstuck during the Bassett affair at Trinity in 1903. John Spencer Bassett had observed, in an article on the race problem, that Booker T. Washington was, with the exception of Lee, the greatest man the South had produced since the Civil War. A storm of abuse broke around his unfortunate head. Public clamor demanded resignation, though the Trinity Board of Trust eventually confirmed Bassett in his job.[30] During the furor, Mims hastened to perform his mediating role. He counseled Northerners on the best tone to adopt and even wrote the account of the struggle that was to appear in Walter Hines Page's *World's Work*. He assured Southerners that no one countenanced the exact substance of Bassett's statement, with its implication of racial equality, only his right to free speech. He worked hard to rally opinion within Trinity itself, so that Bassett's vindication might impress Northerners and provide an example to other liberal Southerners. That Trinity and Bassett survived, at a time when several Southern academics had suffered expulsion for their views, was rightly seen as a success for academic freedom. But it was a local victory, a model for private colleges, more immune than state universities to public pressure. But Mims and others grasped at the triumph with an illuminating fervor. Progress there was in Southern education, but painfully slow and inadequate. Liberals needed the catharsis of tangible advance, the more so in Mims's case because he had decided to remain in the South.[31] Their correspondence has an air of enthusiastic unreality, a whistling in the dark.

This being so, Mims was to be charged with the taint of Yankeeism. A cultural liaison agent with the North he certainly was. But he did not pick up ideas with unguarded eclecticism. Like those before him in the Old South, he demanded that ideas be relevant to his culture, while having a feebler sense than antebellum Southern intellectuals of the idiosyncrasy of that culture. The most arresting example of this was his choice between the educational precedents of Britain and Germany.

At Cornell Mims studied with Hiram Corson. For the *ingenu* Southerner, the professor of English Literature who had known Browning and Emerson was an overwhelming figure. Any man who had been to Europe fourteen times had to be a titan. Old and isolated in a younger faculty dominated by the graduates of German seminars, Corson took Mims as a solacing companion and enlisted him in a private crusade against German education. For Corson, the spiritual and moral value of literature took precedence over its technical aspects. Education should be designed to promote the student's awareness, not his capacity for memorizing facts. The object of the university was to create men of culture, "not to make the head a cockloft for storing away the trumpery of barren knowledge, a greediness for which may increase, does often increase, as true intellectual and spiritual vitality declines." It was a doctrine that Hugh Legaré had preached seventy years earlier. Mims, little inclined towards German philology if only through a lack of intellectual stamina and rigor, took up the creed. Once he proposed to write an article on Corson that would make the German-trained scholars of Cornell "wince." "*Germany has done incalculable harm:* we have lost the richness of English culture," he declared in vehement mood.[32]

This was a defiance of the conventional wisdom of his generation, North and South. Most bright young Southerners interested in graduate study were going to bastions of the new German scholarship such as the Johns Hopkins University, if they did not go to Germany itself. The editor of the *Sewanee Review* wrote in 1901: "So far as the Southern states are concerned, one might almost say that their educational history for the past quarter of a century has been largely that of the Johns Hopkins University." Mims's own mentors at Vanderbilt, William Baskervill, the professor of English; Charles Forster Smith, the professor of Greek; and James H. Kirkland, the professor of Latin, had all gone to Leipzig.[33]

There is some evidence that the mid-1890s began to see a deepening reaction to German scholastic habits. At least Trent spoke in 1901 at Princeton of a "trend in our colleges and universities from purely philological to literary courses." But this was unclear to Mims in 1897, and he felt uneasy about his dissent. He looked at Harvard, where he spent the summer of 1897, and noted that scientific scholarship had become its creed. His new colleague in English at Trinity was William Preston Few, a Harvard Ph.D., "filled with the Harvard spirit, which is essentially technical and critical." As Few discoursed on the gerunds of Middle High German or mentioned his thesis, "On the -ing Suffix in Middle English with Special Reference to Participles and -ing Verbals," Mims wondered at his own ignorance. Occasionally he was beset by doubts.[34]

But a crucial factor in his rejection of the German tradition was its apparent uselessness for reform in the South. Philology had no rhetorical charms in the missionary pulpit of "culture" and severed the connection between literature and society. So Mims set aside doubts and decided to "stay among my own people and try to do for my students and for the people what a mere investigating student cannot do."[35]

This animus against Germany helped, in turn, to sharpen his Anglophilia. Corson did not create it, though he set the seal. Baskervill had introduced Mims to Tennyson and Browning. But enthusiasm for England was all around Mims in the South, in marked contrast to the Anglophobia of the Old South.[36] Near Vanderbilt, there was an "English Club" at Sewanee, mostly of ladies laying siege to Elizabeth Barrett Browning and Matthew Arnold, threading their way gamely through the obscurities of "Sordello." Late in life, Mims wrote in his autobiography of his "love of the English countryside" and his passion for "the necessity of the union of the English speaking peoples in all essential principles and ideals." He was to sit on the first selection committee in North Carolina for the new Rhodes Scholarships in 1902.[37]

Such Anglophilia did not intrude upon indigenous racism, as it had in the Old South, when Britain—host to abolitionists—had stood as the foremost enemy of slavery and the slave trade. British South Africa endorsed the South.[38] Charles B. Aycock's governorship in North Carolina rested on two premises, public education and disfranchisement of blacks. Mims did not dissent from this, as can be seen from an article on Theodore Roosevelt in 1905, where Roosevelt was reproached for having dined with Booker T. Washington.[39] After the First World War, Mims was to launch an antilynching campaign in Tennessee and help along Will Alexander's Southern Interracial Commission. But this was firmly within the framework of a belief in black social inferiority. During the 1950s he was to deplore the "demagoguery" of black leaders who opposed segregation.[40] In this he was quite typical of his generation. For him, segregation *was* social progress.

It is more striking that he dwelled little on the race problem. In all his youthful letters, he mentioned it only once, despite all the contemporary heat on the subject. In Ithaca, an acquaintance had a black girl for a friend, and Mims lightly observed: "She is not in any of Dr. Corson's work—shall I say I am glad? But I must remember that I am in the North again. It did look so funny to see her come into the chapel this morning with a white girl. De gusti bus non disputandum est."[41] Racialism did not weigh upon his mind nor vitiate his sense of community with the traditions of Gladstonian liberalism, on both sides of the Atlantic. He was grateful that the political activism of others had removed the issue from immediate consideration. This relative apathy made him vulnerable. Josephus Daniels commented on speeches by Mims and Walter Hines Page in 1905: "The only men who talk 'nigger, nigger' now are those who traduce the men who have now made it possible to go forward without the menace that full negro suffrage put upon the state for thirty years. When the real statesmen in North Carolina were straining every nerve to remove the negro from politics, they got no help from Mr. Page or Mr. Mims." It was a logically uncomfortable point.[42]

The most important friend made by Mims in these years was, indeed, Walter Hines Page. Page, firmly established in liberal publishing circles in New York, kept his eye on promising young Southerners and adopted Mims as a disciple. They met when Mims went North or on the less frequent occasions when Page traveled South. Page invited the young professor to write for his *World's Work* and tendered advice on the course of Mims's career. Page had the more precise mind, demanding to know the where, when, and how of progress, when Mims too often allowed the hortatory generalization to suffice. With this impulse, Page nudged Mims into writing a series of articles on social change in the South, which obliged Mims during 1911 to travel around the region and actually talk to the industrialists whom he had celebrated.

But Page was anticlerical. He had vetoed Kirkland's place on the Southern Education Board because he thought that Vanderbilt was too close to the Methodist church. When Mims was thinking of returning to Vanderbilt, Page cautioned him to ensure that the post was free of ecclesiastical influence, for bishops were "a pestiferous lot."[43]

This coincided with Mims's own growing disillusionment with the Trinity of Kilgo. The small denominational college seemed to have little future in comparison with large state institutions such as the University of North Carolina. So when Chapel Hill offered him a place in 1909, he accepted.

He had scarcely settled back in Chapel Hill before Kirkland asked him to return to Vanderbilt. Since Baskervill's death in 1899 the English department had been undistinguished. The university itself had been plagued by a protracted dispute with the Methodist church over control of the Board of Trust. At first Mims refused. Kirkland persisted, and in 1912 Mims capitulated. He left North Carolina after eighteen years of involvement with its nascent liberalism. Nashville, by comparison, was a leap in the dark.

For some thirteen years he was deeply involved in the internal affairs of Vanderbilt and seldom published. The English department had to be reconstructed, Vanderbilt was integrated with the nearby George Peabody College for Teachers, the disruptive force of the First World War had to be handled on campus, the curriculum was revised, women's status was haggled over and decided in favor of coeducation. Always there was the need to raise money, and Mims's talents as an orator proved useful in squeezing cash from reluctant alumni.

In North Carolina Mims had been a man in harmony with his times, content that his social beliefs were the wave of the American future. With Woodrow Wilson's election to the presidency—Wilson the scholar, the Anglophile, the stern Christian, the Southerner—the quality of Mims's life seemed translated into political triumph. His friends were called to office: Walter Hines Page went to London, Thomas Nelson Page became ambassador to Rome, David Houston became secretary of agriculture.

The war did not break the mood, for he was enthusiastic about the alliance. With his old beliefs about Britain and Germany, that was not hard. But aftermath damaged exuberance. Wilson, his political hero, failed to win the fight for the League and went from office broken in health. "I have never known a greater disillusionment than the failure of his hopes and plans," Mims later told a Scottish audience.[44] Walter Hines Page died in 1918, worn down by the strain of the war in London. Edward Graham, Mims's old colleague in English at Chapel Hill and latterly its president, fell victim to the influenza epidemic of 1918. Edwin Alderman, whom he knew and respected from summer schools in Charlottesville, had contracted tubercular laryngitis in 1912, from which he recovered only painfully and slowly. Charles Aycock, Edgar

Gardner Murphy, William Baldwin, and Robert Ogden all had died before the war. Mims had been younger, an apprentice progressive. He survived armed with the beliefs he had shared with them. The 1920s did not prevent his continuing in the old way, but a new generation began to challenge his assumptions.

The first onslaught was an attack on the progressive consensus he had helped to form. The years after the war saw racial violence and an increase in lynching. They witnessed a new emphasis upon religious fundamentalism and the rising power of the Ku Klux Klan. Mims was appalled to see the South become a standing joke in Northern intellectual circles, as Mencken chuckled his way through the decade and pointed to Mims and his like as citizens of a cultural wasteland.

He did his best to meet the challenge. When the judicial circus at Dayton had scarcely ended, he sat down in an Appalachian mountain retreat and wrote a refutation of Menckenism. Published in 1926 as *The Advancing South,* it was an *apologia pro vita sua,* serving to remind the postwar generation of the progressive achievements of his own. Was there not more industry, a better educational system, a literature that could boast an Ellen Glasgow, an improving agricultural system, a better status for women and Negroes, a more liberal Church? Was this not a long way from the South of the 1890s? This being so, liberal leaders on whom rested the responsibility for leadership should not be disheartened. They were stronger than they knew, scattered in isolated bands around the region.

Mencken was not impressed. He dismissed Mims and his ilk as "amiable obfuscators" and "mere windjammers." Dr. Mims, he thought, "is better than most, but he is still far too much the orthodox Southerner to see what is the matter with the South." But the book was a remarkable popular success. Mims later claimed that it nearly secured him a Pulitzer Prize, and it is not improbable.[45] On the wave of interest, he took to the lecture podium again and scored a well-publicized success by an address to the Southern Society of New York. He was fleetingly established as an expert on the South.

All this was well, and along old lines: educating the North and encouraging the liberal South. But Mims was facing a more subtle and intimate challenge from his own colleagues in the English department at Vanderbilt. It began as an aesthetic challenge to his view of literature and ended as a repudiation of his social philosophy.

Both John Crowe Ransom and Donald Davidson had been hired by Mims to bolster the department. Both were Vanderbilt graduates, both mildly progressive. Ransom's Rhodes Scholarship doubtless did not hinder Mims's choice. In time, the young men gathered disciples from among the undergraduates, began to meet of an evening, to write and discuss poetry.[46] Ransom and Davidson were respectable enough, but younger men such as Allen Tate and Robert Penn Warren were a touch more bohemian. In his English classes, they scoffed at Mims's views on poetry and thought his teaching techniques—which included the learning of many lines from Tennyson and Browning, plus the composition of a "spiritual autobiography" as a class paper—idiotic.[47] The reputation of the young poets on campus was a little scandalous. They met in the house of a Jew. It was said that young ladies had been seen creeping from their bedroom windows.[48] Since the same was often said of Mims, this brought the name of hypocrite to their lips when the old man declaimed on morality and literature. But respectability had to be officially maintained, so Mims was concerned when the possibility of founding a little poetry magazine was mooted. Everyone, after all, knew about little poetry magazines and their morals.

So he asked the young men to lunch and attempted to dissuade them from their course. His main argument was, as Tate was to recall, "that if we were good we would be published in the Eastern journals."[49] The opinion was not greeted with enthusiasm, though it was the natural reflex of a man whose position had long rested on an intellectual alliance with the North. In his youth this had been the route to fame, and he did not see that as yet another path was open. Besides, though it is doubtful that on this he was candid, he had seen some of the poetry and did not much like it. It had no moral vigor, it was just irony. To give a premature backing to the magazine seemed foolish. But since they persisted, he did not veto it or throw his considerable administrative power against them. When the *Fugitive* made its unexpectedly successful way, he encouraged them, flattered them in lectures and print. Mims had not acquired power without knowing how to back a winning horse. In *The Advancing South*, he cited the Fugitives as evidence of growing literary prowess. "Ransom," he noted, "may never be popular; but for a combination of intellectual subtlety, refined sentiment, originality, boldness of poetic diction, and withal a certain whimsical imagination, his poetry is destined to increasing recognition." He had a few words of praise for Davidson's lyricism.[50]

With Tate his links were miserably sour. With Warren they were little better, especially in the early 1930s. Warren was kept on a low salary as a temporary professor, and then released, because Mims had a low opinion of his teaching. Tate and Mims had had a running battle in classes. Despite this, Tate applied for a graduate fellowship and rested his claim upon his literary progress. He observed to Davidson that most professors would dismiss such a consideration, "with the exception of Mims. . . . Literature, to most of these Profs, is about as remote as Timbuctoo." But he was shocked to discover that Mims refused to recommend him until Tate offered "some sort of apology for past irreverences!" After that, their relationship deteriorated permanently. He and Warren liked to exchange insults of Mims in their letters, such that Tate observed to Davidson in 1927: "I understand from Red that Dr. Mims is now one of my admirers. I am coming to Tennessee, and I prefer not to humiliate him; yet if he speaks to me, I shall insult him."[51]

With the lesser figures of the Fugitive group Mims was on better terms. Ridley Wills wrote of him: "Let young men with burdenous minds say what they care to—I'll stick up for Dr. Mims. . . . He's a Don Q. and he finds many windmills. He knows they are windmills and wishes they weren't." William Yandell Elliott corresponded without rancor with his old professor. Jesse Wills was offered a graduate fellowship by Mims but declined and entered the insurance business.[52] Stanley Johnson, however, ruffled a few tempers. Despite a scholarship, he opted to follow Tate to New York and freelance work. There he wrote *Professor*, a satirical piece mocking the follies of academic life. Its reminiscence of Vanderbilt was obvious, and its central character was a blend of Mims and Walter Clyde Curry, the department's Chaucerian scholar. Unsubtle hints were dropped of dalliances with female undergraduates. News of its publication agitated several Nashville sensibilities, needlessly, Tate thought: "Alas, they will be sadly disappointed; for the thing is harmless as a bromo-seltzer, at least as far as local reference." But the impression was not diminished when its dust cover showed a man with a goatee, Mims's distinguishing mark.[53]

As for Ransom, the matter was more complicated. It is doubtful that he ever liked Mims. The older man was so different in temperament from the cool young poet and philosopher. For a while Ransom seems to have been grateful for the toleration granted him. Mims made a point of using Ransom's achievements as a poet as a valid ground for recommending promotions. In this Mims was breaking ground not followed by most other universities until after the Second World War. The same was true in Davidson's case. But later, in his Agrarian phase, Ransom's feelings hardened. After his departure from Vanderbilt, he observed of the likes of Mims, Kirkland, and O. C. Carmichael, Kirkland's successor, that they had "done nothing for me, these many years, except not to fire me."[54]

Davidson's view was more sunny. He was consistently grateful to

Mims for academic patronage, even after his opposition to the New South ideology crystallized. In 1930 Davidson wrote to John Gould Fletcher, when Mims was about to spend a summer in Europe and proposed visiting Fletcher in London. "Dr. Mims has been a great friend to all of us, especially to myself; in fact, I owe to him most of the opportunities I have had since the War left me high and dry. As an older man, rather of the Walter H. Page generation than of our own, he might well be shocked by the heterodoxies that Ransom, Wade, and I, in his department are continually indulging in; but, to the contrary, he gives us free rein and keeps an attitude of friendly tolerance, give-and-take, or approval for which we think we should be grateful."[55] Tate once playfully suggested to Davidson that since Mims was his boss, he was obliged to be gentle. There is some truth in this. Davidson was the least adventurous of the Fugitive-Agrarians, a shade frightened to step outside the security of Vanderbilt. But more than that, Davidson was to become isolated within the Agrarian group itself, as his peers grew to think his poetry too literal and polemical. These were vices that were virtues to Mims.[56]

During *Fugitive* days the aesthetic differences between Mims and the young poets were as clear as the gulf between Browning and Baudelaire. The rift was the deeper because Mims himself was not a practicing poet. Moreover, they were eager to ignore politics and provincialism in their verse, and he regretted their blind spot about the South. Ransom, he observed in 1926, "like the other poets of the group, has little or no local color, is not conspicuously Southern except in an indirect protest against a sentimentalized South and a commercialized South."[57]

Tate objected in 1925 of Mims, in a piece that paid the old man a backhanded compliment in taking him with some seriousness: "The South of the first generation after the Civil War has had at least one social critic not wholly ancillary to the idols of the tribe. Yet the vigor of his attack, in the *South Atlantic Quarterly* and elsewhere, was not alone sufficient to the purpose. Mr. Edwin Mims's writings betray an inadequate sense of the ante-bellum Southern consciousness, and a sensitiveness to that temperament is the critical requisite prior to all scholarship. His criteria are obscured by a cultural deficiency due, probably, to the influence of the secular and vulgar and moralistic churches. So when he came to summarize Southern poetry, in 'The South in the Building of the Nation,' this cultural astigmatism, in a specific form of unrealized moral and social values, permitted the tribal sentiment to emerge in him almost pure; he succumbed to the sentimental local-color fallacy—the ingenuous opinion that a particular setting is intrinsically more 'poetic' than another. And this is the best in criticism the South of the old school can offer." Elsewhere, after the publication of *The Advancing South*, Tate noted to Davidson that the book had a basic flaw: "It isn't criticism *in vacuo* that will prepare the way for literature; it is the literature itself which creates the state of mind for its acceptance. Moreover, it is impossible, ultimately, to distinguish between the critical act and the creative act."[58]

But Fugitive became Agrarian, and the South became a very live issue. With this, Mims was pleased. He was not happy that the Agrarian critique of Southern culture was so diametrically opposed to his own. But by so representing the New South school on the Vanderbilt campus, he had stimulated the reaction. He had told his budding social critics of the phenomenon in his classes. Davidson confessed that he knew nothing about the New South until he learned of it from Mims.[59] The letters that crossed between Ransom and Tate in 1926, suggesting that they turn their attention to the South, were offshoots of the Scopes Trial controversy. They were also precipitated by the publication of *The Advancing South*. The New South of the Agrarian dissent was peculiarly the New South of Edwin Mims. It was no accident that their most savage attack upon its literature was aimed at Sidney Lanier.[60]

Yet there were continuities between Mims and the Agrarians. They did not entirely distance themselves from the myth of a leisured, gentlemanly Old South that formed a subplot to the New South ideology. Their racial views were similar. They shared the central mystique of the writer as the highest ideal of a civilization. They put religion at the core of their analysis of social health. Even Mims's Anglophilia informed *I'll Take My Stand*. But in each of these, crucial nuances wrecked the unanimity. Ransom argued for a fundamentalist religion, not a social gospel. Tate took to an England earlier than Macaulay's, preferred France, and his man of letters was a literary professional deeply involved in technical problems, not an amateur gentleman scholar reading *The Idylls of the King* to ladies' clubs. The Agrarians did not cheerfully assume that the polite manners of Charleston could be grafted onto a bourgeois class, but wrote gloomily about the destruction of a feudal society by a leviathan industrial world. Above all, they differed about industrialism. In his early essays Mims had been emphatic that industrial change was the necessary prelude to a literary flowering; the Agrarians held exactly to the contrary.

Mims did his best to answer the challenge when his children, his colleagues, and others began to call him outdated. A concerted effort to understand the shift was made, as he turned from his well-thumbed volume of Palgrave's *Golden Treasury* and looked at William Faulkner, Henri Bergson, T. S. Eliot. He tried to understand them, but the book he produced, *Adventurous America,* was a gesture of incomprehension.[61]

He summarized the pessimism in the new writing but insisted on its needlessness. Surely, he said, there were signs of progress everywhere in America. He could call upon his own experience: of Nashville, of Chautauqua, of Yaddo (the writers' colony in New York where he spent the summer of 1928), of Pasadena and the Huntington Library. In the most unlikely spots one could find poets, symphony orchestras, libraries, and new architecture. He was sure—this on the eve of Herbert Hoover's inauguration, Hoover the veteran of Belgian war relief and business success—that American business was culturally benevolent. Had not Mims's universities been firmly wedded to industrial philanthropy, the coffers of the Dukes and Vanderbilts? Had not the *Fugitive* itself been paid for by the largesse of Nashville businessmen? All this being so, why be pessimistic?

Upon reading this, Tate was appalled. "My God! The man is hopeless. It is impossible even to discuss the main issue with him; he doesn't even see its actual terms, but he writes a book about it! His book gives me the feeling of looking at something that lives under a damp log." But events spared anyone the need to answer Mims. *Adventurous America* was published in the same week as the Wall Street Crash.[62]

The Advancing South and *Adventurous America* had the same strategy and the same analytical problem. Mims shared the assumptions of the critics of provincialism more than the beliefs of those he defended. Whilst he did give some sense of cultural vitality in the United States, its hinterland as well as its metropolitan centers, he was convinced that philistinism was undesirable. As he could not have stomached an America indifferent to "culture," his defense of the South and America had to prove that, indeed, it was cultured, somehow approximating to the beau ideal of European civilization. He could not afford to defend America on its own terms. It was not enough to say that capitalism was right; one had to insist that it was good because it endowed libraries and symphony orchestras. He could not accept the integrity of Southern mores but had desperately to demonstrate that "Southern" and "provincial" were not unrelated to the accepted intellectual merits of Boston and London. This was difficult; the raw data were refractory, and his attempt was necessarily ambiguous and unsatisfactory. His long years of effort for "progress" weighed heavily when he judged "achievement."

The Depression punctured even his optimism. Someone remarked to him that ever since the publication of *The Advancing South* the region had been retreating. To cope with this, he took conventional refuge in a cyclical theory of history and the reiterated cry to liberals not to lose heart.[63] But even on the score of Southern liberalism Mims found the world slipping away from him. It was bad enough to have Agrarians swarming over his Vanderbilt, but the younger liberals seemed to have a new credo. He had been shocked to discover, on the publication of *The Advancing South,* that his position was viewed skeptically by the younger men of Chapel Hill. Howard Odum, Gerald Johnson, Edgar Knight, and the cohorts of the Institute for Research in Social Science had embraced a sterner sociological creed of liberalism than that of Mims and Edward Graham. Mims thought of leaders when he considered the agency of social change. This new breed went around amassing statistics and talked of using government power, which Mims was convinced would subvert the rights of the individual. And there was the New Deal. Did it not go too far? Mims always liked to think of himself as holding the center; it was habitual with him to split the difference. But was he any longer in the center?

The Depression contributed to another misfortune. It helped to break up the English department of which he was so proud. For years, there had been financial difficulties between the department and the university administration. One is tempted to say that the central struggle on the Vanderbilt campus in the 1920s and 1930s was not intellectual, but fiscal. Chancellor Kirkland was insensitive to the claims of literary distinction and aware of the need to make ends meet. Ransom, Davidson, and others were not well paid and were irked to be laden with heavy classroom duties when their reputations were so markedly in the ascendant. In the midst of this conflict was Mims. He was devoted to Kirkland and close enough to the counsels of the administration to know the force of Kirkland's demands for financial restraint. Equally, he could hear the laments of his colleagues. So he tacked carefully between the two. In 1925, for example, he was extended a lucrative offer to go back to the newly revamped Duke University. Mims informed Kirkland to gain a raise but also tied the plight of his junior colleagues to any decision to remain. Would the chancellor help him to keep his talented department together? For the moment, it worked.[64]

But this was an awkward business. John Wade could not be held, not because, as Tate later charged, he was driven out by an unforgiving Mims, but because he missed his Georgia home. Randall Stewart went North to Brown University to be closer to his sources for a study of Nathaniel Hawthorne. Davidson, however, Mims did retain when the University of Alabama tried to woo him away in 1935, by talking the chancellor into cutting Davidson's teaching load. But by 1937, when Ransom was tendered an enticing offer from Kenyon College, the balance of forces had moved decisively. Vanderbilt, hurt by the Depression, had less money. Ransom had become too important to respond to low offers backed by Vanderbilt sentiment. Moreover, he was tiring of Agrarianism, intimately associated with Vanderbilt. A foray into university politics, in which he had tried to pick an amenable successor to Kirkland, had come badly unstuck.[65] Mims tried the old formula, the quiet negotiation away from public gaze. He pointed out to Kirkland that Ransom had for several years been getting, by an oversight, less money than Walter Clyde Curry. Perhaps if the chancellor could give Ransom some back pay with a raise, he might be persuaded to stay? The chancellor could not: he had an old rule that a raise should never elevate one faculty member in salary above those of comparable standing. In the meantime, Allen Tate had mounted an aggressive public campaign to force Vanderbilt to retain Ransom. Mims was deeply irritated by the misrepresentations of his position, the accusations that he had been systematically dismantling the English department for years and hurling dissident Agrarians out on their ears. So when a compromise was suggested by Kirkland that involved giving Ransom an increment, funded from an alumni gift, Mims did not concur.[66]

This bitter affair had come quickly after Mims had spent one of the happiest years of his life. He had gone as a visiting professor to Britain for a year in 1935. He traveled about various universities and reveled in British social life. He became a member of the Athenaeum Club, spent a weekend at Cliveden with Lady Astor, dined with a small coterie of friends in the Dean's Yard at Westminster Abbey, gave speeches to the English Speaking Union, and enjoyed himself.

He was disturbed, however, by the indifference of the British to American culture. It was hard to find books on American literature or history. There were not many courses on the subject in universities. Whilst his hosts were politely interested, they were not knowledgeable. So, ever the activist, he upbraided them on their ignorance and tried to persuade his sponsors, the Carnegie Foundation, to increase appropriations of books to British libraries. He even agitated the central oracle of English life, the correspondence columns of *The Times*. A new friend, Sir Josiah Stamp, had repeated Mims's strictures on the condition of American studies and thereby precipitated dozens of letters to the editor. The burden of opinion held that the United States had little culture worth studying and so the omission was insignificant.

Unlike on his earlier trip to Europe in 1910, he was now closer to the social elite. But his long years as a worshipper at the shrine of English culture made him credulous. Oxford dazzled him. He gleefully name-dropped in his letters, and one is reminded of Mencken's malevolent gibe: "The American don is lifted to bliss by the imprimatur of Oxford or Cambridge."[67] But it was in the logic of Mims's intellectual position that he should have placed the "climactic year" of his life, not in the South or even in New England, but dining where Matthew Arnold had once sipped his port. He had always wanted to associate the South with that mystique, and his dinner at All Souls was a small token of success in that dubious venture.

It is perhaps best to leave him there. He stayed on at Vanderbilt until 1942, though that by no means marked the end of his activities. He produced another four books: a biography of Kirkland, a history of Vanderbilt itself, and two brief studies of literature and religion.[68] He tried to write his autobiography, but by the 1950s, well into his eighties, he could not find the resources to produce a compelling narrative; only a disjointed collection of letters and passages, lifted from old books, resulted. He eagerly presented it to publishers, who all politely declined it.

He lived long enough to see himself pass, parenthetically, into historical accounts. They did not please him. He most frequently turned up in unkind asides to the history of the Fugitives and Agrarians, a slightly comic, occasionally sinister figure representing the gloom before the dawn of the Southern Renaissance. He left no disciples devoted to his memory, save the businessmen who attended his classes and can still recite, at the merest drop of a strophe, great chunks of Browning and Tennyson. At alumni reunions, it is said, one can sometimes see old men, gathered on lawns, hurling stanzas at one another and stopping only to chortle uncontrollably at the reminiscence of it all.

Yet the creation of a climate within which literature seemed again worthwhile in Southern society was not a slight achievement. In details the euphoric ambitions of the 1890s failed. Nashville did not become another Oxford, his religious renaissance never came, his kind of literary criticism rapidly lost ground. For even in his youth he had been a little behind his times. He could as well have listened to Oscar Wilde as to Browning. Even when his hopes were realized, in the spread of academic freedom or the strengthening of the educational system, they did not take the forms that pleased him. That was a strain, but he lived with it surprisingly well. In his last days, he even named Wolfe, Hemingway, and Faulkner—the Faulkner whose *Sanctuary* he had first dropped in disgust—as the greatest novelists of his time in America, though doubtless he once more had an eye on his audience.[69]

To look at Edwin Mims's thought is to wander through the commonplaces of the bourgeois nineteenth century eerily extended into the mid-twentieth. What started as a strong firm voice, with something pertinent to say to his times, drifted into anachronism. From the standpoint of Allen Tate, Mims was history repeating itself as farce. From the cruel standpoint of the historian, this has a value: it has left us with a startlingly sharp metaphor of a shift in the mind of the South.

CHAPTER 7

A Heterodox Note on the Southern Renaissance

I T IS A curious process, that by which an explanation self-evident to one generation ceases to hold meaning for the next. We are in the midst of just such a process in historical explanations of the Southern Renaissance, that cultural awakening variously dated but deemed to be well launched by 1930. The traditional explanation is that of Allen Tate. It is familiar, but will bear repetition: "With the war of 1914–1918, the South reentered the world—but gave a backward glance as it stepped over the border: that backward glance gave us the Southern renascence, a literature conscious of the past in the present. . . . 'From the peculiarly historical consciousness of the Southern writer has come work of a special order; but the focus of this consciousness is quite temporary. It has made possible the curious burst of intelligence that we get at a crossing of the ways, not unlike, on an infinitesimal scale, the outburst of poetic genius at the end of the sixteenth century when commercial England had already begun to crush feudal England.'"[1] This explanation served to clarify the standpoint not only of Tate's generation but of the next, young during heady days.[2] It no longer serves.

The explanation has failed for a number of reasons, some empirical,

This essay was originally given as a paper to the Organization of American Historians in Los Angeles in 1984, after I was asked by the program committee to address the question of "recent historical perspectives on the Southern Renaissance." There it received useful criticism from Morton Sosna, James C. Cobb, and Anne Goodwyn Jones. Later Daniel Singal, with admirable dispassion, read and improved it. It was then published in *Perspectives on the American South: An Annual Review of Society, Politics, and Culture, Volume 4,* ed. James C. Cobb and Charles R. Wilson (New York, 1987), 1–18. I have added passages from "The Last Theologians: Recent Southern Literary Criticism," *Michigan Quarterly Review* 17 (Summer 1978): 404–13; and from "Mentalité and Southern History," ibid. 21 (Summer 1982): 515–19.

some generational. It will be helpful to start with the legacy of recent Southern literary criticism, the custodian of Tate's perspective. The first essay of this book, in addressing the mind of the Old South, had occasion briefly to characterize that legacy, especially its attempt to combine, by means of a theory of alienation, the ascending theme of literary improvement with the descending theme of a lost Gemeinschaft culture. It will be self-evident by now that I believe the root of this critical precept of necessary and nourishing alienation lies in Romanticism, an opinion shared by Robert Penn Warren, who has observed in conversation with Cleanth Brooks that the main theme of literature since the Romantic period has been alienation.[3]

True to this perspective, writing Southern literary history and criticism has devolved into gauging the margin of alienation and delineating the nature of community. As has been seen, Lewis P. Simpson has argued that the Old South chose to defy history by forging the image of an integrated pastoral society, a dream world too unalienated to be creative. In so doing, it severed itself from the mainstream of Western literature and was thus impoverished.[4] Other critics have suggested that the imperatives of slavery and the Lost Cause handicapped the South's nineteenth century, with two exceptions: Poe and Twain. And their distance from Southern mythology is explained by their non-Southern connections: Poe's New England birth, the border Southernness of Missouri, and Twain's sojourn outside the region in his mature years. Louis Rubin has made a half-hearted plea for Sidney Lanier, with the crippling proviso that Lanier might have become an important writer if he had but lived longer and stayed away from the South. Similarly, Rubin has puckishly argued that the Renaissance flowered chiefly in the Piedmont South because Tidewater communities gave a genteel approval to literature that throttled creativity.[5]

Such logic was designed by Tate to explain the Southern Renaissance, and it is not surprising, therefore, that it seems to work most efficaciously when applied to the interwar years. One of the most acute chapters in Rubin's *The Writer in the South* is his discussion of the Fugitives and Agrarians. He is understandably eager to dispel the legend—partly fostered by the Agrarians themselves—that they were but simple country boys, possessed of the old values and writing out of a shocked dismay at the modern world. They did not have an identity so much as they asserted one. As Simpson has shrewdly put it: "They more or less successfully convey the impression that their inheritance is something solidly given; although the trouble that they take to give this impression reveals how much of their inheritance is artifice, how little merely 'passed on.' If I read them at all correctly, I would say that no American writers ever worked harder at inheriting their inheritance than the Agrarians."[6]

Alienation may be the critical key, but the Southern critics have had a moderate taste for it. Taking their stand with Tate, they have had a low opinion of an irreligious, existential modern world. The remarkably gloomy Walter Sullivan, in *A Requiem for the Renascence,* has discoursed on "our day of disorder and faltering belief" with scathing distaste. For the inadequacy of their faith in God, the likes of Walker Percy and William Styron have been summarily dispatched.[7]

Rubin has been most explicit about this religious approach to literature. The distinctive approach of the South is "an attitude toward the nature of man in society that can best be described by the word 'religious'—though I hasten to add, by no means sectarian." Later he elaborates: "The image of human life that it represents is one in which the values embodied in it—love and honor and pity and pride and compassion and sacrifice, to adopt Faulkner's memorable assessment—have not been relativist, arbitrary, materialistic, but absolute, unswerving, spiritual." Sullivan is most insistent upon this. "Fiction," it seems, "is a moral art." If recent writing is bad, it can be improved by transcending "the past and the present by the pursuit of values that are metaphysical and therefore eternal." In this vein, there has been much talk that literature embodies "ultimate truths." Thus history has been deemed a lower truth than religion. The most euphoric statement of this sentiment concludes Holman's assessment of Faulkner: "To the limited view of the scientific historian . . . Faulkner, with all his reverence for the past and its meaning, does not give a place of highest honor. That high place is reserved for the imagination of the artist, which can transmute the data of history into the enlarged reality of art, which can translate sociological data into the eternal problems of human culpability and compassionate feeling. Faulkner's 'postage stamp of earth' has stretched out to the four corners of the world, and the middle class planters and farmers and storekeepers of Yoknapatawpha County can body forth man's enduring tragedy."[8]

Even if one grants the force of such a religious analysis, there are difficulties of internal logic. One can understand why Rubin should have added his demurrer about sectarianism. It would have been awkward to have Methodists, Baptists, and Jesuits falling to dispute in the midst of his lecture. But one wonders how it is possible to have a religious attitude without defining and articulating a collateral theology. Without such explicitness, offering the opportunity of debate, religion becomes a vague incantation upon those authors of whom one approves. But this evasiveness commenced, in fact, with the Agrarians themselves. Tate was an agnostic who migrated into Catholicism. Ransom was a Methodist who flirted very briefly and unconvincingly with an eccentric God of Thunder and ended up a polite Episcopalian. Davidson never cared for religion at all. Warren is a sort of existentialist, henpecked by friends into guilt about living off the capital of Christian morality. *I'll Take My Stand* is eloquent about religion but never specifies which religion. Indeed, when the Agrarians met in council with Seward Collins in 1933 at Andrew Lytle's Alabama farm, Cornsilk, to plan their contributions to the new *American Review,* they were careful to advise against a specific religious position even as they endorsed religion as a special concern of the periodical.[9]

This simultaneous interest in history and religion has necessarily led to certain distortions of history itself. Rubin has written, in a spirit, apparent from the context, defensive of a transcendental theology: "The historical sense, the assumption that what human beings have done in time is meaningful and that men are creatures of time and are molded by what has transpired before them, rests absolutely upon the conviction of the importance of what men can achieve; for if human life ultimately means nothing, and if there are no values which transcend the requirements of the moment, then the past is indeed a bucket of ashes, and only what *is,* and not how it came to be or what it may one day turn out to be, is of any interest."[10] This is dubious intellectual history. The centuries in which a transcendental religion held most absolute sway, the Middle Ages, were not remarkble for a historical sense. Nor should one expect this. The point of absolute values, fixed on man by a god, is that they are not dependent upon time and place. While there was latent in Christian teleology a sense of time, it was secularization that sired the modern obsession with history. For history is what defines the relations in which man lives, and the existentialist is deeply concerned with it. Robert Penn Warren, who admits diffidently to a certain paganism in a published conversation with Cleanth Brooks, knows this full well.[11]

Such a universalist theology is especially incongruous in a modern literary critic. His theme of alienation is irredeemably relativist, since the legacy of that Romanticism was precisely a "natural supernaturalism." Lewis Simpson and Walter Sullivan, in castigating and understanding modernism, have liked to cite the conservative philosopher Eric Voegelin, for whom modernism is a "gnostic madness" in which man has arrogated the prerogatives of God in seeking to redefine human nature. Unfortunately, it would seem that literature is intimately involved in such gnosticism. The doctrine does not merely apply to man's action upon his fellow man: it also implies that man can *understand* man in his entirety. Yet it is such understanding that is the chief vanity of literature. In the high place Faulkner gives the artist and the critic gives Faulkner, gnosticism is firmly lodged. To his credit, Sullivan has thought this through: "Beginning with the ascendency of romanticism and increasingly in our own time, we have come to think too highly of literature. Barzun reminds us that in the nineteenth century art supplanted religion in the mind of artists, then in the minds of their followers, as the revelation of ultimate truth, the repository of the highest reality."[12]

One of the strategies by which this transcendentalism has been maintained was the insistence of the New Criticism, following and adapting Symbolist aesthetics, that literature embodied a special and superior order of knowledge. Ransom, in his abortive philosophical study of the late 1920s, claimed that literature went a step beyond the accomplishment of scientific knowledge. Naturally, to maintain such a distinction, science and history had to be expelled from the domain of literature. So was born, though not with Ransom alone, the curious modern distinction between "imaginative literature" and the rest. Crucial to the argument was the insistence that art was ultimately separable from "propaganda." This was an offshoot of the theology of "ultimate truths." To note that a literary production was caused by and aimed at local social issues seemed to diminish its universality, and thus an oration, a satire, a proslavery argument, a history, was deemed irrelevant to the concerns of literary criticism. It is a distinction necessarily opaque to the historian. (It is an irony, by the way, that the word *propaganda* has a religious origin. It formed part of the title of the Congregatio de Propaganda Fide, the missionary arm of the Roman Catholic church, and only acquired a pejorative meaning in the nineteenth century among anti-Catholic zealots.) But one might usefully quote Edmund Wilson here, lest the historian be thought too partial. In a letter in 1931, fittingly to Allen Tate, he discussed the meaning of the distinction between propaganda and art, as well as the range of the word *literature:* "I'm looking back to Shaw, Wells, Bennett, France, Flaubert, Dostoevsky, Ibsen, Renan, et al. You call some of these people propagandists, but I don't see how you could . . . if by propaganda you mean the kind of thing which is put out by governments, political parties, etc. If by propaganda you mean, on the other hand, merely attempts to persuade people of one's point of view or particular way of seeing things, every writer is a propagandist. . . . If scientists like Descartes, Newton, Einstein, Darwin and Freud don't 'look deeply into experience,' what do they do? They have imaginations as powerful as any poet's, and some of them were first-rate writers as well. How do you draw the line between *Walden* and *The Voyage of the Beagle*? . . . You are still, I think, too much impressed with the dicta on this subject of the Aquinas of *The Criterion,* who has an obvious interest nowadays in disparaging scientific revelation in order to fortify religious revelation."[13]

All these are arguments directed at the internal logic of the standpoint of recent Southern literary criticism. But history itself, particularly social and intellectual history, has cast further doubt upon the descending theme of social disintegration, the Gemeinschaft / Gesellschaft motif. It has, no doubt, been an image of great potency for novelists and poets, but it will scarcely serve as a serious sociological proposition. It is doubtful that, as Tate claimed, the South's presence in the modern world was drastically altered by the First World War, that the region was any more in and of that world in 1920 than it had been in 1910. Indeed, it is arguable that the Southern economy in 1850, before the decline of cotton, was more a part of a modernizing world than it was to become in 1920. There is scant evidence that industrialization was sufficiently intensifying in the 1920s to posit a special moment of economic transition, least of all from a noncommercial to a commercial economy. Woodward has called this social explanation nonsense, and the repudiation has been echoed by Daniel Singal, who bases his study upon the premise that ideological change preceded social change in the region. Richard King has half resisted Woodward and Singal on this but concedes the economic point, while insisting that intellectual Southerners felt themselves in the midst of a fundamental economic change. This is a distinction without a difference.[14]

Moreover, the evidence is clear that Tate's claim—that Southerners were newly conscious of the past in the present—was scarcely a novel discovery in 1930, though his generation obviously modulated the definitions of what past in what present. George Washington Cable, as much as Faulkner, was obliged to meditate upon the interpenetrations of then and now. Further back yet, this sense of a vanishing world was a crucial part of antebellum thought. If one but turns to the first Southern novel, *Swallow Barn,* one can find this in its 1853 preface: "Swallow Barn exhibits a picture of country life in Virginia, as it existed in the first quarter of the present century. Between that period and the present day, time and what is called 'the progress,' have made many innovations there, as they have done every where else. . . . An observer cannot fail to note that the manners of our country have been tending towards a uniformity which is visibly effacing all local differences. . . . The country now apes the city in what is supposed to be the elegancies of life, and the city is inclined to value and adopt the fashions it is able to import across the Atlantic, and thus the whole surface of society is exhibiting the traces of a process by which it is likely to be rubbed down, in time, to one level, and varnished with the same gloss." One could with no great difficulty parallel from Southern history the procession of laments for a vanished integrated agrarian society that prefaces Raymond Williams's *The Country and the City*.[15]

It is particularly improbable to locate the Eden of community in the years in which the Agrarians were growing up. The 1890s, racked by depression and the social conflict of agrarian populism, were scathing times of social disunity. In the nineteenth century the South was a socially mobile and divided society. Thus the perception of community, inherited by the twentieth century, was as much a fiction of alienation for the Old South as for the 1920s. For Christians in the 1970s, uncomfortable in an apparently agnostic intellectual society, it may seem like harmony to note that antebellum Southerners were religious. In the clamor between Methodist and Baptist, Roman Catholic and Protestant, the unity was more opaque. For the urbanite, to note that most nineteenth-century Southerners lived on farms may seem like community. For the sharecropper desperately arguing with his landlord, the slave quietly sabotaging his tools, the tenant farmer fighting to keep down his rent, the sense of integrated values was less apparent. In short, it is doubtful that the South has ever been in other than what social historians have taught us to think of as at least the early modern, and possibly even the modern, world.

Only Lewis P. Simpson has sensed the difficulties posed by this fact, partly because he has been persuaded by Eugene Genovese's argument that the Old South, though precapitalist, was implicated in that modernity as, in Simpson's précis, "being within the realm of a possible interpretation of a complicated and paradoxical epoch in modern history."[16] No doubt much of Simpson's critical writing rehearses the familiar eschatology of the Southern literary critic. He does mechanically offer us that inevitable quotation from Allen Tate about the Southern Renaissance being a special consciousness born of historical change, and that from Quentin Compson about the past not being dead, and that from Stephen Dedalus about history as a nightmare, all of which should be sealed up in concrete and deposited in the

Tombigbee River. Half his perspectives—and most of his heart, I suspect—are orthodox, nothing that could not have been learned in the English department of the South for the last thirty years.

But half are not. Simpson has made the most concerted effort to reassess the legacy of Allen Tate. But he is very diffident about it, so polite and gentle in his disagreements that one could almost miss the heterodoxy. Simpson does not stoop to the slashing phrase. He simply says, "Let me raise another possibility," and does not bother to explain, perhaps not even to himself, that the possibility is entirely destructive of the orthodoxy. He would, I think, be uncomfortable in the role of the rebel. Yet his argument is this: since the early modern period self-consciousness has moved progressively to the center of both society and the literary vocation; history has become mind; in the South this displacement has been coincident with the growth of the region itself; there has never been a moment of Gemeinschaft wholeness in Southern history from which later writing has taken its fruitful literary awareness. He observes, in writing of Richard Beale Davis's *Intellectual Life in the Colonial South,* that Davis has raised "the possibility [of] tracing in southern colonial culture what Hegel describes in his *Philosophy of History* as the essential cultural consequence of the modern subjectifying of history: a secularization of the spiritual, which issues in a spiritualizing of the secular." Yet nothing has been more crucial to traditional Southern literary criticism than the belief that once upon a time there was an undifferentiated Southern society, which is now lost. The demise has been variously dated: at the Civil War, with the rise of the New South, at the First World War. But everyone has agreed that it happened at some moment. Simpson does not believe it. That is a heterodoxy of fundamental importance. It means that the Southern writer, always regarded as the self-aware survivor of the transition, never had a transition to survive. He, like the rest of us since the Middle Ages, made it up. He invented the South and therefore himself.[17]

This theme of self-invention is not peculiar to the Southerner. Simpson sees it in Henry James, whose observation in *The American Scene* on the Capitol in Washington sets the motif and title of Simpson's *The Brazen Face of History:* "One rubbed one's eyes, but there, at its highest polish, shining in the beautiful day, was the brazen face of history, and there, all about one, immaculate, the printless pavements of the State." The last sentences of *The Brazen Face of History* chillingly summarize Simpson's viewpoint and gloss the James quotation: "With singular perceptiveness James saw himself as the embodiment, we may say, of the secularization of the spiritual . . . in, that is to say, his self-willed, yet deeply unwilling, deformation of the reality of God. Ten years before World War I, when he had seen the shameless, detached, and no doubt Satanic visage of history looming above the American Capitol, James had looked, we may suppose, on a face palpably his own. There is a kind of terror in thinking that he was a survivor looking upon what he had survived, and still must survive." [18]

Simpson is not happy about this self-invention. It makes his vision of Southern literary history unmitigatingly bleak. There is no cozy corner of Southern history where the Southerner can curl up with his kinfolk. He is left, as Simpson seems to be, unhappily chatting with the likes of Hegel, Dilthey, Nietzsche, who are liberally sprinkled through his essays. He is left with phrases—"the subjectification of history in the individual consciousness," "the secularization of the Third Realm"—which seem to come from a primer of German Romantic philosophy. Lewis Simpson stands oddly before us, the Schlegel of the Louisiana State University Press.

But here one must tread very carefully. Simpson has quoted Baudelaire's "the man of letters is the world's enemy" as a motif for the theme of literary alienation and implies that it can be used as an adequate characterization of the Romanticism of the early nineteenth century. [19] This is a half-truth. Those earlier formulations were double-edged. The artist was to forge a dialectical relationship with society, but his task was as much to bring back his alienated vision and reintegrate it with society, thus creating a richer texture for life, as it was to stay permanently aside. In short, Romanticism was not just Baudelaire, it was also Herder. Modern thought has lurched between these polarities, the psychology of alienation and the sociology of community. Southern literary criticism, heir of that tradition, has done likewise. It is fair to say that Allen Tate began with the premise of alienation and moved, unsuccessfully, towards community. His successors have begun with community and been obliged to echo the pieties of alienation. Yet it is difficult not to resist the conclusion that though their head has been with alienation, their heart has remained with community.

This yearning for community has given rise to one of the more half-baked myths of Southern literature, the conventional wisdom that the Southern mind is "concrete." There has been much confusion among the Southern critics over the delimitation of the Southern Gemeinschaft. Categories by no means synonymous have been run together: the discrete social communities of localities—Faulkner's northern

Mississippi, Ellen Glasgow's Richmond, or Thomas Wolfe's Asheville—and "the South." Hugh Holman has sensed this and has tried to split the South into the three social categories that might explain the standpoints of Faulkner, Glasgow, and Wolfe: Delta, Tidewater, and Piedmont. If Gemeinschaft has any meaning beyond the metaphorical (and even Ferdinand Tönnies, the author of Gemeinschaft / Gesellschaft theory, used it chiefly as a metaphor, not as an argument for the historical existence of actual Gemeinschaft communities), it applies to such localities. By no stretch of anything but a phenomenological imagination can so huge and diverse an area as the South be designated a community. The South is a metaphysical construct, born of the interaction of an intellectual tradition, historicist Romanticism, with social and political history. Indeed the Southern mind may be quite the most metaphysical on the North American continent. It is the student of metaphysics who can take the greatest pleasure in the discussions among Southern critics about the meaning and scope of *Southern*.[20] Much of the history of the Southern mind is such a debate: not how many angels may dance upon the head of a pin but how many and what manner of men may crowd upon the word *South*.

ALLEN TATE was confessedly the master spirit of this critical legacy, and it is important to remember that his analysis was partisan. He was staking a claim for himself and his contemporaries. Mencken and his ilk needed refutation, and the refutation was successful.[21] No one now doubts the existence of a respectable body of Southern writing in these years, though in less careful hands than Tate's the claim was substantiated by counting up Pulitzer Prizes, Guggenheims, and, *mirabile dictu*, the Nobel, a method of analysis notoriously subject to skepticism and refutation, since Pearl Buck preceded William Faulkner to Stockholm.[22] But Tate was partisan in a deeper, more important sense. By defining the characteristics of the Renaissance, he was delimiting a canon, of those who exemplified his definition. The logic was circular, made possible for Tate because he was both inside and outside the canon, both poet and critic, using the standing of the poet to justify the authority of the critic, the acumen of the critic to justify the strategy of the poet. It is an old and respectable sleight of hand, nowhere better done than by Coleridge in the *Biographia Literaria*, a precedent of which Tate was abundantly aware. In urging the necessities of intellectual imperialism, Tate was an honest partisan. "A sound critical program has at least this one feature: *it allows the reader no choice in the standards of judgement*," he wrote in 1936 in commenting upon the function of the critical quarterly. The need was, "not to give the public what it wants, or what it thinks it wants, but what—through the medium of its most intelligent members—it ought to have."[23]

Tate's Renaissance was a Christian eschatological drama, after the fashion of T. S. Eliot, embodying, to use Frank Kermode's phrase, "the sense of an ending."[24] Matters in Tate, and among his disciples, are always dying. They wait on their senatorial chairs for the barbarians to come, the Gnostics to subvert religious rectitude. This vision has faltered, not just because we Visigoths are less Christian, but because the Renaissance is now seen less as an ending, more as a beginning. It is studied often to explain the origins of the sea change of the 1950s and 1960s, to make intelligible Selma, black enfranchisement, civil rights. This rationale is expecially clear in the recent writings of Morton Sosna and Richard King: the first became aware of the South by watching in Chicago the television images of the civil-rights struggle; the second was in Chapel Hill when the sit-ins began in Greensboro. If the culture of the South awoke, Selma is what it awoke to do.[25]

This has altered criteria and, with them, the canon. Look at, for example, the influential anthologies of Louis Rubin and Robert Jacobs, *Southern Renascence: The Literature of the Modern South* (1953) and *South: Modern Southern Literature in Its Cultural Setting* (1961). They include Allen Tate, William Faulkner, Robert Penn Warren, Ellen Glasgow, James Branch Cabell, Stark Young, Katherine Anne Porter, Thomas Wolfe, Eudora Welty, Erskine Caldwell, Caroline Gordon, John Crowe Ransom, John Peale Bishop, Donald Davidson, Cleanth Brooks, Merrill Moore, and Carson McCullers. Of these seventeen, six are directly Fugitives or Agrarians, ten are so by connection of friendship or marriage. Others are present largely to point the moral: Cabell and Glasgow as flawed portents, Caldwell and Wolfe as liberal horrors, Welty, Porter, and McCullers as successors. It is a coherent canon, tightly conforming to Tate's standards, themselves duly elaborated in thematic essays.[26] Look now at recent studies of Southern thought. Some names have dropped from sight: Caldwell, Gordon, Bishop, Moore, even Wolfe. More important is the appearance of new names, of different hue: James Agee, Howard Odum, Rupert Vance, Gerald W. Johnson, Frank Owsley, C. Vann Woodward, Lillian Smith, John Wade, Broadus Mitchell, William Couch, Guy Johnson, Jonathan Daniels, Wilbur Cash, George Fort Milton, William Alexander Percy, V. O. Key, Margaret Mitchell.[27] There are more political liberals here, previously beyond the pale of a conservative literary criticism. But that is an insufficient clue, for it would not explain the presence of conservative figures like Owsley, Wade, and Percy. More crucial is a different sense of the legitimacy of ideology and of genre. Politics and social analysis seem to be far more acceptable, even crucial, for even in the discriminations of well-established figures such as Faulkner, Tate, Davidson, the emphasis now falls far more upon their social than their aesthetic achievement. This is a heresy, often rebuked by the orthodox. For remember that Tate and Ransom, Warren and Brooks, in their incarnations as New Critics, argued that ideology was death for the writer, because it bred polemic, propaganda, the perils of explicitness. Rather we should honor irony, tension, ambiguity, resolution only in the technique, never in the world.[28] This emphasis had, in fact, required them to disown not only the Erskine Caldwells and Mike Golds but even their younger selves. *I'll Take My Stand* was edited into a metaphor, as though John Ransom had never written that party politics were necessary, as though Allen Tate had never spoken of taking hold of tradition by violence, with the *Action Française* in his mind.[29]

That so much of this recent historical writing has been instigated by the 1960s has several consequences, not least a greater interest in the problem of race. But most important is that the 1960s, whatever their disappointments, seemed to teach the efficacy of ideology and politics. Matters did change, they did move, whereas the lesson for Tate had been that matters did not change, or only for the worse. No Agrarian marched with thousands to the Lincoln Memorial and saw an American president endorse his program. Thus, recent writing is more interested in the social discourse of change, the direct confrontation with society, exemplified in such as Woodward on Tom Watson, Odum on regionalism, Vance on the cotton economy, Cash on the Savage Ideal, Agee on the sharecropper. Those who hazarded the mire are honored. This affects the sense of genres. Sociology, historical narrative, political analysis, these become legitimate, coequal with the lyric or the novel. This is striking in, for example, Singal's attempt to conjoin Odum and Faulkner as literary figures, or in Richard King's grouping in a single chapter Warren, Key, and Woodward, or in Fred Hobson explicating Lillian Smith, James McBride Dabbs, and Cash, as well as reaching into the political discourse of the nineteenth-century South through Edmund Ruffin, Hinton Rowan Helper, and Daniel R. Hundley.[30]

So the canon is mutating. It needs to change much more. It still fails to accommodate black writers, a fact note uncomfortably in the prefaces to many of these works.[31] Charles Johnson, Ralph Ellison,

Richard Wright, Jean Toomer, Mary McLeod Bethune, these are acknowledged, not assimilated to the analyses.[32] But the omissions run
deeper. Woodward has written that the Renaissance was confined "to
the literary arts—poetry, fiction, and drama. It did not spill over to
any significant degree to the visual or performing arts. There was no
Southern Renaissance in music, painting, sculpture, so far as I am
aware."[33] I am puzzled why drama is not a performing art but let that
pass. I detect faint rumblings of reappraisal about painting, largely in
studies of the WPA, but little on the score of architecture. But music?
The major contribution of Southern culture to the world in this century is, beyond a doubt, music. Southern writers have given us rich
and interesting variations upon established literary genres, but the
forms of modern literature would be much the same if Tate and Faulkner had never lived. We would lack *The Sound and the Fury,* but we
would have *Ulysses.* We would miss the "Ode to the Confederate Dead"
but could rub along with *The Waste Land.* It would be a shame to be
without *Understanding Poetry,* but there would still be I. A. Richards.
But take away W. C. Handy, Louis Armstrong, King Oliver, Duke
Ellington, Dizzy Gillespie, and you deprive the world of something
that only the American South could give. Go to Moscow, Hong Kong,
Lusaka, Buenos Aires, Edinburgh, and try to engage the local population in a discussion about *All the King's Men,* and unless you blunder
across an academic or a student, you will meet blank stares. Mention
the "St Louis Blues" or "Take the 'A' Train," and they will whistle it
for you. Jazz is the music of the twentieth century, and it is chiefly
Southern, by origin and expatriation. We would distort less to write
cultural histories of the South by including Armstrong and excluding
even Faulkner than to do the reverse, which is our practice.

What if we included jazz in our syntheses of the cultural awakening
of the American South? What would it do to the analysis? It would,
for one thing, further call into question the simple insistence that historical consciousness and rootedness are characteristic of the South.
Jazz, though a traditional form, is not remarkable for historicism.
There is little history in the lyrics of the Mississippi blues except personal history. Verses are marked by Woodward's familiar list of Southern qualities—defeat, despair, frustration—but lack his other *sine qua
non,* the explanatory power of time, chronology, public events. Jazz is
an existential form, individual not social,[34] defining for the moment,
seeking the induplicable. It flirts with the texture of place, as in a song
such as "Darkness on the Delta," but the imagery is fleeting, thriving
upon dissonance and the variety of standpoint. Only in rare formal

compositions such as Ellington's *Black, Brown and Beige* can a historical vision be found, assuming that one disallows as historical consciousness the habit of musical allusion characteristic of the jazz solo. In short, the progress of evolution from Robert Johnson to Charlie Parker is alone evidence enough to upset Tate.[35]

A new synthesis of the Renaissance would need to cope with these problems of the canon. Yet I detect a loss of interest in the central question, Why the Southern Renaissance? With the partial exception of Singal, to whom I must return, no recent work sets itself the task of answering the question. Richard King pokes at it, by offering the notion of a Southern family romance, a repudiation of the fathers, but the idea is haphazardly applied, often disappears from the analysis, is never historically demonstrated. King is useful as a reader of texts, the utility of which he has often urged, but he is bored by context. Upon the individual text he is often illuminating, usually fresh, welcomely independent. He thinks *I'll Take My Stand* is flat and hysterical, he regards Faulkner's Nobel Prize speech as so much "tedious humanism." But he is not quite a historian by temperament, for after Nietzsche he wants to use hermeneutics to abolish history, to free us from its nightmare. His own technique is brute intellectual force, and I go to his book as I might go to a boxing match, appalled by the violence, impressed by the skill and training. Yet even Woodward has given up on explaining the Renaissance. He has surveyed the usual explanations and dismissed them all, thereby leaving nothing but a vacuum, a mystery.[36]

Mystery is a useful word because it catches the mood of 1940, now dissipating. The Renaissance was a wonder, a puzzle, a mystical experience. It needed an explanation the way the ecstasy of Saint Theresa needs one, that is, very little, since those who believe in the miracle understand that rationality would only dissipate its force. To define it, you need, not a rationalist, but Bernini. For Tate, even for Woodward, the fact that the South had produced a literature able to face the world was a spectacle so novel that it needed a special order of explanation. It is unsurprising that they lurched into mysticism, because they were thinking in the attitude of prayer, their heads suffused with incense, their knees not yet sore. Given the economic and intellectual poverty of their point of reference, the South of 1900, all this was understandable. But is it in retrospect necessary? When we talk of the Southern Renaissance, all we need and should mean is the emergence of an ordinarily competent literary culture, a stock of good writers, the occasional very good one, the rare genius. An ordinary investment in literacy, universities, publishers, journals, is likely to yield that. There is no mystery: Western culture swarms with such people.

We have mingled two distinct issues in analyzing the Southern Renaissance. There is, firstly, the quantitative fact of more and abler Southern writers. This is chiefly an economic problem, of the condition of education and the consumption of literature. That the intellectual culture of the Old South was truncated by the Civil War, that its ideology needed reappraisal, that the Southern economy, especially its educational system, needed rebuilding—all these seem sufficient to explain the belated emergence of the Southern Renaissance.[37] There is, secondly, the question of themes. Here there is no single renaissance, but several, because there are many individuals and groups of differing persuasions. We should not jumble these issues of theme and substance, which it has been characteristic of Tate and his disciples to do, as though you have to believe in certain things to be creative at all. Different standpoints serve the energies of different people at different times. If this is so, there is no good reason to accept Tate and Walter Sullivan's gloomy apprehensions that the Southern Renaissance was temporary. The Agrarian themes of 1930 are dead or moribund, but a lively culture goes on.

I mentioned that only Daniel Singal hazards the general problem, the origins and nature of the Southern Renaissance, though even he prefers to regard his book as a study of the nature of modernism, only incidentally written about the South, because there the transition was belated and contracted. *The War Within* has been much hailed, and one is glad to have it, to add to the canon, to fuel the debate. It is a book of many merits, notable for its solid expository prose, grave in pace, earnest in standpoint. Since it is the nearest to a synthesis that the new generation of historians has offered, it bears close scrutiny, the more so because its analysis is flawed.

Singal believes that the South underwent a successful transition from Victorianism to modernism between 1919 and 1945. Victorianism is regarded as a systematic intellectual paradigm, as is modernism. The former is held to be characterized by a passion for moral discipline, a hierarchical view of culture, a need to distinguish firmly between the barbaric and the civilized, a desire to establish innocence as a cultural goal. The latter is marked by cultural relativism, a recognition of the necessity of evil, a rejection of psychological repression, a stamina in the face of moral uncertainty, a disdain for gentility, an admiration for dialectical conflict.[38] These are deemed firm categories, strong enough to be laid as a rubric upon individual figures. Thus Ulrich Phillips, Broadus Mitchell, Ellen Glasgow, and James Branch Cabell are post-Victorians; Howard Odum, William Faulkner, and the Agrarians are "modernists by the skin of their teeth"; William Couch, Rupert Vance,

Guy Johnson, Arthur Raper, and Robert Penn Warren are modernists. This is admirably tidy, but it has the clarity of consistent error.

It is the burden of this book that modernism is a modulated version of Romanticism, but I will not insist upon that point here. Whether modernism is a full and original intellectual paradigm is open to genuine doubt, so let us give Singal the benefit of Peter Gay's case.[39] Romanticism does not exist on Singal's intellectual horizon. The word occurs rarely and inconsistently in the book: Carlyle, otherwise called a Victorian, appears fleetingly as a Romantic thinker, without any discussion of whether these are or are not mutually exclusive categories; the *Fugitive* is said to bear the marks of "the old romanticism," by which is meant the myth of the wanderer; and Donald Davidson's poetry is said to be romantic, here apparently implying lush exoticism. Similarly, as Richard King has noticed, Idealism is abruptly dubbed the culminating philosophical expression of Victorianism, as existentialism is to modernism, though it is puzzling how Idealism, which predates Victorianism, can be its culmination. Yet Idealism nowhere features in Singal's exposition of Victorianism. Nor could it, because Singal is insistent that Victorianism is incapable of fathoming the nature of "shifting polarities," and it would be a matter of some ingenuity to prove that Hegel, Marx, and Darwin did not understand the idea of the dialectic.[40] But one must set aside the destructive possibilities of ideas that do not occur in Singal and confine attention to those that do, Victorianism and modernism.

Singal does not describe Victorianism, he condemns it: it is a "genteel cultural omnibus"; it lacks cultural self-criticism, "the discontent with civilization [having] largely dissipated during the nineteenth century"; it is marked by "incorrigible naivete," "false optimism," and "complacent self-deception"; it has the "conception of a universe composed of timeless, abstract truths." In short, the nineteenth century is a wasteland, upon escaping from which we may congratulate ourselves. Now I thought we had long got beyond this kind of caricature, that it had been laid to rest with the sardonic ghost of Lytton Strachey. But apparently not, because Singal does not even blush to use that old chestnut, the piano leg with curtains. Generations of study by Victorian historians go for little. Walter Bagehot has no critical realism; Ranke does not grasp cultural relativism; Charles Fourier flees from man's sexual nature; Darwin is opaque on man's rootedness in the animal; Anthony Trollope is given to fantasy; Engels is innocent about society; Carlyle is handicapped by gentility. It is important to stress that while Singal correctly observes that the Victorianism of the

New South is far from subtle, his is an indictment levied against the general phenomenon.[41]

Now, Singal is better at defining his version of Victorianism than at specifying his Victorians, so the thesis is slippery. One gathers that Darwin is not a Victorian but T. H. Huxley is, though how this can be is obscure.[42] Only one Victorian text is discussed, Stevenson's *Dr. Jekyll and Mr. Hyde.* Singal's exegesis will serve to point up his difficulties. He argues that the Victorians inordinately stressed personal morality because they felt repression of man's animal nature must not be relaxed. He writes: "Nothing illustrates this imperative better than Robert Louis Stevenson's famous novella of 1885 . . . in which the eminently respectable Dr. Jekyll transforms himself into an alter ego, the pleasure-seeking Mr. Hyde, in order to experience a few of the indulgences he had always denied himself. The experiment soon goes awry, however, culminating when Hyde commits a succession of unusually sadistic crimes purely on impulse. Jekyll, who had always assumed that he could regain control at will, finally resorts to suicide to stop the insatiable Hyde from usurping him forever. The lesson is clear: a civilized man must not unleash the animal within, even for a moment." This is a symptomatic misreading. For Henry Jekyll did not deny himself pleasures, though he was not proud of them, and he understood "that man is not truly one, but truly two," that he has a "thorough and primitive duality." Jekyll undertook his experiments to sunder the halves, to rid man of his lower and bestial side, so that "the unjust might go his way, delivered from the aspirations and remorse of his more upright twin; and the just could walk steadfastly and securely on his upward path, doing the good things in which he found pleasure, and no longer exposed to disgrace and penitence by the hands of this extraneous evil." That is, the experiment was undertaken precisely to test the validity of that aspiration to innocence that Singal claims is the essence of Victorian values. The result was disaster, murder, the enfeeblement of Jekyll, suicide. "I have been made to learn," Jekyll says, "that the doom and burden of our life is bound for ever on man's shoulders; and when the attempt is made to cast it off, it but returns upon us with more familiar and more awful pressure." The lesson of the novella is certainly that man errs in isolating and releasing the animal to walk the streets uninhibited but that, more important, he needs the animal within to function at all. Yet we are informed that such an insight is reserved to the modernist[43] and does not occur fully in the South until Robert Penn Warren's *Night Rider.*

I dwell on this not because I wish to dismiss Victorianism as a useless concept. To use the phrase does connote something, a sensibility, a knot of problems, a stance, a tone. But it is not a consistent enough body of ideas to constitute a paradigm equal to the Enlightenment, Romanticism, or even modernism. It existed, not so much as a world view, as a debate about the implications of Romanticism, most notably a debate about the relevance of Romanticism to industrialism. To hazard a crude parallel, one can suggest that Victorianism was to Romanticism what we are to modernism; that is, it was a sober postprandial weighing of the wisdom of the reigning and overly bold paradigm. Macaulay asked, Do we really wish to be Byron, just as we ask, Do we really want to be Joyce? In both cases bets are hedged. This being so, Victorianism cannot be made to bear the weight of Singal's analysis. Yet even if we set aside the issue of Romanticism, the analytical difficulty of Singal resolves itself into this: he takes the worst of Victorianism and the best of modernism. That is, he replaces Tate's partisanship with Strachey's. This is not a step forward.

What of Singal on modernism? Singal has an eccentric definition, evident when we note that it makes William Faulkner and Allen Tate less than full modernists, yet bestows the accolade on William Couch and Guy Johnson. What rubric will perform this trick? Singal sees modernism as a realist doctrine, direct, candid, culturally relativist, grasping the necessity of evil, open to and welcoming conflict. When his dramatis personae falter in these qualities—as all do, it seems, but Robert Penn Warren—Singal sadly marks them down on the grade sheet he carries through his book. But is this modernism? If it is, it is not the modernism I thought I knew, for Singal's rubric puts a question mark not only against Faulkner but against Eliot, who makes an appearance in *The War Within* as someone who had "set himself up as a gentlemanly man of letters in London and had joined the Anglican Church." As I understand it, modernism was precisely *not* a realist doctrine.[44]

Malcolm Bradbury and James McFarlane's anthology *Modernism* offers a contradictory definition. "One of the word's associations is with the coming of a new era of high aesthetic self-consciousness and non-representationalism, in which art turns from realism and humanistic representation towards style, technique, and spatial form in pursuit of a deeper penetration of life. . . . human consciousness and especially *artistic* consciousness could become more intuitive, more poetic; art could now fulfill *itself*. It was free to catch at the manifold—the atoms as they fall—and create significant harmony not in the universe but within itself (like the painting which Lily Briscoe completes at the end of *To the Lighthouse*). The world, reality, is discontinuous till art comes along, which may be a modern crisis for the world; but within art all becomes vital, discontinuous, yes, but within an aesthetic system of positioning."[45] It is by this rubric that it has been customary to define as modernists Eliot, Woolf, Picasso, Pirandello, Faulkner, Pound, Tate, Dada. Modernism is about the necessity, not of realism, but of fiction. The informing social ideology of the fiction is largely irrelevant. The modernist is not defined by his conservatism or reformism, by being a High Anglican or an atheist, a liberal or a fascist, but by the stance that sees the private myth of art as a solution, however unstable, to the crisis of the times.

This is not Singal's modernism. So it would be prudent to inquire, What *is* Singal's modernism? Does it not look remarkably like reform liberalism, with a little psychology and anthropology thrown in for good measure? How else can we fathom the otherwise unfathomable proposition that the logic of modernism, according to Singal, should have forced William Couch "to entertain the possibility of racial integration in the South"? How else can we explain that Singal believes Southerners would have "to break with the Victorian ethos," because "*only then* could they begin finding solutions to the region's multitude of social problems" (my italics)? How else does it make sense that the modernist impulse of "integrating thought and emotion" was related to the desire "to bridge the existing gaps between classes and races within the South, as well as the gap between the South and the rest of the nation"[?] Is this not an old-fashioned Whiggish analysis, where the drama is the process by which the innocent, mythic, and socially repressive nineteenth century, its brain befogged by Cavaliers, racism, and gentility, is swept aside by brisk, realist, sociological, bleak liberals? It is a good yarn, but it has little to do with Victorianism and modernism. Philosophically there is almost nothing in Couch, Raper, Vance, and Johnson that a Victorian could not have believed and acted upon.

Instead *The War Within* is most interesting for its implicit messages. Almost always Singal distributes praise and blame, modernism and Victorianism, according as his characters embrace the implications of politics and reject the timidity of stoicism. The dying fall of his chapters on "modernists by the skin of their teeth" comes when Odum will not face "the political implications" of his regionalism, when Faulkner becomes reactionary but "curiously apolitical," when Tate prefers ambivalence to action. Conversely, it is the political vision of Couch, Vance, Johnson, and Warren that Singal admires. "Stoicism," and "restraint" Singal deprecates, "freedom from ambivalence" and "the world of spontaneous feeling" he celebrates.[46] In short, the 1960s are very alive in the intellectual strategy of *The War Within* in ways it is difficult not to respect, whatever one's doubts about its account of Southern thought.

So Singal does not help us much in escaping from the toils of the Southern Renaissance. As with many such historiographical problems, our difficulties are partly semantic. Indeed there has been much puzzlement over the relevance of the term *renaissance,* when all concur that this marked no rebirth. Why is it used? For us, the answer is that we are stuck with the word because our predecessors used it. But this just pushes back the problem. Why did our predecessors use it? The answer provides a useful sidelight on the Southern Renaissance.

It has been customary to think the Renaissance unexpected by Southerners. The record does not bear this out. The Southern Renaissance was predicted, noted just as it happened, hailed as it proceeded, celebrated as it changed. The paradigm was available long before there was something to which it could be attached. Southerners had been predicting a renaissance for several generations. William Gilmore Simms and George Fitzhugh had done so, William P. Trent and Edwin Mims had done so.[47] Each expected a different renaissance, according to his own lights, but few generations declined to expect the fitting efflorescence of their culture.

The roots of the paradigm run deep. The late eighteenth and early nineteenth century had reified the concept of the renaissance. It is omnipresent in the historical typology of Romanticism, in Schlegel, in Sismondi, in Madame de Staël. The idea reached its fruition with Jacob Burckhardt. But the notion also had been extrapolated from the immediate occasion, the Quattrocento, to other cultures: France, the Netherlands, Germany, England. Each extrapolation required adjustments in emphasis, in notions of genre, in theories of continuity or discontinuity, as national cultures varied.[48] But every culture was supposed to have had this progression out of barbarism into light. In the United States the idea was most energetically applied to the antebellum culture of New England, the more so because, like the Quattrocento, it was said to mark a liberation from a stifling theological precedent by a vigorous commercial and urban culture. Dante was much on the mind of Lowell and Emerson, just as Emerson and Lowell were much on the minds of the New South generation of 1910. This, for example, is William Preston Few, then a young English professor at Trinity College, later president of Duke University, writing in 1904: "From time to time in the history of the world there have come epochs when the ordinary processes of national development have been superseded by more rapid methods and when civilization has gone forward at a bound. Such epochs were seen in England in the last half of the sixteenth century and in New England in the middle and later decades of the nineteenth century. Such an epoch, I believe, is dawning upon us here in the South." Does that sound familiar? Do we not catch an anticipatory whiff of Tate's 1935 reference to the Southern Renaissance as like, "on an infinitesimal scale, the outburst of poetic genius at the end of the sixteenth century, when commercial England had begun to crush feudal England. The Histories and Tragedies of Shakespeare record the death of the old regime, and Doctor Faustus gives up feudal order for world power"?[49]

Three ideas were crucial to Tate's interpretation of the Southern Renaissance: the mutation of economic and social order, the decline of religious coherence, the briefly energizing value of witnessing these changes. All were available to him by 1935 in contemporary interpretations of the Italian and English Renaissances. Historians such as Ferdinand Schevill, Henri Pirenne, and E. P. Cheyney were offering a socioeconomic interpretation of the Italian Renaissance that popularized the insights of Alfred von Martin and, obliquely, Max Weber, who saw the problem of the Renaissance as that of an emergent capitalism that destroyed feudalism and established a rational, urban, individualist order. These had grafted economics onto Burckhardt's case that the Renaissance had instigated the modern world.

Available too was the idea that the Renaissance was inexplicable without the precedent of the Middle Ages. In the hands of a Roman Catholic historian such as Christopher Dawson, it had been argued that an organic religious community had disintegrated, releasing new and temporarily vital intellectual forces. As Wallace K. Ferguson has put it, Dawson had conceded to the Renaissance "a certain reprehensible originality," one that was ultimately destructive. Dawson, it should be noted, was a friend of John Crowe Ransom and closely linked to the Catholic and Anglo-Catholic intellectual community of Eliot, Christopher Hollis, Hilaire Belloc, and G. K. Chesterton, with which Tate himself was connected. Indeed few phrases better describe Tate's sense of the Southern Renaissance than Ferguson's "a certain reprehensible originality."[50]

Lastly, the migration of the paradigm from the Quattrocento to sixteenth-century England had made it respectable to confine the meaning of a Renaissance to belles-lettres, since England had seen no appreciable achievements in painting, sculpture, or architecture. If one rereads Tate's 1935 essay with these interpretations in mind, the parallels are everywhere apparent. We find him writing, "The trouble ultimately goes back to the beginnings of finance-capitalism and its creature, machine-production. Under feudalism the artist was a member of an organic society." We find references to the Old South as aristocratic, feudalist, and possessed of a religion "nearer to Aquinas than to Calvin." We find, too, that Tate thought the Old South intellectually deficient, because it had not been feudal enough, taking its cue too much from a post-feudal, eighteenth-century England and having the inspiration of a rooted peasantry choked off by the intervention of African slavery.[51]

Little of this need surprise us. Of the Agrarians, Tate was the intellectual poacher. He believed in the efficacy of importation. "The arts everywhere spring from a mysterious union of indigenous materials and foreign influences," he once observed. His standing as a critic of the South has derived, to no small degree, from this exoticism. His essays abound in resonant and dignified parallels and allusions. There is a sweeping charm in a sentence like this: "Nor do we doubt that the conflict between modernism and fundamentalism is chiefly the impact of the new middle-class civilization upon the rural society; nor, moreover, should we allow ourselves to forget that philosophers of the State, from Sir Thomas More to John C. Calhoun, were political defenders of the older religious community."[52] By force majeure Tate had welded Southern culture into the wide and intoxicating problem of Western culture. The difficulty for us is that he had welded it into the wrong problem, or one of chief interest to literary and historical theologians, and in raising his eyes to the world, he had turned them away from grasping the various and complex facts of the South itself. His Renaissance paradigm had not been intended originally to describe the cultural economy of the region, so it is little wonder that the euphoria of its explanatory power abated, we begin to notice an inaptness.

CHAPTER 8

A Private Passion: W. J. Cash

W. J. CASH's *Mind of the South,* with its claim that the South has had no mind, only a hedonistic and irrational temperament, is something of a nuisance for intellectual historians of the South, and the temptation to assist in its repudiation is very great. The book has been a primer for students of the region for more than two generations, and while it might be said modestly to have assisted Southern political, social, and economic history, *The Mind of the South* has immeasurably inhibited the study of the mind of the South.

The ammunition for such a repudiation is ready to hand, more than sufficient. Cash took his own life in Mexico City, because he thought himself stalked by Nazi agents, whereas in fact, after a respectful silence, it has been historians who have preyed upon him. Merely to summarize the criticism will make the point. It is said that *The Mind of the South* ignores the colonial history of the South, scants the Old South, and misunderstands the New South. It barely mentions slavery and is more or less racist in its characterization of blacks. It neglects women, except as totemic objects of Southern mythology. It diminishes the existence of class conflict in the Old South and insists upon its relative impotence after the War. It misunderstands the nature of aristocracy. It overstresses both the unity and the continuity of Southern history. It has very little grasp of political history and has no co-

This essay is largely new, though I have taken pages from "W. J. Cash, Hegel, and the South," *Journal of Southern History* 44 (August 1978) : 379—98. The passages of that article that recommend Hegel to Southern historians strike me now as an unsatisfactory exposition ("gangling" was Richard King's adjective, and he is probably right) and used Cash rather shamelessly as a peg on which to hang my own thoughts, which were then bent upon finding an analytical standpoint for my *The Idea of the American South, 1920—1941.* This is intended, by way of redress, to focus more resolutely on Cash and his book.

herent explanation for the Civil War. It is provincial in its emphasis both upon white males and upon the Piedmont of North Carolina as the archetypal South. It exaggerates the guilt of Southerners over slavery. It shows little understanding of the formal ideas of generations of Southern intellectuals. Its view of Reconstruction is primitive. It overestimates the static quality of agricultural society.[1]

So the corpse is riddled, and it would require a necromancer to piece together the shattered bones, torn sinews, and spilled blood. It may be objected that the book does live. In the sense that it is still widely read, this is true. But with not even the robust exception of Bertram Wyatt-Brown, it is doubtful that there are left any disciples of Cash *tout à fait*, only those who admire his prose or are persuaded by isolated aspects of his analysis. His influence on the debate about the persistence of planter influence beyond the Civil War is still marked, for example.[2] Yet his partisans have been driven to begin their defenses of the book by remarking that Cash must be read by the standards of the historiography of the 1930s, a just remark that concedes the point of his diminishing exactitude.[3] But asset-stripping in *The Mind of the South* is an unsatisfactory procedure. It is a book that stands or falls by the coherence and integrity of its cumulative argument. While I think it true that the book is most coherent in its early pages, which Cash rewrote most often, and most diffuse in its later pages, nonetheless Cash intended a carefully articulated and constructed book.

A number of years ago I attempted to breathe life into the corpse by arguing that *The Mind of the South* can be seen as a quasi-Hegelian book and that Hegel offered useful counsel for students of Southern history. It is worth rehearsing part of that argument briefly, as a preliminary to a closer examination of the book's narrative strategy.

The Mind of the South is a book about the Southern *Zeitgeist* and its ability to transform both the perception of the individual and socioeconomic realities. Cash was a philosophical Idealist, not only in the crude sense of believing that ideas can be forces in the historical process but also in a more specific dialectical sense. There is the movement of thesis-antithesis-synthesis in the book.

The thesis was the agricultural condition of antebellum society. The climate, the lushness, and amiability of the land were themselves "a sort of cosmic conspiracy against reality in favor of romance." The frontier had discouraged intellectuality and loosened social bonds by creating an individualism free of "the close-pressing throng . . . , rigid class distinctions, the yoke of law and government, economic imperatives." Thereby there had emerged a series of discrete social groups.

For Cash, the plantation was "an independent social unit." "The farmers and crackers were in their own way self-sufficient too." The Southerner's world was "a simple aggregation of human units, of self-contained and self-sufficient entities."[4]

To this thesis of an atomized, unself-aware society Cash offered an antithesis: the race problem, slavery, and the dispute with the North. From these tensions came the synthesis of Southern self-consciousness. "It was," Cash asserted, "the conflict with the Yankee which really created the concept of the South as something more than a matter of geography, as an object of patriotism, in the minds of the Southerners." Under the pressure of the dialectic, the South drew together around racial loyalty, a paternalistic myth, a more severe and Calvinistic religion. Cash's name for the synthesis was "the savage ideal, . . . that ideal whereunder dissent and variety are completely suppressed and men become, in all their attitudes, professions, and actions, virtual replicas of one another."

Cash was asserting that the image of the planter "actually came to be" the planter. He was saying that a society with no little differentiation had by the act of perceiving unity actually come to be unified. "The delicate implication that this Southerner was somehow any Southerner at random" was internalized. The Southerner "so absolutely identified his ego with the thing called the South as to become, so to say, a perambulating South in little."[5]

The synthesis of feeling and social reality was, for Cash, the central issue of continuity between Old South and New. It is probably unfair to suggest that his repudiation of the Old South–New South distinction was a denial of historical change. In fact, *The Mind of the South* is very rich in a sense of change, especially in the industrial history of the New South. Cash was saying something more complex and distinctly Hegelian: the perception generated by one set of social conditions survived to inform and influence the younger society, itself being forged dialectically by changing conditions.[6]

A central example in this argument was the supposed relationship between "the savage ideal" and the development of class consciousness in the South. Cash assumed that class loyalty was the natural product of an industrializing society. Logically, Southern industrialization ought to have produced such a feeling. It seemed to Cash from his vantage point among the cotton mills of Charlotte that it had done so only imperfectly. His explanation was the transforming power of the savage ideal, which united race, Southern patriotism, and religion against a dissident force such as unionization. Discrete social issues had become so intertwined in the ideology of Southernism that to touch one aspect of Southern society was to initiate a chain reaction that touched all issues. Thus, although Cash thought he detected in the 1920s "powerful forces . . . toward the development of class consciousness," the Southern myth proved too powerful to permit a victory at Gastonia. That strike served "to clench the matter, to fix solidly in the minds of the great mass of Southerners the equation: labor unions + strikers = Communists + atheists + social equality with the Negro."⁷ So time and again Cash dragged the reader and his Southerners to the brink of the breakthrough, time and again his millworkers seemed about to break into "The Red Flag," and time and again he shook his head and let them sing "Dixie" after all.

Cash had some sense of the formal influence of ideas. He made something of the influence of Romanticism, as engendering "an age of nostalgia," and of the force of "the *Zeitgeist* . . . the great tide of sentimentality which, rolling up slowly through the years following the French Revolution, broke over the Western world in flooding fullness with the accession of Victoria. . . . Nowhere, indeed, did this Victorianism, with its false feeling, its excessive nicety, its will to the denial of the ugly, find more sympathetic acceptance than in the South." He was adamant that such Romanticism had persisted in Southern culture. Yet his definition of Romanticism confounded it with Victorianism, and was thin at best. "Or am I mistaken in thinking," he writes at one point, "that the essence of romanticism is the disposition to deal in the more-than-life sized, the large and heroic, the picturesque and vivid and extravagant?" To which one can only reply, yes, you are mistaken.⁸

More usually in Cash's analysis of Southern history, ideas grow indigenously, out of the whirl of society and discourse. For example, he observes of the Civil War and Southern identity that Southerners, "in their years together, [had] a hundred control phrases . . . burned . . . into their brains. . . . And of these phrases the great master key was in every case the adjective Southern." Such analysis gives *The Mind of the South* an irritating fuzziness, especially of chronology. One is constantly shown change and then told it amounts to little. Cash's Southerners are always acting without full awareness, "groping," or "in some dim manner . . . beginning perceptibly to respond to the logic of the circumstances." His constant reference to "a tendency rather than a rigid set of facts" is archetypal Hegelian language. To hold that there are complicated interpenetrations between awareness and the social process, that there are no hard edges to individuality or group identification, that events occur without conscious intent, is to assert a historical philosophy that is in opposition to the positivism character-istic of American historians. The puzzle is not that Cash has been re-cently censured but that he escaped criticism for so long. He was a very odd historian by most American standards.[9]

So Cash wrote an ingenious book about the development of South-ern identity, while he thought he was writing a book about the South. There is a great difference: it is one thing to trace the dialectical rela-tionship between perception and society; it is another to merge the two. The essence of Hegelian dialectic is that the discordant elements that go into the synthesis are not abolished; they remain alive. It is only in the mind of the observer, the philosophical historian, that they are resolved. Cash, however, destroyed the opposing elements in his synthesis. His Southerners did, in fact, become uniform versions of the savage ideal.

One could salvage a little of *The Mind of the South* by substituting "the Southern idea" for "the South." Many propositions in Cash marked down by Woodward as error have much more vitality when applied only to Southern self-consciousness. While it may be not true that the South is a kind of nation, temporally and spatially united, or that the Southerner is a miniature South, it is clearly true that many Southerners have believed such things and sometimes acted on the presumption. But it would be absurd to make such a substitution. If Cash had wanted to write a coherently Hegelian book, he would have done so. Being half in and half out of an Idealist approach to Southern history, *The Mind of the South* was a confused book.

But was Cash a philosophical historian? By lenient standards, he was. The 1930s saw a growing awareness that mythology was a forma-tive influence on Southern history. John Crowe Ransom had begun to see it. Howard Odum spent much of his 1930 volume, *An American Epoch,* brooding on the significance of intersectional images. John Donald Wade was moving towards his admission in 1954 that for him the South was "one of the really great abstractions of our race." Cash went much further, much faster, with more sophistication than any of his contemporaries, and thereby helped to make possible postwar symposia such as *The Idea of the South.*[10] But by more rigorous stan-dards Cash falls short. For while he grasped how ideas had formed others, he did not grasp how they had formed him. That is, to use Hegel's distinction, he had understanding but not reason.

To use one illustration, he did not grasp that his own historical analysis embodied a Romantic image. After all, *The Mind of the South* is about the emergence from simplicity of an increasingly complex, alienated, and burdensome society, out of which is being fashioned a useable self-awareness. To a degree surprising for 1941, it makes much of the influence of climate and landscape, sensuous and formative. "The dominant mood," Cash insists, "the mood that lingers in the memory, is one of well-nigh drunken reverie—of a hush that seems all the deeper for the far-away mourning of the hounds and the far-away crying of the doves—of such sweet and inexorable opiates as the rich odors of hot earth and pinewood and the perfume of the magnolia in bloom—of soft languor creeping through the blood and mounting surely to the brain." There is much more of this kind of thing, an urban man's reverie, appreciative yet also condescending, since nature is held only to encourage simplicity, the misleading intoxications of imagination. Romantic, too, is his stress upon the integrity of the South as a national culture, evolving within its own social and ideological logic. The power of the analysis greatly lies in documenting the strain and agony of that necessary evolution. But it is a Romantic spiral as yet without closure, though Cash is tolerably clear that the savage ideal cannot survive indefinitely, that it will break. Nonetheless, Cash was fascinated with the topic of Romanticism. It is one of the largest entries in the index, and he once proposed to write a study of Lafcadio Hearn, to be titled or subtitled "The Anatomy of a Romantic."[11] But he felt that Romanticism was alien to himself, except as it clung to him like the simplicity of childhood.

It is not fanciful to ask whether Cash was a sufficiently detached and philosophical observer, because he himself poses the issue. It must be remembered that he identifies the emergence of a critical intelligentsia as the most hopeful sign in Southern history, and the "final great tragedy" as the inability of those realists to reach those whom they should lead. In a book singularly devoid of heroes, the nearest thing to praise is lavished on "the complexity of mind, the knowledge, and, above all, the habit of skepticism essential to any generally realistic attitude."[12]

The Mind of the South is a bitter book. Cash is harsh towards both planters and industrialists. He is hard on the brutalizing effect of slavery. He denounces the ordinary Southerner as childlike and uselessly hedonistic. He sees no hope in religion. Politicians put on the mere hypocrisy of a puppet show. He does not admire the frontier, nor its successor. He deprecates the failure of class consciousness to emerge, yet he shows little enthusiasm for societies where it has. Blacks are only primitive and sensuous, and he does not advocate sensuality, even as he regrets Puritan guilt about hedonism. This bitterness is why it is unsatisfactory to place Cash within the Southern liberal tradition. For while Cash himself did move from a sentimental conservatism about Southern culture into a scathing denunciation of its faults, he never quite laid hold of a useable reform tradition, because he could repose faith in no one. His biographer notes significantly that Cash was "ashamed—for he was no hypocrite—at the way the local Negroes idolized him as their champion when his book came out. He knew only too well that he was no activist."[13]

So while Richard King is right to say that *The Mind of the South* is a moral book, its morality is at the expense of others.[14] It is deeply evasive about Cash's own morality. Even in those scathing and amusing passages where he reviles and caricatures the crimes and folly of others, bitterness is the language of his morality. We are offered no vision of an alternative order, except the slim hope offered by critical realism. And in a book that makes much of the necessity of realism, Cash is singularly uninterested in the content of the ideas held by his critical realists. He sweeps aside the intellectual culture of the Old South, which might matter little to his own world, but he chiefly considers his intellectual contemporaries, not as creators, but as victims.

There is evasiveness, too, in the voice of Cash, the narrator. Much has been made of Cash as the heir of the extravagant rhetoric that he himself identifies as Southern, and certainly there are purple passages. He has a great gift of mimicry. But he seldom identifies with his subjects, and he makes sure the reader knows that this is so much mummery, that a firm line is drawn between ordinary Southerners and Cash. And the identity of Cash himself is the book's little secret. It is true that he sometimes uses the personal pronoun, though far less often than some critics have insisted.[15] True references to himself are all in the latter pages of the book, when he is discussing recent social developments, as when he remarks that he himself has heard university graduates boast of burning a Negro.[16] For the rest, he refers to himself only as the fashioner of his narrative, the debater persuading his reader, anticipating his objections, making sure that points are understood. The reader knows, therefore, that this book is not the product of an impersonal sociologist but the thesis of an impassioned man. What he does not know is who this man is. Wilbur Cash himself is anonymous.

The book has no personal preface, no acknowledgments, no footnotes, all mechanisms by which historians traditionally situate themselves in a community of discourse. In an earlier draft there were footnotes, but in a desire to reach the ordinary reader they were omitted.

But the absence of these rituals testifies to a need deeper than popularity and influence. The book lacks explicit confessional, which makes *The Mind of the South* unusual in the modern Southern tradition.

Cash's contemporaries, especially the journalists, took a different tack in informing the reader not only of the South but of themselves, the Southerners. Clarence Cason, whose *90° in the Shade* Cash admired and whose suicide he mentioned (and was perhaps to emulate), begins with, "Inasmuch as propriety requires that an author give warning as to what is to be met with in the pages of his book, I think it would be well for me to begin by repeating a story. My father was a physician. . . ." Carl Carmer's *Stars Fell on Alabama,* whose story of a University of Alabama fraternity toasting the Southern Woman over a cake of ice Cash cited, has in its second paragraph, "As I came down the car steps, I felt a sudden burning gust. The train had been hot and still but this heat was alive and virulent. My tweed suit was oppressive and it made me a marked man." Jonathan Daniels, whose *A Southerner Discovers the South* Cash called "calm, good-humored criticism," begins with "We Southerners are, of course, a mythological people" and by its second page is remembering that "my first guide was Harriet, yellow and wise, who could look all that the conventional Mammy was supposed to be but who possessed knowledges and interests which made childhood under her guiding a dark excitement of endless variety." There is no such reminiscent directness in *The Mind of the South*.[17]

Which is not to say that the reader with an acute ear, even a dull ear, cannot begin to infer the identity of Wilbur Cash. He will begin to suspect, for example, that the author comes from North Carolina, because he talks about it so incessantly. But this is not knowledge Cash has candidly given the reader. In this sense, it is wrong to place Cash in the tradition of Southern storytellers, for he masks his own face. He does not tell us that so-and-so was his grandfather, that when he was a boy this happened or he remembers reading that book. Though, for example, he does describe his great-great-grandfather coming to the Carolina backcountry in 1800, he is carefully rendered as an anonymous Irishman. So the book's voice has no confessed body.

Yet no one will doubt that implicitly *The Mind of the South* is confessional, a private agony mediated into an abstract historical analysis. Its central appeal has been to intellectual Southerners, oppressed by isolation in a culture they feel inhospitable to their own kind. Cash takes his reader through the cast of Southern types—the yeoman, the planter, the industrialist, the cracker, the black—and each time makes clear that here there can be found no home, no sympathy. He celebrates analysis, hospitality to new ideas, "the capacity . . . for detachment, without which no thinker, no artist, and no scholar can do his work." But the price of detachment is loneliness. No passage expresses this more than his description of a Saturday in a city of the New South: "To go into the town on Saturday afternoon and night, to stroll with the throng, to gape at the well-dressed and the big automobiles, to bathe in the holiday cacophony; in the case of the women, to crowd happily along counters and finger the goods they could not buy; in the case of the males, maybe only to stand with the courthouse habitués and talk and spit tobacco juice, or in the press about a radio loud-speaker blaring a baseball or football game from the front of the store and let off steam with the old hunting yell; maybe to have a drink, maybe to get drunk, to laugh with passing girls, to pick them up if you had a car, or to go swaggering or hesitating into the hotels with their corridors saturated with the smell of bichloride of mercury, or the secret, steamy bawdy houses; maybe to have a fight, maybe with knives and guns, maybe against the cops; maybe to end whooping and singing, maybe bloody and goddamning, in the jailhouse— it was more and more in the dream and reality of such excursions that the old romantic-hedonistic impulses found egress, and that men and women were gratefully emptied of their irritations and repressions, and left to return to their daily tasks stolid, unlonely, and tame again."[18]

It requires no especial insight to be aware that Cash himself had not been able to manage successfully such excursions, could not yell with conviction, or laugh with passing girls, or fight with knives, and so was left with his repressions and irritations, with his loneliness unappeased. A look at Cash's own life, the life he carefully omitted from his book, will only confirm this impression.

One finds that though capable of bursts of merriment, he was an ordinarily ebullient youth but a very unhappy man, solitary, shy, "rarely cheerful and basically pessimistic," odd and grim. He disliked crowds except as an observer. He would sit on a bench outside the courthouse, or by a window in his favorite drug store, to watch the people. Immured in a crowd, he would struggle, often unsuccessfully, to find a single person with whom earnestly to converse tête-à-tête. He was awkward with women and feared impotence. He had bad depth perception and was physically clumsy, famous enough for knocking things over that a hostess felt obliged to tape down her tablecloth, lest he wreak havoc. He dressed badly, had a pot belly, went bald. He was "a terrible storyteller" and even suffered from an odd constriction of the throat that occasionally rendered his talk unintelligible.[19]

All societies are cruel to such people, but Southern male society especially so, because it makes much of fitting in, of ostentatious masculinity, of the gift of entertaining the crowd, of sharing values. Cash analyzed this cruelty better than any one, because he had experienced it more than most, which makes his book a cry of pain. It is little wonder that *The Mind of the South* took a long time to write and that, by his own testimony to Alfred Knopf, he always approached the continuation of his narrative with "extreme depression and dislike." Little wonder also that he most admired Thomas Wolfe, the Southern bard of alienation and loneliness.[20]

Cash was a more intellectual man than the reader might guess. Repelled by Southern society, like many others, he tried to find refuge in other traditions. He bicycled through Europe, to weep at the beauty of the rose window at Chartres Cathedral. He dabbled in the writing of a novel, "in the manner of Dostoevsky." He listened to Beethoven, Mozart, and Sibelius; read Lytton Strachey, Karl Marx, and Remy de Gourmont; was persuaded by the glooms of Spengler, Henry Adams, and Darwin. These appear, lovingly, and irrelevantly evoked, in *The Mind of the South* as so many reproaches to his region, which had given him a childhood informed only by Thomas Dixon and an abundance of dishonest Baptist sermons. He had, indeed, intended to make the final segment of his book a commentary on "the South and the Modern Mind." Fragments of this ambition survive in the final version, as when he gaudily summarizes the effect of the First World War in training a generation apprehensive of disaster, but they are diminished by his sense that his own time testified to the miscarriage of modernism in the South. And there is pathos in the knowledge that Cash saw modernism as exclusively a Yankee and European phenomenon, and himself more or less as a modernist. That is, he had no place in his own culture.[21]

As I have remarked, *The Mind of the South,* though it celebrates intellect, is inattentive to the content of ideas, preferring to scrutinize the social position of the intellectual, his isolation. "The young man returning to his native place," he writes of the modernist intellectual, "particularly if he lived in the larger towns, might now and then find a few people tolerant enough by education or native temperament to listen to him amiably and quietly and perhaps to encourage him in some of his notions. But the general effect on the community, in all classes, was to produce terror and anger in one degree or another." This construction helps to explain why he speaks of his love and hatred for the region, and why he holds up his claim to being a "loyal son," on the last page of the book, as a talisman to ward off the savage ideal. It may also explain why only the Agrarians excited in Cash a sharp desire to examine ideas in detail. He admired them for their intellectual sophistication and gladly rolled off his pen the great names who, he claimed not very accurately, had influenced them: Aquinas, Spinoza, Hobbes, Kant, Donne, Maistre, Ruskin, Brunetière, Eliot. Acknowledging these gifts, he was angry that they had failed to see the point and could instead find succor in the Southern tradition, where he had found none. "Being poets . . . ," he wrote, "they longed for a happy land into which to project their hearts' desire." Having the same longing, Cash regarded with astonished bitterness men who could, however unstably, succeed in that projection.[22]

In all this resides the essential power of *The Mind of the South* for succeeding generations of intellectual Southerners. He has spoken to the loneliness of those many who have grown up asserting themselves in the face of an unsympathetic society, obliged to surmount an anti-intellectual religious tradition of great and emotional power. Cash publicly reenacted a very private passion, and evidence abounds of the start of recognition that a first reading, usually in youth, has brought to Southerners of sensibility. While Cash's non-Southern readers have reacted to an analysis of great verve and apparent coherence, the book for them uncovers the errors of aliens who excite curiosity, anger, or amusement. Donald Davidson was partly right when he observed that Cash was not above pandering to such people.[23] But for Southerners the monologue of *The Mind of the South* is internal, the more powerful because its confessional is displaced and masked and can present itself, not as a private truth, a mere subjectivity, but as a public fact of painful reality.

CHAPTER 9

From a Chase to a View:
C. Vann Woodward

C. VANN WOODWARD is not easy to catch. He knows that there are taxidermists who would nab him for the display cases of historiography, and so he has taken to hovering near his critics, close enough to encourage the chase, far enough to evade capture. He has often said that it is better to be criticized than to be forgotten. There is a cunning in the quarry who courteously offers the chase, runs on, doubles back, feints, leaves a half-concealed trail, yet manages to be back in his lair at night, safe in the knowledge that the woods echo with blundering hunters, who exclaim to one another that the old fox is here somewhere, if only they knew where. The elusive quarry makes the hunter his accomplice in sport, though they play a different game. The quarry plays for survival, the hunter for blood. The term Woodward has coined for the sport is *gerontophagy,* the eating of elders.[1]

But this is Woodward in old age. The young C. Vann Woodward was very different and played a game that had higher stakes, not mere personal survival but no less than improvement for his society. The old Woodward has given us some insight into the young, though through the selective sensibility of memory, and should be given due weight as

---

I have used passages from "C. Vann Woodward and the Burden of Southern Liberalism," *American Historical Review* 78 (June 1973): 589–604, but this essay is partly new. On some issues, most notably the closeness with which Woodward may be understood to stand in the liberal tradition, I have changed my mind. Woodward has gone to the trouble of telling me I was wrong, and on a matter of self-perception he should know. Other problems, unapparent to a twenty-three-year-old living in England, now draw my eye. There has been a considerable body of writing on Woodward since 1973, some of which has made my own contribution supererogatory or mistaken. Most importantly, Woodward has contributed his own *Thinking Back,* with its distinctive combination of autobiography, memoir, and critical discourse. The book is dedicated to his critics, "without whose devoted efforts life would have been simpler but less interesting." I would not wish Professor Woodward's life to become uninteresting.

the best witness we have but one scarcely detached and decidedly reserved.

He was born in Arkansas in 1908, the son of a Latin teacher and school principal, in the flat delta whose landscape was then crowded with black and white sharecroppers, mules, tumbled shacks, cotton, poverty, and is now almost devoid of people, being instead the empty domain of soya and the occasional Japanese company. Vanndale stands on the Arkansas side of Memphis, as Faulkner's Oxford stands on its Mississippi side, and the juxtaposition is worth bearing in mind. Woodward's own family was scarcely indigent, nor utterly obscure. His birthplace bore his maternal family name, his forebears had owned slaves, an uncle was a sociologist at Southern Methodist University, and governors of Arkansas might come to call. The family was Methodist, and seriously so, enough that one of Woodward's dissents was a reticent agnosticism. Religion is conspicuously absent from his vision of Southern history.[2]

His family moved on to Morrilton, a small market town in the Arkansas River valley, a far different landscape, wooded, gentler, a town with more decided amenities, such as a railroad and a Carnegie Free Library, where the inquiring adolescent son of a schoolmaster might extend his learning. The town was mostly beyond the state's black population, fading into that limbo between South and West that marks the indeterminate culture of western Arkansas. But it had the Ku Klux Klan, whose leader, in full regalia, might drop in to church to make a welcome donation and whose members Woodward once saw gathering to commence a lynching.[3] Woodward was a junior member of the modest and small Southern bourgeoisie, and his father was moving up, not down, from crossroads to small town, from teacher to college dean. Implicitly Woodward's own youthful act of gerontophagy was a repudiation of the class that had bred him and a conscious reaching out in sympathy for those with whom he had little in common, the dirt farmers and blacks who were far from his own parents' front parlor. This moral education seems to have been accidental in a young man whose career drifted into a vocation. Certainly his formal education seems to have been unrewarding. Little was to be expected from two years at Henderson College in Arkadelphia, and little more, on his own testimony, was received from Emory. More might have been expected from Columbia University, but this Northern foray was brief and unsatisfactory. He wobbled in his intellectual interests: philosophy as an undergraduate major, sociology for two days at Columbia, political science for a master of arts degree, literature as a hobby. He worked on farms, taught English at Georgia Tech, traveled to the Soviet Union, all the while observing.

Woodward has become a calm and reserved man, but there is reason to think that he was an intense and reserved youth. He took social injustice as a personal affront and, if he was not formally a socialist, adopted the passionate language of class warfare. His biography of Tom Watson freely speaks of "capitalist expansion," of the Old South as a "feudal system," of "class conflict," of "crushing oppression," of "reactionary capitalist allies," of the "southern urban proletariat" being only "an embryonic class," not yet "class conscious." A favorable comment upon Watson by Eugene Debs occurs on the final page as a sort of benediction.[4] It is no surprise to learn that Woodward later thought about writing a biography of Debs. Labor organizers felt free to use his couch in Atlanta, he was glad to lend support to the young communist Angelo Herndon, absurdly indicted on a charge of raising an insurrection against the state of Georgia. With such an education, and with less reserve, he might have made a serviceable apparatchik. Instead, and improbably, he decided to write a book, a collective biography of seven Southern demagogues, portentously entitled *Seven for Demos*. He had studied little history and had been bored by that he had read, and the venture was undertaken outside the apparatus of the academy.[5]

In his memoirs Woodward has made much of the barrenness of the historical writing of his youth. There is no reason to doubt that reading the old American Nation series was a rigidifying experience, leading a young historian to think he was entering the vocation, not of necromancer to others, but of undertaker to himself. As for Southern historians, the precedents were unencouraging. Ulrich Phillips applied the supposed ethic of New South efficiency to the Old South, Douglas Southall Freeman wrote hagiography, the spirit of William Archibald Dunning presided over Reconstruction. The very small band who had written the history of the New South offered little but the propaganda of the middle class.[6] The reform tradition was the liberal tradition, which then meant segregation, an alliance with Northern industrialism, disfranchisement for blacks and poor whites alike, many empty promises, emptier for the starkness of the Depression. Yet the liberals had their moments: some, such as Will Alexander, could fight lynching; others might rally to save Angelo Herndon; some, such as Howard Odum, might care for social justice. Rupert Vance, an old friend from Morrilton, had written eloquently and in detail about the failures of the cotton economy and would try to make sociology a humane discipline.[7] And the national liberals had moved to embrace Roosevelt's peculiar and reluctant radicalism. Woodward himself supported the second New Deal and spent the summer of 1935 surveying the backcountry of Georgia, to be moved and shocked by the rural poverty for which James Agee was later to find words. So liberalism was a tradition that had alternately to be embraced and pushed away, depending on the time, place, and issue. There were to be moments when Woodward would proclaim himself a Southern liberal, moments when he would not, but always it was a tradition with which he was obliged to maintain a fruitful tension.[8]

If little had been done by historians, more was being achieved by Southern poets and novelists. Woodward was to become one of the great celebrators of the Southern Renaissance, doffing his cap in the direction of Faulkner, Warren, Welty. His *Origins of the New South,* though showing some sympathy for the naturalism of Theodore Dreiser and Jack London, otherwise judges the literature of the late nineteenth century by the critical standards of the 1930s.[9] His memoirs reinforce the impression of a young man eagerly devouring the fresh new books that came gleaming from the press to testify of the possibilities of achievement by a Southern intelligence.[10] Unfortunately, the evidence from the 1930s does not entirely endorse this impression and suggests a refinement.

In 1938 Woodward gave a Phi Beta Kappa lecture at the University of Florida, "The South in Search of a Philosophy." Much of it expresses the Beardian analysis of the New South that his *Tom Watson* was concomitantly embodying. But there are passages about contemporary Southern letters that now read oddly. He speaks dismissively of the literature of the 1920s as "in flight from realities, or in obsession with the more nauseating realities." James Branch Cabell and the Fugitives are said to have "sought sanctuary in the ivory tower and fled to the French Quarter of New Orleans, or, when they had the money, to the Left Bank in Paris." Faulkner is characterized as one "who seemed to draw most of his subjects out of abandoned wells." To which is added, "One can only speculate with misgivings upon what future literary historians will make of the earth-departing fantasies and the neurotic grotesqueries that constitute the literary output of the South from 1919 to 1929."[11] We fortunately need not speculate, since one of the future literary historians was to be C. Vann Woodward, and his verdict reads very differently.

There are passages, too, from 1938 that discuss the Agrarians. Woodward was never to find them plausible, except as they condemned the inhumanity of industrialism. But his explanation for their origins as romantic poseurs holds especial interest. He notes correctly that *I'll Take My Stand* was a product of revulsion at the materialist faith of the 1920s and less correctly that it was a product of the 1930s and their "extreme disillusionments." But this is his chronology for the Agrarian movement: "On the Boulevarde de Montparnasse, Southern esthetes of the Fugitive school sat around the same sidewalk cafe tables with Northern esthetes of the Humanist school—both convivial in a self-imposed exile—as long as their stocks and bonds returned dividends. When dividends began to fail in 1929 the Northern expatriots returned to New York to find themselves sudden converts to communism, while the Southern expatriots returned to Louisiana and Tennessee to find themselves sudden converts to agrarianism." This is bizarre both as criticism and history. The only person to whom it remotely applied was Allen Tate, of whose arrogance and incivility Woodward had had a sight in 1936, when Tate had grandiloquently walked out of a session of the Southern Historical Association in which the Agrarians had been criticized.[12]

What is more important, Woodward gives evidence here of an inattentiveness to and lack of sympathy for contemporary Southern literature. Unusually for him, he seems to have been taking stereotypes from American history—in this case, from Malcolm Cowley's *Exile's Return*—and imposing them on the South. But his logic is clear enough from later passages where he extols the Chapel Hill Regionalists as seekers after "facts, facts, facts, dug out, tabulated, and analyzed by professional students of society." He wanted then, whatever he was to want later, stern social realism, not irresponsibility, not art for art's sake, not art for the wrong social causes, but men who might grasp "the possibility of using industry under social control for the achievement of a better society under a new type of political and economic government."[13]

So Woodward's recent version of his intellectual apprenticeship in the 1930s needs to be taken with a grain of salt. He speaks lightly of his engagement with Chapel Hill, of mixing with the wrong set, the aesthetes of Franklin Street, but such hard evidence as we have (itself, of course, selective) shows a more earnest young man, emotional, self-consciously dissident.[14] It is true that his interracial friendships, his sympathy for organized labor, his distaste for the bourgeoisie, placed him well outside the mainstream of Odum's thought. But Woodward lived in a time, the 1930s of the New Deal, and a place, the Chapel Hill of Frank Graham, when dissidence was acceptable and brought few punishments. Odum arranged a fellowship for him and helped to find a publisher for his biography of Tom Watson. Many around, including Wilbur Cash of Charlotte, spoke confidently of the utility of critical realism, and of themselves as the useful critical realists. The University of North Carolina had fashioned a breathing space for dissidents such as Woodward, and he used the maneuvering room to seek out other dissidents in the Southern past.

He turned to Populism, a step not entirely original, for there had begun to be scattered studies by historians such as Benjamin B. Kendrick, Alex Matthews Arnett, and Francis B. Simkins.[15] As Woodward himself was to remark: "It was easier in the 1930's than it is in the 1950's to understand the 1890's. For the look of things in the South in the trough of the Great Depression did a lot toward making the desperate mood and temper of the South of the nineties wholly credible."[16] But no one made Populism as central to modern Southern history, welded it into a Beardian analysis that was applied in turn within Southern society, or showed such respect for the bottom rail, the gesture and hope of rebellion. *Tom Watson* is a book perhaps most marked by its distaste for the powerful and rich, who usually appear as hypocrites, charlatans, a "grim and bearded lot" never to be trusted.[17] In Watson, Woodward found a man who resisted the divisiveness of racism and sought to yoke together poor white and black in a common front against economic oppression. In this, Woodward may have been lucky. Watson was not entirely typical in his sympathy for the black.[18] As Woodward himself was later to establish, poor-white democracy went hand in hand with the elimination of blacks from politics and the rise of Jim Crow. But there was a difficulty on this score even in Watson's career. The tribune of the underdog in the early 1890s, Watson became in the twentieth century the foremost vilifier in Georgia of Negro, Jew, and Catholic. Woodward faithfully chronicled both aspects of Watson's story but kept them distinct, thereby neatly avoiding a considerable difficulty for himself as a Southern dissident. If the bitterness of Tom Watson was the logical and necessary consequence of his disappointed crusade, the moral was an uncomfortable one. By splitting the first part of Watson's career off from the second, Woodward neutralized the issue. He did admit that the two might be related but not that they were an organic whole. For it was crucial to Woodward to believe that Watson could have succeeded.

Woodward has consistently stressed change in the Southern past, because he has wanted change. If Southern history is a remorseless unity, unbroken in its social conservatism and unchallenged by a significant radicalism, the task of the Southern reformer is futile. He is trying to sow on ground so stony that it is not worth buying the seed: one might as well go off to a better plot, as did many liberals of George W. Cable's day. On the other hand, if Southern history is ferment and change, in which conservatism has triumphed only after a desperate struggle and holds an insecure victory, there is hope. It has been Woodward's insight to point to this volatility. Woodward has charged as the central fault of Cash that he overestimated the unbroken flow of Southern history: "The history of the South . . . would seem to be characterized more by *dis*continuity, one trait that helps account for the distinctiveness of the South and its history. . . . Southerners, unlike other Americans, repeatedly felt the solid ground of continuity give way under their feet."[19] Hence he was to deplore, in 1964, the stereotype of the conservative South and point to examples of Southern dissent, such as the abolitionism that existed below the Potomac before the Civil War and the writings of George W. Cable after it. "It would be a tragic decision to make intransigence and desperate adherence to a discredited code the test of southern loyalty."[20] Alternatives were sanctioned by the lessons of the Southern past and by the thoughts and actions of Southerners.

Woodward sought out those "forgotten alternatives"[21] that would have created a more liberal South if they had succeeded. *The Strange Career of Jim Crow* is perhaps the most sustained example of this search. There he examined the history of Southern race relations and noted that segregation, the Jim Crow of the statute book, was not the immediate sequel of emancipation. Dating from the 1890s, it was an institution scarcely old enough to encompass the life span of a single individual: it was not the immutable system that Southerners imagined in the passions of the 1950s. There was no golden age, but there was a moment of some flexibility in the relationship of black and white in the South. Now that the crisis over the dismantling of segregation has passed, and with it the need to prove the transience of Jim Crow, the book reads less compellingly. It looks the most wistful of Woodward's attempts to find a useable past, as well as the most successful in reaching a wide and active audience. As he himself has been forced to recognize, segregation was only the structure of a relationship and not the heart of the matter. His glimmer of hope seems a faint light beside the fact of consistent discrimination.[22]

It is important to remember that Woodward has always sought the indigenous solution, obliged to find his glimmers within the Southern tradition. Whatever his flirtations with socialism, they gave him no

taste for the solidarity of the oppressed of all nations or the opportunities offered by the insights of Marx or Gramsci. His opinions of
those who lingered on the Boulevard Montparnasse have already been
cited. His experience of Oxford is mentioned in *Thinking Back* without enthusiasm, with the commentary, "I knew that I would never
be a Christ Church princeling and would never feel comfortable in a
Sorbonne beret." He has been inclined to poke fun at the North,
whose Emersons have condescended to the South as the "less-civilized
portion of the country," and one detects a note of satisfaction in his
essays of the 1960s, which observe a historiography that punctured the
egalitarian myths of the abolitionist and neo-abolitionist. Though he
has offered his patronage to comparative history, he has written little
of it himself, rather puckishly rejoicing in the title of a provincial. Maneuvering room has been constricted because he has so consistently
adhered to the Chaucerian sentiment that serves as an epigraph to
Thinking Back, "But trusteth wel, I am a southren man." [23]

If one sets aside the diversion of the Second World War, the period
from *Tom Watson* to *The Strange Career of Jim Crow,* and including
Origins of the New South, 1877–1913 and *Reunion and Reaction,* may be
regarded as a unity. The biography served as an introduction and apprenticeship. The commission to write the New South volume for the
History of the South series obliged him to synthesis, which being established generated his lectures on segregation and his detective story
on the Compromise of 1877. They are very much of a piece, which is
partly because they were researched and written, if you eliminate the
years of the war, within a relatively short span, just twelve years from
1938 to 1954. The edifice was essentially complete by the time Woodward
was forty-six. *The Strange Career of Jim Crow* may, it is true, be regarded as a transitional book, in that it draws on the hard work for
Origins but begins to ease Woodward into the role of his maturity,
that of the critical essayist.

This pattern had several causes, but one is worth noting. The
task of fulfilling his commission from the Littlefield Fund forced
Woodward into extensive manuscript research, rather against his temperament. As he confessed in the bibliography to *Origins of the New
South,* "The historian is driven to manuscripts by necessity rather than
zeal." [24] The admission is candid and is borne out by the rest of his
career. With the partial exception of his edition of Mary Chesnut, neither the necessity nor the zeal to penetrate archives seems to have re-
curred, even though the span of the New Woodward now far exceeds
the chronological span of the Old Woodward. [25] The commission may

even have forced him into the role of synthesizer more than may have been native to him.

The analytical standpoint of his magnum opus was partly borrowed from Charles Beard, though Woodward made intrasectional class and racial conflict more important than intersectional strife. Nonetheless, however much it marked a beginning for Southern thought, *Origins of the New South* stood at the end of a national tradition. In many ways the book was the last triumph of the progressive school, though declaring the bankruptcy of the middle class. Woodward carried the tradition to its logical conclusion, purging naiveté and methodological shortcomings, understanding the force of myth.[26] Above all, he wrote in the modern manner, with sharp irony. But his passion for synthesis has had its limits, and they are suspiciously congruent with the obligations imposed on him by that commission. He has never, for example, felt the necessity to elaborate a coherent vision of the Old South, except to declare that whatever it was, it was different from the New South. His reviewing of recent works on the New South, while always generous, is pointedly vigilant, whereas his comments upon the historiography of the Old South have conferred his blessing upon a bewildering range of contradictory viewpints, from Robert Fogel and Stanley Engerman, to Eugene Genovese, to Bertram Wyatt-Brown, strange bedfellows.[27]

Origins of the New South is a complex book. Not the least of its merits was the closing of a gap. On the eve of its publication in 1951, Woodward wrote of a new book on Mississippi politics: "Falling between the period when the historians generally leave off and the period when the sociologists take over—between the end of Reconstruction and the very recent past—the half century studied by Mr. Kirwan represents the most neglected cycle of Southern history. It is therefore a compliment of a dubious sort to say that he has written the best political history of the period covered so far available for any state of the region. The fact is he did not have a lot of competition."[28] Woodward's bibliography, itself the first of its kind, was a tale of woe: "Biographies of this period have only recently emerged from the commemorative stage and published correspondence is all but non-existent," he lamented and then added, "A list of prominent figures of the post-Reconstruction South who have yet to find competent biographers would probably be longer than a list of those who have been so fortunate." Seldom has a subject been raised from such obscurity to such illumination at a single bound. Just as a piece of technique, an effort of research, the book was a virtuoso performance.[29]

More than that, *Origins of the New South* was the fulfillment of his new image of the Southern past, the fresh moral geography at which he had hinted in the 1930s. And the vision is moral, maintained throughout the work with a tenacity whose coherence makes the book one of the few works of art that Southern historical literature has produced. The vision is expressed not merely in conclusions but in the structure and style of the analysis.

Woodward used irony, that idiom most complex, phenomenological, and evasive. Irony is a mood that often occurs in his writing and needs careful discussion, for Woodward has used it in two senses, one rhetorical, the other philosophical, though the two blend imperceptibly. Irony's rhetorical purposes will become evident from an examination of Woodward's writings. Its philosophical meaning is less elusive, being used in the manner of Reinhold Niebuhr. By this usage, men are deemed free to choose their acts but not to control the consequences of action. Human nature is inescapably a compound of virtue and vice, and history so unpredictable that virtue can generate vice and vice can generate virtue. Precision of vision is impossible, though illusions can sometimes be detected and, by commentary, mitigated. So irony denotes both the situation of those caught in history and the awareness of the historian, who sees irony and is condemned to express it.[30]

At the level of rhetoric, irony has served many purposes in conveying Woodward's voice. On one level, irony in his narrative has discriminated between heroes and villains for a mind too subtle to want to name heroes and villains. Of Robert Dabney, for example, Woodward commented: "Never, of course, was there the remotest chance of Dabney's goose quill prevailing against the clattering presses of Grady and Dawson, Tompkins and Edmonds. Anyway, the New South had no ear for pessimism—not with Georgia boasting eleven millionaires in 1892, and Kentucky twenty-four, and New Orleans alone thirty-five!" Or note his scathing characterization of the myth of the Old South, created in the 1880s: "What bittersweet tears washed Nashville's grimy cheeks over Page's *In Ole Virginia!* 'Dem wuz good ole times, marster—de bes Sam ever see! Dey wuz in fac'! Niggers didn' hed nothin' 'tall to do.' Embarrassing race conflict dissolved in liquid dialect, angry Populist farmers became merely quaint in Billy Sanders' vernacular, depression rolled aside, and for a moment, 'de ole times done come back again.'" Such passages contrast strongly with the seriousness of tone in the chapters on Populism. One can sense the satisfaction in a sentence like "Not until the New South was confronted by the Populists did it meet with a challenge that set it back on its heels for a spell." Irony thus expressed the morality of a man who elsewhere directly remarked of a progressivism for whites only that it "no more fulfilled the political aspirations and deeper needs of the mass of the people than did the first New Deal administration."[31] This phrase, "deeper needs of the mass of the people," neatly expressed Woodward's basic moral precept.

A central tradition of American historical literature has been its moralism. As one social morality has succeeded another, interpretation has supplanted interpretation with a remarkable fidelity. Consistent with this, Woodward's writing represented a shift in the morality of Southern thought. He turned its concerns from the bourgeoisie to the Southern masses. He widened it to include blacks, whose social inferiority had been a central assumption of earlier generations. He raised the broad issue of social responsibility in Southern politics. Woodward has had to fight his battles among a Southern historical profession that has scarcely been radical, as when he desegregated the annual banquet of the Southern Historical Association in 1952, the year of his presidency. But on the whole, his views on race generated surprisingly little outcry among his Southern contemporaries, however much they doubtless grumbled in private. It is hard to imagine that he would have escaped so unscathed or proceeded so laden with honors if he had written forty years earlier.

Yet the meaning of irony was more complex than just advancing the purposes of morality.[32] The mood had been present in his *Tom Watson*. Sometimes irony was just pleasure in a phrase well turned, perhaps influenced by Gibbon, who once nearly tempted Woodward into Roman history. The spirit of Lausanne may linger in a sentence like this: "He [Watson] was attracted and repelled at the same time: it was magnificent to be incorrigible, but it was practical to be conciliatory."[33] Sometimes irony expressed itself in a Menckenian joy at the absurdity of humanity. Woodward was then beginning to be, as he has remained, a comic writer of suppleness, with gifts of timing and bathos. Sometimes irony became so heavy that *sarcasm* seems the better term.

Tom Watson was a more rambling, more linear book (longer by five pages, if you exclude the paraphernalia of bibliography and index) than *Origins of the New South*. The later need to compress seems to have had the effect of making irony leaner, more businesslike. In *Origins of the New South* irony is less in the phrasing, more in the structure of the book. More fundamentally, the will to believe had been stronger in the young dissident, writing when the second New Deal was fresh.

The desire to believe was as strong in 1951, but evidence for the possibility of progress was more mixed, the intractability of history more apparent. Irony became more insistent as detachment from the hopes of dissidence grew.

There was little bleakness in this. After all, there was sometimes hope of progress. Involved in legal cases that would help to remove the legal barriers of segregation, Woodward knew matters could change. Even so, like many others, he was to be surprised at the rapidity of change once launched in the civil-rights movement, enough to be lured temporarily into speaking of a national commitment to equality not only in his own times but in the first Reconstruction.[34] Thus irony became a stance of dissidence, less for society, more for the satisfaction of the ironist, a kind of quiet testimony. This transition has much to do with the special power of *Origins of the New South*. The young Woodward supplied the stamina and indignation to make research worthwhile, the older informed the voice of the book.

The 1950s were not years of encouragement. Charles Beard's vision of American history as a record of social struggle was not one to conjure with in the intellectual atmosphere of the 1950s. It was, after all, the heyday of consensus, of the attempt to find the common denominators of American culture. When Richard Hofstadter wrote of the "common climate of American opinion" and remarked that its existence "has been much obscured by the tendency to place political conflict in the foreground of history,"[35] he gave a new mandate to the historical profession in America, which Woodward ignored. Right in the middle of his foreground was the angry Populist farmer, though Woodward has always been more interested in the forces that damaged the farmer than in the farmer himself. Though his work has immensely impelled the development of Southern social history, and made possible the Carlo Ginzburgs of a recent Southern generation, he himself, perhaps from a desire to avoid condescension, has avoided recreating the *mentalité* of anonymous Southerners.

Woodward kept up a running dialogue with the consensus perception, though muffled by his friendships with Hofstadter and David Potter, until the events of the 1960s reasserted the impression of social division. He insisted upon the validity of dissent, whether of an under class from a business culture or of the South from the national pattern. In 1959 he published a critique of the new hostility towards Populism, partly exemplified in Hofstadter's *The Age of Reform*. Woodward conceded the existence of nativism among Populists, their hatred of the Jew and the foreigner, their provincialism. But the Arkansan in

Woodward clearly rose against the New Yorker in Hofstadter. He pointed out that these were not characteristics peculiar to Populists, nor were they always true of Populists themselves. He referred to the case of Tom Watson, seeing positive value in this tradition of revolt: "One must expect and even hope that there will be future upheavals to shock the seats of power and privilege and furnish the periodic therapy that seems necessary to the health of our democracy. But one cannot expect them to be any more decorous or seemly or rational than their predecessors." Moreover, the intellectual has a role to play, as he did during the New Deal: "For the tradition to endure, for the way to remain open, however, the intellectual must not be alienated from the sources of revolt."[36] Later Woodward returned more explicitly to the consensus school, in an essay called "The North and the South of It." He asserted that "what America lacked in the way of class tensions she made up in the indigenous tensions of her peculiar heritage. Americans have characteristically thought in terms of regional, religious and racial or ethnic rather than class conflict." He added, "We have been somewhat hasty in sweeping under the rug of liberal consensus this ancient question."[37]

But what was the dissident to offer in reply when Populism had so dwindled? If the present was unencouraging, history might give some useful testimony. In this mood, Woodward wrote in the 1950s his most influential essays, "The Irony of Southern History" and "The Search for Southern Identity." He examined previous attempts to capture the essence of the South: Ulrich Phillips, who saw the resolution to maintain white supremacy as the cardinal test of the Southerner; and the Agrarians, for whom the South was the agricultural way of life. He found both to be at fault. One can be a Southerner without believing in black inferiority—on Phillips's logic, Woodward himself would not be a Southerner, an obviously intolerable conclusion—and to live in a city like Atlanta does not disqualify one from that identity. What then is different about the South? Woodward pointed to its variance from the norm of American experience. As the nation has been characterized by economic abundance, success, and the legend of innocence, so the South, in counterpoint, has been a land of poverty, failure, and the bitter realism born of such experience. "In that most optimistic of centuries in the most optimistic part of the world, the South remained basically pessimistic in its social outlook and its moral philosophy."[38] In a nation without a heritage of feudalism, the South had slavery. In a country rootless with social mobility the South and its literature are firmly tied to place. But what is the use of this peculiarity? Scarred like

Europe with war, the South has a sense of realism. It may be that the irony of the Southerner's position may make him more adept in an international world where American innocence is no asset.

In a revised edition of *The Burden of Southern History* Woodward was to return to this problem. At the end of the 1960s he was forced to note how that decade's events had dismantled the national myth of innocence and success. His case might have been strengthened if the South had been innocent of the disorder of Vietnam and the black revolt, but "the irony of history had caught up with the ironist—or gone him one better. For in this fateful hour of opportunity history had ironically placed men of presumably authentic Southern heritage in the supreme seats of national power—a gentleman from Texas in the White House and a gentleman from Georgia in the State Department. And yet from those quarters came few challenges and little appreciable restraint to the pursuit of the national myths of invincibility and innocence. Rather there came a renewed allegiance and sustained dedication."[39]

The curious thing about Woodward's initial essays on Southern identity, tacitly recognized in the revision, was his reliance on the consensus theory—the same idea he had so resisted in his own work on the South. However much the region had bred in him a pessimistic skepticism, it departed when he raised his eyes to the nation. He accepted the homogenized version of the American past contained in books such as David Potter's *People of Plenty*. His insight about the South gave him no advantage over Northern historians in seeing suffering north of the Potomac. In truth it could not. His idea needed the counterpoint of Southern realism and Northern innocence, Southern poverty and Northern wealth. Without it the distinctiveness of the South melted away. And it was part of his task to establish that singularity.

As the 1960s dealt savage blows to the consensus school, so they undermined Woodward's definition of the South. He was left only with the conclusion that "Americans might still have something to learn, if they would, from the un-American and ironic experience of the South with history." With that phrase, "if they would," his case slipped away. Woodward could only claim that although there are lessons in the Southern past, they are there only for those who care to learn them. Thereby he lost the one point that would prove his theory: something in the Southern milieu compels Southerners to learn these lessons; it is the unavoidable burden of Southern identity. In *Thinking Back*, Woodward has had to concede the point, to indicate his use of the subjunctive in these essays, not to what was, but to what might be.[40]

These essays also testify to the peculiarity of Woodward's stance. Those Southerners most marked by the pessimistic resistance to panacea, to which Woodward gave his approval, are Southern conservatives. It is they who have felt most sharply the sting of defeat and drawn lessons from it. But they were conservative lessons. Southern liberals took the same events with comparative lightness because they were not intellectually involved in them. If one examines the genteel historians whom Woodward himself supplanted, one sees that the very things they ignored in the Southern past were those episodes richest in social disappointment. Their task, after all, was the Southern future and a judicious edition of the Southern past, not the responsibility for Jefferson Davis's aberrations.

Their vision of that future was euphoric. Liberals such as Walter Hines Page were constantly heralding the dawn of a new age. Edwin Mims's *The Advancing South* was as far removed from social pessimism as one can imagine: "No one can have too high a hope of what may be achieved within the next quarter of a century. Freed from the limitations that have so long hampered it, and buoyant with the energy of a new life coursing through its veins, the South will press forward to a new destiny."[41] A main task of Southern liberalism has been to assimilate the South to the nation. It has been an impulse towards, not away from, innocence. If the Vietnam misadventure can be seen as an exercise of American innocence, the role of Lyndon Johnson in it was entirely faithful to that Southern tradition of liberalism. He was more typical of it than Woodward himself, who by his own testimony has drifted in and out of that tradition.

Rather Woodward has blended the pessimistic moral diagnosis of the conservatives of the Southern Renaissance with his own Populist variant of Southern radicalism. Perhaps it is little wonder that he found it natural in 1960 to sympathize with George Fitzhugh, the intellectual *sui generis*.[42] The idiosyncrasy of the vision needs emphasizing because it has been masked by its apparent triumph among the recent generation of Southern historians.

Nonetheless, components of the synthesis command varying degrees of respect. The account of the Compromise of 1877 is more or less intact. The claim that the New South was run by new men is looking frail but is still workable. The theory of the taking of a political right fork, an alliance with the Northeast, has been badly dented. The analysis of the origins of segregation has been so qualified, its chronology so revised, that little of its original pungency remains. The account of Populism, though his version of its racial attitudes has been softened, remains definitive, as does his explanation for the origins of disfranchisement and character of Southern progressivism. His definition of the South as a colonial economy has been powerfully reinforced.[43] The house of Woodward may have peeling paint, the odd room may be unuseable, but it is still the only hotel in town worth the price.

And yet the triumph of *Origins of the New South* was always curiously illusory, since what Woodward most cared for, the centrality of the Populist vision, is what most of his readers, though they were polite, could not follow. Like Turner's frontier, celebrated because it was dying, Woodward's Populists were given their proper due, but it was posthumous. The synthesis was founded on a regret and a hope, and now the hope is gone.

This has given him the status of an outsider, the essayist carefully following the upheavals of the 1960s and still commenting on current affairs. The civil-rights movement brought him fleetingly into the mainstream of Southern liberalism, the moment when, in debate with a Marxist, he felt able to call himself a "liberal, even more, a southern white liberal." Martin Luther King himself read passages from *The Strange Career of Jim Crow* before the state capitol at Montgomery, as Woodward watched.[44] The historian marched at Selma.

An outsider in politics, he was the insider among historians. As the upheavals of the 1960s reverberated through scholarship, Woodward found himself a critic of new views. Once outflanked by Cold Warriors to his right, he was now bedeviled by existential presentists to his left. With sane irritation, he strove to represent the nature of "mixed motives, ambivalence, paradox, and complexity."[45] It was in these years that his writings began to show a sharp awareness of the conflict of intellectual generations and to develop rules by which the genteel brutality of that campaign may be conducted. He has played his role with firmness, but with compassion, encouraging debate, indulging the raw and young. Power has brought responsibilities, which have been scrupulously discharged. But the role has served others better than it has served Woodward, for the reviewer has tended to supplant the historian, to the point where he has come to review himself.

The shift may even be located as far back as the 1950s. His "The South in Search of a Philosophy," the lecture of 1938, was a search for an energizing praxis. His search for Southern identity twenty years later was a meditation upon the self-critical voice, a scrutiny of the nature of experiencing, a denoting of the quality of irony. This transition from an emphasis upon action to a concern with the private voice was, for the discipline of Southern history, a fruitful step, for it promoted the historical study of Southern self-awareness. But it marked a turning inward.

The role of the essayist has existed in counterpoint with that of the teacher, both functions of a desire to help others grow. Of his teaching one can say little, except to note that in his time and at his behest, first Johns Hopkins, then Yale, became the focus of advanced graduate studies in Southern history. The quality of his students has scarcely been matched; their devotion to him is fierce.[46] They have policed and marked out the boundaries of his achievement, though they are of motley complexion, a diversity of liberals, socialists, conservatives, all different, yet all believing that they sustain Woodward. He has become a kind of pope, with the gift of spotting talented young parish priests, and giving them the confidence to become themselves bishops and archimandrites. A few have become archbishops. One or two may be *papabile*. But upon the evidence of *Thinking Back,* they will have to wait until a Cardinal Camerlengo taps his silver hammer in New Haven. This is no Celestine V, who retired before his time.

CHAPTER 10

Intellectual History and the Search for Southern Identity

I TAKE AS MY text two propositions—the novelty of a self-conscious and rigorous Southern intellectual history and the traditional structure of the search for Southern identity and distinctiveness—to puzzle briefly over their interrelationship. Some may dispute the originality of a Southern intellectual history. Certainly there has been a rich tradition of Southern literary history and criticism that dates at least from William P. Trent's 1892 biography of William Gilmore Simms (if not from Simms himself), that carries on through John Wade upon Augustus Baldwin Longstreet in 1924, that finds a summary in Jay B. Hubbell's *The South in American Literature, 1607–1900* in 1954. I need not rehearse the achievement in our own time, both for strength and weakness, of such as Hugh Holman, Louis Rubin, and Lewis P. Simpson. Certainly there has been a strong tradition of writing upon Southern political thought, whether upon Thomas Jefferson or Edmund Ruffin or Tom Watson or upon ideologies of States' rights and secession, a tradition most notable for being grounded in political circumstance, as though political discourse were only a way of talking about the ballot box. Certainly there have been persistent histories of racist thought, in former times benign, in later times critical, presently turning confusedly benign again. Sympathizing with slaveholders is rather common just now (I am not innocent of the charge myself), partly because we live in Thermidorean times. These traditions have been incidentally intellectual history, on their way to answering more

---

This essay was given as a lecture to a symposium on Southern distinctiveness held at the University of Alabama in 1984, in whose proceedings it is being published. I have retained the informality of address appropriate to such a genre and added some passages included when I repeated myself before the Center for Arkansas and Regional Studies at the University of Arkansas.

pressing questions. But the great traditions of Southern historical literature have rested firmly upon literary, political, and social history, and it is logical that the first systematic attempt to define the mind of the South, that by W. J. Cash in 1941, should have found it natural and axiomatic to disdain mere intellectuals, in a style itself unintellectual, and that it took nearly thirty years before the omission was noticed and reprimanded.[1] But intellectual history itself—that is, the history of the social function of the intelligentsia, or the history of particular intellectuals, or the scrutiny of texts, or all three—is a latecomer to the South, and we are in its younger days.

It is proper to mention antecedents, work by Rollin Osterweis, Clement Eaton, William R. Taylor, and Paul Gaston. But Taylor and Gaston saw themselves as contributors to a different debate, in Taylor's case the nature of American provincial life and imagery before the Civil War, in Gaston's case offering a Kantian gloss upon the mythology of the new South. The cases of Osterweis and Eaton are more delicate, since they regarded themselves as intellectual historians. But they labored under the marked disadvantage of not being themselves intellectual, so their work was flawed, less by premise, more by accomplishment. While it used to be argued that one could not write political history without having been a politician (this was the familiar argument of Machiavelli and Bolingbroke), that case has, for good or ill, weakened in recent years. Yet it seems incontestable that intellectual history written by nonintellectuals is an unhappy affair. But matters have been more crisply commenced in the recent work of Drew Gilpin Faust and Robert Brugger on the Old South, Richard King, Morton Sosna, and Daniel Singal on the New South.

Why is it so late a development? Intellectual history itself is a latecomer everywhere. Perry Miller has been credited with using the term first in 1939 in his preface to *The New England Mind: The Seventeenth Century*.[2] Jumbled up with "American Studies," with which it maintains a friendship like that of Byron with Augusta Leigh, it gained a secure place in American historical literature during the 1950s, even if, being written not only about intellectuals but by intellectuals, it grew doubtful and neurotic during the 1970s. It has yet to be accepted as a subdiscipline in Europe, which prefers to talk about the history of political thought, or the history of ideas, or the history of philosophy and resists the notion of a "European intellectual history" as the phantasm of the European wing of American history departments.[3]

As for the South, there has been and is a widespread apprehension that the South is a peculiarly unintellectual place. Here the influence of Cash has been greatest, with his captivating claim that Southerners have been romantic and brainless. But Cash was not alone. Gerald Johnson observed in 1926, "As for the Intelligentsia, it doesn't exist and never has existed in the South as one of the ruling castes. The South has produced thinkers, but it has never honored them. . . . The Intellectual in the South is merely an eccentric."[4] Such perspectives produce the situation to which Richard King addresses himself in *A Southern Renaissance:* "While working on this project I often encountered friendly skepticism when I described what I was doing as an intellectual history of the South between 1930 and the mid-1950s. Typically the response would be, 'Is there one?' It was as though I had proposed a study of Spiro Agnew's political ethics or of Norman Mailer's poetry."[5] I smiled with recognition when first reading that passage. The intellectuality of the South, improbable to New York, is inconceivable to Cambridge, which still has difficulty with the intellectuality of New York, even as it rifles the coffers of the *New York Review of Books*. "I am interested in Thomas Wolfe," I once said as an undergraduate to a don of wide erudition and some flexibility, and he firmly corrected me. "Not Thomas. The name is Leonard, Leonard Woolf." Provincialities have a way of colliding.

But intellectual history itself has mutated in ways that make a Southern branch more plausible. The older tradition of Arthur Lovejoy and the philosophy of the history of ideas emphasized the grand sweep of ideas from Plato onwards. His pages swarm with ponderings of ontology, epistemology, phenomenology, and march along with the agreeable notion that the great books explain, if not everything, then at least everything that a civilized man should aspire to know. Such a tradition was not likely to look kindly upon a South that, whatever its merits as an intellectual culture, has no systematic and original philosophers to boast. Until the twentieth century, perhaps until very recently, perhaps even now, the South has imported its ideas, though it has often exported its style. The Johns Hopkins University and Herbert Baxter Adams once sent scholars of the South out into its hinterland, but Lovejoy sent none, and it is a pretty and parricidal irony that the Johns Hopkins University Press has taken a special interest in patronizing Southern intellectual history, which has taken the repudiation of Lovejoy as a first order of business. Singal's preface talks about finding a middle ground between the Neo-Platonism of Lovejoy and the notion that objective social causation explains everything. I myself wrote in 1979, "In the dispute between the disciples of

Arthur Lovejoy, who hold that the history of ideas can be written without close reference to those who held the ideas, and intellectual historians, my sympathies lie with the latter."[6] Both of these quotations, these artifacts, demonstrate the novel pressure of the new social history upon intellectual historians. Intellectual history, though not without much grumbling and agonizing, has heeded the siren imperatives of the new social history. We are all social historians now, with more or less enthusiasm and grace. Intellectual historians have become cultural historians, historians of mentalité, historians of meaning, social historians of ideas, call us what you will. Ideas and intellectuals are studied in institutional and social context. Clifford Geertz is cited, Thomas Kuhn is pondered, systems of discourse are reflected upon, structuring wits are frightened by the elegant anarchy of Michel Foucault.[7] Being thus less metaphysical but more social, we offer a face towards the older tradition of Southern historical literature and can sneak in the back door in the footsteps of black historians who have advanced to the front parlor. For the moment, I suspect that intellectual historians are still in the kitchen. But doors are ajar, and they will widen.

Two facts about the new Southern intellectual history are striking. It is inclined to be biographical in its narrative strategy, at a time when John Higham has singled out biography as a fading part of American intellectual history.[8] The reasons are partly strategic. Intellectual history elsewhere can turn single-mindedly social and archaeological because it has a generation and more of biographical and textual work for which a social context cries out to be defined. We do not urgently need a new biography of Voltaire, so Robert Darnton can set about the publishing history of the *Encyclopedia*. To the contrary, we do need a hatful of biographies of Southern intellectuals, which has influenced the biographical strategies of *A Sacred Circle,* of *A Southern Renaissance,* and of *The War Within.* Moreover, the decision by younger historians to interest themselves in biography may be a reproach to Higham's generalization. Daniel Singal has argued, as the rationale of his study, "I turned to the concrete sensibilities of the intellectuals—to the structures of their minds and their ways of perceiving the world. For it is within their sensibilities, formed through individual life experiences, that abstract thought and social conditions must be fused."[9] An intellectual history where minds became but epiphenomena, but artifacts of social context, would be profoundly impoverished, and I, for one, would wish to have nothing to do with it. In fact I suspect that Southern intellectual historians may be anticipating, rather than lagging behind, trends in American historiography. They do not seem markedly less new-fangled as a consequence of the structure of Southern history, if I can anticipate those who think the South especially hospitable to conceding the individual life's importance. I see a variety of new-fangled intellectual preferences, ranging from Brugger's interest in psychohistory, to Faust's sociological tastes, to King's Freudian and Nietzschean standpoint, to my own neo-Hegelianism. This is no school. The subdiscipline has been eclectically established, partly because it has radiated from no single mentor or center.

The second salient point is that this intellectual history is being written partly by non-Southerners. The South has not only imported its ideas, it seems to be importing its intellectual historians.[10] Several years ago C. Vann Woodward observed a similar but far larger invasion of social and economic historians, spearheaded by the likes of Robert Fogel, Stanley Engerman, and Eugene Genovese, and counseled a wary hospitality: that Southerners should observe and learn but count their spoons. He also noted that they fought out their battles in the South though not for the South: "It has not been North versus South, but rather a battle waged on Southern soil between factions of an alien army. A few Southerners were recruited in their ranks, but mainly Southerners have remained noncombatant if fascinated spectators."[11] In many ways there is an equal exoticism in the questions and style of Southern intellectual history. It worries about the paradigms of intellectual revolutions, it applies the hermeneutics of Freudianism, it frets about the intellectual respectability of cultural nationalism, all questions that adhere to the structure of Southern history but have not been generated self-consciously by the indigenous tradition of self-analysis. That local tradition has stuck with literary history or, what may be more significant, has interested itself in religious history, which is or can be a variety of intellectual history, is much written by Southerners and reflects the survival of Christianity among the Southern intelligentsia at a time when it has diminished elsewhere. To the agnostic outsider religion is one of the interesting objects of Southern history, to the insider it is often a motive of great intensity, leading to extended meditations upon the South as a "sacred society."[12]

Yet there is a more fundamental reason why the South has not generated its own intellectual historians. The Southern intelligentsia does not like to think of itself as one, with the consequence that it sees no reason to write its own history. This is a crucial fact. The tradition of seeing the South as merely instinct, unreflective and remorseless, has

two sources. There is a non-Southern, what one may call an abolitionist, tradition, still alive and finding of late an energetic and persuasive exemplar in Bertram Wyatt-Brown, who has walked off with a
good many spoons.[13] That he has done so to the applause of many
Southerners, who find congenial his portrait of antebellum Southern
culture as trapped in a debilitating and violent system of honor, indicates a second source, the South itself, which is much attached to the
idea that it is a place hostile to abstraction. Mencken the outsider
scoffed at the mind of the South, yet Cash the Southerner erected the
joke into a dogma. He would have done so, I think, if the influencing
Mencken had never noticed Dayton and stuck to swigging German
beer in Baltimore. The theory of the antimetaphysical South knows no
political boundaries, but arises on the lips of the liberal, the populist,
and the conservative alike.

Let me cite private evidence to illustrate how Southern thinkers resist their own intellectuality. My first book, *The Idea of the American
South, 1920–1941,* was variously reviewed, often with kindness, sometimes with puzzlement, occasionally with irritation. Reaction from
non-Southerners showed no discomfort with the proposition of a
Southern intellectual history worth writing, which indicates that the
old Menckenian and abolitionist tradition has grown enfeebled. Those
who were most resistant to its claim that ideas have had a formal and
vital role in creating Southern culture were Southerners. My favorite
is James J. Thompson, Jr., in a journal called *The Southern Partisan,* a
conservative periodical friendlier to Jesse Helms than to Hegel, who
observes that I promise "to wreak more destruction than all the John
Browns the North has marshalled against the South in the last hundred years or so" and offers a summary of my thesis as, "There is no
South; it exists only in the minds of those oddly misnamed creatures
known as 'Southerners.'"[14] The article was entitled "Does the South
Exist?" and before it was placed a map of the region, over which was
superimposed an immense question mark. This bizarre misreading of
my thesis is a common one among Southern readers, and instructive.
For, of course, I never denied the existence of the South. But I certainly did say that perception has had an indispensable and continuing
dialectical role in the creation and sustenance of that culture.[15] That
such an assertion is hastily misread as relegating the region to the
status of an idea, and *therefore* to unreality, is symptomatic of a desire
among the Southern intelligentsia to see its South as a hard empirical
fact and—this implication is important—Southern intellectuals as,
not molders, but registrars. "The South is as real and as amenable to

discussion as are France, Hollywood, poetry, capitalism, astronomy, or corn," a recent conservative symposium declared in its introduction.[16] That it is real the intellectual historian will not deny. That it is amenable to discussion the intellectual historian is delighted to concede. For it is peculiarly the business of the intellectual historian to debate such matters. We have the late and good, though occasionally tedious, C. E. M. Joad constantly on our shoulders, asking, and saying whenever something is proposed, "It depends what you mean by. . . ."

The modern Southern intelligentsia has developed relatively unselfaware, rather populist, rather positivist. The reasons will be obvious. A self-conscious intellectual class is the product of an affluent and self-assured society, manifesting itself in and permitting Madame du Deffand's Paris, Matthew Arnold's Oxford, Ralph Waldo Emerson's Boston, or Lionel Trilling's New York. It requires wealth, it requires a tolerated social role for critical intelligence with defensive ramparts, which, while they often prove far from impregnable, offer a breathing space for speculation. It is true, as Daniel Singal reminds me, that Trilling's New York produced, and needed to produce, the closest study of American philistinism in Richard Hofstadter's *Anti-Intellectualism in American Life*. Nonetheless, the depredations of McCarthyism upon the New York intelligentsia, while agonizing and claiming victims, left a culture with incomparably greater resources than those available to their Southern cousins, in the form of universities, libraries, periodicals, endowments, presses, and patrons. In short, an intelligentsia requires precisely the society the South since 1865 has lacked. The Southern intellectual has had to look over his shoulder; he has often been poor; he has been fired for critical independence; he has been pilloried by press or pulpit; he has been harried by state legislatures more interested in corn than poetry and unimpressed by Matthew Arnold's claims for the function of criticism. The anti-intellectualism characteristic of American culture in general has been amplified in the South by the social exigencies of poverty, only of late lessened, and by the demonology of evangelicalism.

One consequence is clear: the Southern intellectual has masked his intellectuality in order to survive. He has become folksy, he tells stories that can be used interchangeably in lecture room or bar, he writes without incongruity novels in which football players quote Vico and enter tobacco-spitting contests.[17] John Shelton Reed is the master of this voice in our own day, although Woodward very occasionally has a line in populist rhetoric, a capacity to say complicated things in the assumed manner of a simple Arkansas boy. At its best this tradition, this pact between trained intelligence and the vernacular, is a remarkable validation of democratic culture, beside which the gawping enthusiasm of those *narodniki*[18] who trooped through Russian peasant villages in the 1870s was a fleeting engagement. At its worst it is a silly deification of the *Volk* that romanticizes and distorts "simpler folk" and betrays the Southern intellectual into a curious self-contempt.[19]

To observe that many intellectual historians of the South come from outside the South, while their subject matter is of interest to Southerners, is to note the potential for confusions of emphasis. The gulf of tone between the indigenous and the exotic may be illustrated by remembering that at a meeting of the Southern Historical Association in 1982 a panel enjoined to meditate upon this very question of Southern identity was composed of one non-Southerner and several Southerners. The former gave a somber and intelligent analysis of literary genres and their influence upon Southern perception. The other panelists discussed religion and country music. But *discussed* is the wrong word. They enthused, they applauded, they stood in reverent admiration at the cultural miracle of the Southern people.

Let me recur to the invaluably naked logic of the *Southern Partisan*. Mr. Thompson begins his critique with this invitation: that I go with him to a bar on the banks of the James River, where he will beg silence for me to declaim my views to the assembled farmhands and blue-collar workers. Then, rather ungraciously, he proposes to flee the ensuing brawl in the direction of Newport News.[20] His wit is instructive, but his logic more so: the final court of appeals for ideas in the South is a bar. Where I used to come from it is a senior combination room. Each has marked disadvantages, but the difference is great, not alone for the distinction between port and prejudice on the one hand, and Pabst and prejudice on the other. One difference is important here: the Southern intellectual has become committed to being an ideologist. It is not enough that he be in contact with other intellectuals, that he rest content in that small corner of society that has an interest or stake in the systematic discussion of ideas. Rather he wishes to be in intimate contact with his society, with his South, with his "native soil."

Which brings us to the search for Southern identity. It is the moment when the Southern intellectual goes looking for his society, puzzles over what it is he is supposed to be looking for, what it is he represents or wishes to represent or hopes to influence, what it is that might be out to nail him bleeding to the state flagpole. As his motives are various, so are his answers. The literary critics wisely tell us, when we wish to understand what is going on in a piece of prose or poetry, that we should listen, not to what it says, but to how it says. By this dictum, consider under what auspices and in what narrative form this search is conducted.

Its form is the essay. It is not in extended and researched works of integrated scholarship. There is no satisfactory account of Southern identity. We have books on slavery, on cotton mills, on quilts in the Appalachians, on discrete social facts which can be researched through discrete evidence, diaries, letters, censuses. Sometimes, as with Howard Odum, someone bravely sticks these facts together and calls it the South.[21] Few are persuaded. Temerity is rewarded with dissident uproar. If the synthesis is genuinely eclectic, it fails to define. If it is definitive, it defines by taking the significant and crucial step of deciding upon value, that one thing matters more than another, that the Black Belt matters more than Knoxville, fundamentalism more than urban sociology, honor more than racism, white more than black, black more than white. But the place where such decisions of value are usually taken or articulated is the ruminative essay. For the essay is ill adapted to collating empirical data. It is too short, too constrained. What is implicit in the long narrative, selection, is openly proclaimed. We grow perfunctory, we cut corners, we become representative, anecdotal, illustrative.

Look at the genre of the "search for southern identity" essay, look at those by Ulrich Phillips, John Crowe Ransom, and C. Vann Woodward. They offer historical arguments or sociological arguments, the more persuasive the better their history or sociology, but their motive and intention is programmatic. They may say, this is how things are. But they are much more concerned with changing or affirming. Phillips believed in white supremacy and was putting his shoulder to its rutting wheel. Ransom hoped the South was agrarian and conservative, but his aim was to keep or make it so. Woodward was attempting to influence his culture, to remind the South of its mixed history and capacity for flexibility.[22] No doubt the historian is always somewhat programmatic, no doubt social concern is an indispensable source of moral energy. Yet, in the search for Southern identity wishes are overmastering. It is ideology, it is to the Southern intellectual what the jeremiad is to the Protestant minister. Whether such sermons are heeded, whether anyone other than other Southern intellectuals is listening, whether the silent presence of the Southern demos denotes rapt attentiveness or indifference, is very unclear and apparently not in the interest of the intelligentsia to clarify. For certainly few social groups have refused to analyze themselves more than that Southern intelligentsia. But the search is the more persuasive as ideology by denying its ideological content. The minister is better able to strike terror or inspire hope if he stands before his congregation as, not a precise theologian, but the livid incarnation of God.

Will the new Southern intellectual history be of much use in the search for Southern distinctiveness? Will we help or hinder? When Southerners mount up for the chase, do we join in or snicker at you from the comfort of the bar? In one sense, I doubt we will offer you much aid and comfort. Our job, though not our only job or even our most important job, is to mount up, but to follow you, not the fox. If you will go off on these chases, I suppose we must follow, even if some of us regard it as the unspeakable in pursuit of the uneatable. Philosophically the quarry is pretty uneatable, and there are grounds for suspecting that you are on a drag hunt. As usually practiced the search for Southern distinctiveness is a logical nightmare.

Southerners are religious, one might say.[23] Yet there are agnostic Southerners, and religious sectarianism has been so marked that it is unclear whether the admission of religiosity advances the premise of cultural homogeneity. Southerners are devoted to place, it is said. Yet Southerners have left the region with abandon, and moved within the region at a dizzying pace. In 1838 Hugh Legaré felt moved to observe on the proclivity of Americans, very much including Southerners, for selling up and moving: "This . . . is a peculiarity of our people. Sir, I do not mention this as a very prepossessing or honorable *trait* in our character—I mention it simply as a *fact*. We have no local attachments, generally speaking—nothing bears the *pretium affectionis* in our eyes. If an estate, a residence in town, a country seat, rises a little beyond what we are accustomed to think its value, it is sold without any hesitation."[24] Southern realtors are not noticeably impoverished, and there were some Southerners who were so unsure about geography that they mistook Saigon for Yazoo City.[25] Southerners are agrarian in their values, you might counter. Yet there are Charlestonians who have echoed Sarmiento's views on the relationship between Buenos Aires and the pampas: "Everything which the city contains is blockaded there, proscribed beyond its limits; and any one who should dare to appear in the rural districts in a frock-coat, for example, or mounted on an English saddle, would bring ridicule and brutal assaults upon himself."[26] Southerners resist the abstractions of pernicious reforming Yankees, you might go on. Yet Southerners could best Thomas Aquinas in their talent for making scholastic distinctions within the miriad niceties of sectional identity.[27] Southerners are Celts who like pork, some of you, I know, will assert. What do we do with Louisianans who prefer to crunch frogs' legs?[28] It is a logical mess. The intellectual historian, obliged by his trade to keep a log of such desperately contradictory assertions, may be driven to quote Francis Jeffrey's protest at Wordsworth's *The Excursion,* that other ambitious Romantic quest: "This will never do! . . . The case of Mr. Wordsworth, is now manifestly hopeless, and we give him up as altogether incurable, and beyond the power of criticism. We cannot, indeed, altogether omit taking precautions now and then, against the spreading of the malady; but for himself, though we shall watch the progress of his symptoms as a matter of professional curiosity and instruction, we really think it right, not to harass him longer with nauseous remedies—but, rather to throw in cordials and lenitives, and wait in patience for the natural termination of the disorder."[29]

Yet the intellectual historian knows that such a vigil would be long and hopeless, and he will be forgiven if occasionally, in the watches of the night, he will be found muttering to himself what Theodore Zeldin recently observed: "Studies of national identity habitually beg the question that they are supposed to investigate. They assume that nations are distinct entities. All our instincts tell us that there is something different between a German and an Italian, but then all our instincts tell us that the earth is flat. The business of scholarship is to question the obvious. I have my doubts about national history as a method of discovering the collective character, soul or mind of people, because national history tries to make political frontiers explain too much, just as in the old days 'crucial dates' like 1485 were supposed to cut off medieval from modern."[30] How much more is this skepticism applicable to the South, which has no political frontiers, only a hazy and recent institutional infrastructure, and is especially reliant for its survival upon an act of emotional and intellectual will?

Does the intellectual historian offer only skepticism? By studying the history of the Southern intelligentsia, we are of use in teasing out the boundaries and dialectics of perception and discrete realities. We can suggest that the debate over Southern identity is the social discourse of intellectuals in the South, to be appraised as such. Even to the positivist historian, unskeptical about the South and sectional identity, this will be of some value, since he will need to distinguish between the idiosyncrasies of individual viewpoint and the society observed. We can discern in the modern South many of the mechanisms that Drew Gilpin Faust has described of the Old South. The intellectual is alienated in a changing and democratic culture that regards him with suspicion, and to keep his place and sanity, he elects to become his chosen society's ideologist, to serve, preserve, and reform the culture. Indeed I suspect that the thesis of *A Sacred Circle* fits the twentieth-century intellectual more neatly than it does James Henry Hammond or Nathaniel Beverley Tucker. If you are uncomfortable at being compared to the despised proslavery thinker, you may take a meager comfort in the fact that both Faust and Bertram Wyatt-Brown have found in the proslavery argument an instrument of self-criticism, capable of both sanguine rationalization and social reform.[31]

None of this is to argue that no Southern culture exists, but that the intellectual historian has usages in defining the shape of that culture. Static sociologies do not work, for time and place are too various. It is instructive, when reflecting upon the South, to weigh the sensible advice of E. P. Thompson, obliged to think about an analogous phenomenon, class. If you substitute the word *South* in this quotation for the word *class,* my meaning will be clear. "There is today an ever-present temptation to suppose that class is a thing. . . . 'It,' the working class, is assumed to have a real existence, which can be defined almost mathematically. . . . But a similar error is committed daily on the other side of the ideological divide. . . . it is assumed that any notion of class is a pejorative theoretical construct, imposed upon the evidence. . . . [But] if we remember that class is a relationship, and not a thing, we cannot think this way. 'It' does not exist, either to have an ideal interest or consciousness, or to lie as a patient on an Adjustor's table. . . . If we stop history at a given point, then there are no classes but simply a multitude of individuals with a multitude of experiences. But if we watch these men over an adequate period of social change, we observe patterns in their relationships, their ideas, and their institutions. Class is defined by men as they live their own history, and, in the end, this is its only definition."[32]

The South, too, is a relationship, not a thing. The intellectual historian can help to measure the many acts of definition by which Southerners have created and sustained their culture. Above all, he can remind the Southerner, in the midst of history, that while it is natural and necessary to want to stop, to judge, and to act, history goes on. The search for Southern identity is a straining for a still point, because humankind cannot bear very much reality, but, to quote further that attentuated Southerner and Heraclitean, T. S. Eliot, in *Burnt Norton:* "Except for the point, the still point / There would be no dance, and there is only the dance."

Notes

INTRODUCTION
The Endeavor of Southern Intellectual History

1. For example, Robert von Hallberg, ed., *Canons* (Chicago, 1984).

2. John B. Boles and Evelyn Thomas Nolen, eds., *Interpreting Southern History: Historiographical Essays in Honor of Sanford W. Higginbotham* (Baton Rouge, 1987), vii.

3. Clive James, *From the Land of Shadows* (London, 1982), 19; Kenneth Tynan, *A View of the English Stage, 1944–1965* (London, 1975), 14.

4. J. R. Pole, *Paths to the American Past* (New York, 1979).

5. On Romantic irony see Lilian R. Furst, *Fictions of Romantic Irony* (Cambridge, Mass., 1984); and Anne K. Mellor, *English Romantic Irony* (Cambridge, Mass., 1980). On irony in general see Wayne C. Booth, *A Rhetoric of Irony* (Chicago, 1974); and D. C. Muecke, *The Compass of Irony* (London, 1969).

6. Herbert Butterfield, *Man on His Past* (Cambridge, 1955); J. H. Plumb, *The Death of the Past* (Boston, 1970).

7. John Emerich Edward Dalberg-Acton, *Lectures on Modern History*, ed. J. N. Figgis and R. V. Laurence (London, 1926), 12; Douglas Southall Freeman, *R. E. Lee: A Biography*, 4 vols. (New York, 1934–35), 1:xiv.

8. Leonard Krieger, *Ranke: The Meaning of History* (Chicago, 1977), 46.

9. George Macaulay Trevelyan, *"Clio, A Muse" And Other Essays* (London, 1913), 160.

10. Ibid., 162; Lytton Strachey, "A New History of Rome," *Spectator* 102 (2 January 1909): 20–21, quoted in Michael Holroyd, *Lytton Strachey and the Bloomsbury Group: His Work, Their Influence* (Harmondsworth, 1971), 162.

11. F. M. Cornford, *Microcosmographia Academica: Being a Guide for the Young Academic Politician* (Cambridge, 1908), 11.

12. Hugh Blair, *Lectures on Rhetoric and Belles Lettres* (1783; reprint, New York, 1826), 359.

13. For example, Hayden White in *Tropics of Discourse: Essays in Cultural Criticism* (Baltimore, 1978).

CHAPTER 1
On the Mind of the Old South and Its Accessibility

1. W. J. Cash, *The Mind of the South* (New York, 1941), 96–97.

2. Drew Gilpin Faust, *A Sacred Circle: The Dilemma of the Intellectual in the Old South, 1840–1860* (Baltimore, 1977); Robert J. Brugger, *Beverley Tucker: Heart over Head in the Old South* (Baltimore, 1978); E. Brooks Holifield, *The Gentlemen Theologians: American Theology in Southern Culture, 1795–1860* (Durham, 1978). [To this can now be added Ralph E. Luker, *A Southern Tradition in Theology and Social Criticism, 1830–1930* (New York, 1984); James Oscar Farmer, Jr., *The Metaphysical Confederacy: James Henley Thornwell and the Synthesis of Southern Values* (Macon, Ga., 1986); Laurence Shore, *Southern Capitalists: The Ideological Leadership of an Elite, 1832–1885* (Chapel Hill, 1986); Elisabeth Muhlenfeld, *Mary Boykin Chesnut: A Biography* (Baton Rouge, 1981); Lester D. Stephens, *Joseph LeConte: Gentle Prophet of Evolution* (Baton Rouge, 1982); Martha R. Severens and Charles L. Wyrick, Jr., eds., *Charles Fraser of Charleston: Essays on the Man, His Art, and His Times* (Charleston, 1983); William B. McCash, *Thomas R. R. Cobb (1823–1862): The Making of a Southern Nationalist* (Macon, Ga., 1983); Betty L. Mitchell, *Edmund Ruffin: A Biography* (Bloomington, 1981); Alison Goodyear Freehling, *Drift toward Dissolution: The Virginia Slavery Debate of 1831–1832* (Baton Rouge, 1982); Dickson D. Bruce, Jr., *The Rhetoric of Conservatism: The Virginia Convention of 1829–30 and the Conservative Tradition in the South* (San Marino, 1982); Michael O'Brien, *A Character of Hugh Legaré* (Knoxville, 1985); Michael O'Brien and David Moltke-Hansen, eds., *Intellectual Life in Antebellum Charleston* (Knoxville, 1986); and Allen Kaufman, *Capitalism, Slavery, and Republican Values: Antebellum Political Economists, 1819–1848* (Austin, 1982).]

3. "The Union and Its Compromises," *De Bow's Review* 21 (August 1856): 177.

4. George Tucker, "Discourse on American Literature," *Southern Literary Messenger* 4 (February 1838): 85.

5. William J. Grayson, "Autobiography," ed. Samuel Gaillard Stoney, *South Carolina Historical and Genealogical Magazine* 49 (April 1948): 98

6. George Frederick Holmes, "The Present Condition of Letters," *Southern Literary Messenger* 11 (March 1845): 174.

7. An anecdote frequently used to illustrate the supposed social inferiority of authorship concerns Lord Morpeth. When visiting Charleston, the Englishman is said to have asked the whereabouts of Simms. His interlocutors confessed ignorance and intimated that Simms was not considered such a great man in Charleston. "Simms not a great man!" replied the visitor. "Then for God's sake who is your great man?" But this story is undocumented. Trent tells it in his life of Simms, but without annotation. It is probable that it came from the survivors of antebellum Charleston with whom Trent conversed. Yet there are good reasons for doubting Morpeth's partiality for Simms, as his tastes were more Augustan than Romantic. Even if the story is true, it scarcely proves its supposed point. That passing strangers should be unaware of Simm's location does not demonstrate the low social standing of the litterateur. And one might consider that in denying Simms the title of greatness, our anonymous Charlestonians merely anticipated the verdict of modern criticism. See Louis D. Rubin, Jr., *The Writer in the South: Studies in a Literary*

Community (Athens, Ga., 1972), 13; William Peterfield Trent, *William Gilmore Simms* (Boston, 1892), 129; and lectures on Alexander Pope and on America in *The Vice-Regal Speeches and Addresses, Lectures and Poems of the late Earl of Carlisle, K.G.,* ed. J. J. Gaskin (Dublin and London, 1865), 406–7. [On Trent see John McCardell, "Trent's *Simms:* The Making of a Biography," in *A Master's Due: Essays in Honor of David Herbert Donald,* ed. William J. Cooper, Jr., et al. (Baton Rouge, 1985), 179–203.]

8. George Frederick Holmes, "Sir William Hamilton's Discussions," *Southern Quarterly Review,* n.s., 8 (October 1853): 289–90.

9. *Southern Literary Messenger* 12 (April 1846): 254.

10. Perry Miller, *The Raven and the Whale: The War of Words and Wits in the Era of Poe and Melville* (New York, 1956), 84.

11. The popular Riverside edition of Emerson was published between 1883 and 1893; that of Lowell in 1891; that of Longfellow in 1895; that of Oliver Wendell Holmes in 1896. This is not to say that these were not noticed before the Civil War, but their earlier reputations were more problematical, less canonical.

12. Paul Hamilton Hayne, *Lives of Robert Young Hayne and Hugh Swinton Legaré* (Charleston, 1878), now obscure; Octavius Brooks Frothingham, *Transcendentalism in New England: A History* (New York, 1878; reprint, New York, 1959).

13. Paul Hamilton Hayne, "Hugh Swinton Legaré," *Southern Review* 7 (January 1870): 122, 156–57.

14. Trent, *Simms,* 51–52.

15. H. L. Mencken, "The Sahara of the Bozart," in *Prejudices: Second Series* (New York, 1920), 137. It is worth pointing out that the *Library of Southern Literature* still has value as a starting point for inquiry into lesser or unjustly obscure writers.

16. Vernon L. Parrington, *The Romantic Revolution in America, 1800–1860* (New York, 1927), 3–125. Some of my remarks on Southern literary critics were used in "The Last Theologians: Recent Southern Literary Criticism," *Michigan Quarterly Review* 17 (Summer 1798): 404–13. [For a more detailed assessment, see Michael O'Brien, "Vernon L. Parrington," in *Twentieth Century American Historians: Dictionary of Literary Biography: Volume Seventeen,* ed. Clyde N. Wilson (Detroit, 1983), 342–50.]

17. [It is less clear now how far we still live in the midst of this school. Some of the leading figures have passed, or are passing, from the scene. Emblematically the coeditorship of the *Southern Review* has passed from Lewis P. Simpson to Fred Hobson, who—though a student of Louis Rubin's—shows a skepticism of the orthodoxy. See Hobson, *Tell about the South: The Southern Rage to Explain* (Baton Rouge, 1983). Other voices are being heard. There is, for example, the feminist scholarship of Ann Goodwyn Jones in *Tomorrow Is Another Day: The Woman Writer in the South, 1859–1936* (Baton Rouge, 1981). Lewis P. Simpson sounded elegiac of his generation when he recently recounted a visit to the grave of Allen Tate in Sewanee and a salutation made "in the name of those of us who in one way or another belong to the second and third generations of the twentieth-century southern literary scene . . . for whom, more than any other figure, Tate had worn the aspect of a field commander of the literary troops." See Simpson, "The Critics Who Made Us: Allen Tate," *Sewanee Review* 94 (Summer 1986): 474.]

18. Louis D. Rubin, Jr., and C. Hugh Holman, eds., *Southern Literary Study: Problems and Possibilities* (Chapel Hill, 1975), 48.

19. See esp. Allen Tate, "The Profession of Letters in the South" (1935) and "A Southern Mode of the Imagination" (1960), reprinted in *Essays of Four Decades* (New York, 1970), 517–34, 577–92.

20. This discussion is distilled from: Rubin, *The Writer in the South;* idem, *William Elliott Shoots a Bear: Essays on the Southern Literary Imagination* (Baton Rouge, 1975); C. Hugh Holman, *The Roots of Southern Writing: Essays on the Literature of the American South* (Athens, Ga., 1972); Lewis P. Simpson, *The Man of Letters in New England and the South: Essays on the Literary Vocation in America* (Baton Rouge, 1973); idem, *The Dispossessed Garden: Pastoral and History in Southern Literature* (Athens, Ga., 1975); and Walter Sullivan, *A Requiem for the Renascence: The State of Fiction in the Modern South* (Athens, Ga., 1976). [See, now, Simpson, *The Brazen Face of History: Studies in the Literary Consciousness in America* (Baton Rouge, 1980); and William C. Havard and Walter Sullivan, eds., *A Band of Prophets: The Vanderbilt Agrarians after Fifty Years* (Baton Rouge, 1982).]

21. Rubin, *William Elliott,* 27; Rubin and Holman, *Southern Literary Study,* 112–13. [An effective criticism and defense of just such a "non-Southern" play by an antebellum Southerner—Louisa McCord's *Caius Gracchus*—can be found in Richard Lounsbury, "*Ludibria Rerum Mortalium:* Charlestonian Intellectuals and Their Classics," in O'Brien and Moltke-Hansen, *Intellectual Life in Antebellum Charleston,* 325–36.]

22. Simpson, *Dispossessed Garden,* 37–38; Tate, *Essays,* 523.

23. Fleetingly, of course, Wilson himself contributed in *Patriotic Gore: Studies in the Literature of the Civil War* (New York, 1962), but Southern literary criticism has been a social circle as much as an intellectual specialty. To the former, Wilson was external.

24. Cleanth Brooks, *William Faulkner: The Yoknapatawpha Country* (New Haven, 1963); Lewis P. Simpson, ed., *The Possibilities of Order: Cleanth Brooks and His Work* (Baton Rouge, 1976).

25. Rubin, *William Elliott,* 256–57; Holman, *Roots of Southern Writing,* 176. The exception is Jay B. Hubbell, *The South in American Literature, 1607–1900* (Durham, 1954), which is marked by a breadth of research and eclecticism of standpoint that are invaluable to the historian.

26. Edd Winfield Parks, *William Gilmore Simms as Literary Critic* (Athens, Ga., 1961).

27. See, for example, John Ward Ostrom, ed., *The Letters of Edgar Allan Poe* (Cambridge, Mass., 1948). The University of South Carolina Press is publishing a centennial edition of Simms's novels, and the John Harvard Library of Harvard University Press has reprinted the same author's *Views and Reviews in American Literature, History and Fiction,* with a preface by Holman; the University of North Carolina Press has had a series of "Southern Literary Classics," with novels by Caruthers, Wirt, Beverley and George Tucker, and Caroline Lee Hentz; the Gregg Press, in its "Americans in Fiction" reprints, has four novels by John Esten Cooke, four by Simms, and two by Caruthers. Richard Beale Davis et al., eds., *Southern Writing, 1585–1920* (New York, 1970), 326–30, has a snippet of Legaré's Byron. [The centennial edition of Simms is now defunct.]

28. Eugene D. Genovese, *The World the Slaveholders Made: Two Essays in Interpretation* (New York, 1969), 115–244; George M. Fredrickson, *The Black Image in the White Mind: The Debate on Afro-American Character and Destiny, 1817–1914* (New York, 1971), 78–82. [Genovese and Elizabeth Fox-Genovese are now engaged upon a study of "the mind of the master class," snippets of which have appeared as articles and pamphlets. See Genovese and Fox-Genovese, "The Religious Ideals of Southern Slave Society," *Georgia Historical Quarterly* 70 (Spring 1986): 1–15; idem, "Slavery, Economic Development, and the Law: The Dilemma of Southern Political Economists, 1800–1860," *Washington and Lee Law Review* 41 (Winter 1984): 1–29; Genovese, *"Slavery Ordained of God": The Southern Slaveholders' View of Biblical History and Modern Politics* (Gettysburg, 1985); idem, *Western Civilization through Slaveholding Eyes: The Social and Historical Thought of Thomas Roderick Dew* (New Orleans, 1986).]

29. For example, David Donald, "The Proslavery Argument Reconsidered," *Journal of Southern History* 37 (February 1971): 3–18.

30. William R. Taylor, *Cavalier and Yankee: The Old South and American National Character* (New York, 1961).

31. The South is given its due in, for example, Henry F. May, *The Enlightenment in America* (New York, 1976); Donald H. Meyer, *The Democratic Enlightenment* (New York, 1976); H. Trevor Colburn, *The Lamp of Experience: Whig History and the Intellectual Origins of the American Revolution* (Chapel Hill, 1965). The most persuasive, if erroneous, proponent of the America-is–New England–writ–large school is Sacvan Bercovitch, in *The Puritan Origins of the American Self* (New Haven, 1975). The attempted riposte is Richard Beale Davis, *Intellectual Life in the Colonial South, 1585–1763*, 3 vols. (Knoxville, 1978), which though successful as archaeological bibliography, is less so as historical criticism.

32. An older example is Merle Curti, *The Growth of American Thought* (New York, 1943); a once standard textbook, Gerald N. Grob and Robert N. Beck, *American Ideas* (New York, 1963), considers thirty-three intellectuals from the "national" period, of which seven are Southerners: Jefferson, Monroe, Taney, Peter Cartwright, Calhoun, Fitzhugh, and Simms.

33. John Higham and Paul K. Conkin, eds., *New Directions in American Intellectual History* (Baltimore, 1979).

34. Michael O'Brien, *The Idea of the American South, 1920–1941* (Baltimore, 1979), 213–27. [I wish I could say that this schizophrenia has significantly lessened, although Thomas Bender's new series at the Johns Hopkins University Press, New Studies in American Intellectual and Cultural History, shows an interest in the South. See Kenneth S. Greenberg, *Masters and Statesmen: The Political Culture of American Slavery* (Baltimore, 1985); and Steven M. Stowe, *Intimacy and Power in the Old South: Ritual in the Lives of the Planters* (Baltimore, 1987).]

35. Clement Eaton, "Recent Trends in the Writing of Southern History," *Louisiana Historical Quarterly* 38 (April 1955): 41. I find since writing this that I have been involved in arranging a conference in a most agreeable spot, Charleston; reality outruns the ironist, as usual. [Though it is now possible to discern a growing sense of a collective endeavor—evident, for example, in Farmer, *Metaphysical Confederacy*–we are as yet spared a newsletter.]

36. Brugger, *Beverley Tucker;* Robin Colin McLean, *George Tucker: Moral Philosopher and Man of Letters* (Chapel Hill, 1961); Neal C. Gillespie, *The Collapse of Orthodoxy: The Intellectual Ordeal of George Frederick Holmes* (Charlottesville, 1972); Faust, *A Sacred Circle;* Clyde N. Wilson, ed., *Selections from the Letters and Speeches of the Hon. James H. Hammond of South Carolina* (Spartanburg, S.C., 1978); William K. Scarborough, ed., *The Diary of Edmund Ruffin,* 2 vols. (Baton Rouge, 1972–76); Holifield, *Gentlemen Theologians;* Harvey Wish, *George Fitzhugh, Propagandist of the Old South* (Baton Rouge, 1943); Clement Eaton, *The Mind of the Old South,* rev. ed. (Baton Rouge, 1967). A useful recent article is Robert J. Brugger, "The Mind of the Old South: New Views," *Virginia Quarterly Review* 56 (Spring 1980): 277–95. [On recent biographies see Michael O'Brien, "Biography and the Old South: A Review Essay," *Virginia Magazine of History and Biography* 93 (October 1985): 375–88.]

37. Quentin Skinner, *The Foundations of Modern Political Thought* (Cambridge, 1978).

38. [There have been useful additions to our store of texts. See Rayburn S. Moore, ed., *A Man of Letters in the Nineteenth-Century South: Selected Letters of Paul Hamilton Hayne* (Baton Rouge, 1982); C. Vann Woodward, ed., *Mary Chesnut's Civil War* (New Haven, 1981); Carol Bleser, ed., *The Hammonds of Redcliffe* (New York, 1981); William Gilmore Simms, ed., *The Charleston Book: A Miscellany in Prose and Verse* (Charleston, 1845; reprint, Spartanburg, S.C., 1983); *The Writings of Benjamin F. Perry,* ed. Stephen Meats and Edwin T. Arnold, 3 vols. (Spartanburg, S.C., 1980). And it was inexcusable not to have mentioned *The Papers of John C. Calhoun,* ed. Robert Meriwether and Clyde N. Wilson, 16 vols. to date (Columbia, S.C., 1959–).]

39. [Since there seems to have been some misunderstanding that this essay argues the equality of antebellum Southern culture with New England culture, I can only stress that this paragraph is unchanged since I first wrote it. Moreover, I can testify that it was written with the firm intention of evading those Southerners who might see in my arguments an opportunity of dancing gleefully on the grave of William Lloyd Garrison. Clearly, I have wished to raise the estimate of antebellum Southern thought, but I have pointedly reserved judgment on where that estimate will conclude. I assume, given the volatility of critical reasoning, that it will rise without settling down anywhere definitively. See my remarks in *A Character of Hugh Legaré,* xii. Cf. Drew Gilpin Faust, "The Peculiar South Revisited: White Society, Culture, and Politics in the Antebellum Period, 1800–1860," in *Interpreting Southern History: Historiographical Essays in Honor of Sanford W. Higginbotham,* ed. John B. Boles and Evelyn Thomas Nolen (Baton Rouge, 1987), 100.]

40. David K. Jackson, ed., *The Contributors and Contributions to the Southern Literary Messenger (1834–1864)* (Charlottesville, 1936); Guy A. Cardwell, "Charleston Periodicals, 1795–1860" (Ph.D. diss., University of North Carolina, 1936); and Frank Ryan, Jr., "'The Southern Quarterly Review,' 1842–1857" (Ph.D. diss., University of North Carolina, 1956), offer suggestions for the *Southern Review, Russell's Magazine,* and the *Southern Quarterly Review,* but not with thoroughness. We badly need a reference volume comparable to the *Wellesley Index of Victorian Periodicals.* [On the *Southern Review* see, now, "Contributors to the Southern Review," in O'Brien, *A Character of Hugh Legaré,* 283–96.]

41. For example, Jan C. Dawson, "The Puritan and the Cavalier: The South's Perception of Contrasting Traditions," *Journal of Southern History* 44 (November 1978): 597–614. [A further illustration is Reginald Horsman, *Race and Manifest Destiny: The Origins of American Racial Anglo-Saxonism* (Cambridge, Mass., 1981), the more telling because Horsman does mingle Southern and Northern evidence. Horsman quotes from George Frederick Holmes some five times—in the guise of a writer in the *Southern Quarterly Review*—without knowing so and thinking that Holmes is five separate authors, none of whom has a name.]

42. Fredrickson, *Black Image in the White Mind*, 54. [Chesnut's views can now be found in three paperbacks: Mary Boykin Chesnut, *A Diary from Dixie*, ed. Ben Ames Williams (Boston, 1949), though bowlderized and unreliable; Woodward, *Mary Chesnut's Civil War*; and C. Vann Woodward and Elisabeth Muhlenfeld, eds., *The Private Mary Chesnut: The Unpublished Civil War Diaries* (New York, 1984).]

43. Rollin G. Osterweis, *Romanticism and Nationalism in the Old South* (New Haven, 1949), 151–52. Gillespie, *Collapse of Orthodoxy*, 251, correctly attributes "Herder's Philosophy of History," *Southern Quarterly Review* 5 (April 1844): 265–311, to Holmes. [In fact this essay, though sympathetic to Herder on the principle of cultural nationalism, is otherwise scathing on Herder's intellectual sloppiness.]

44. *The Letters of William Gilmore Simms*, ed. Mary C. Simms Oliphant et al., 6 vols. (Columbia, S.C., 1952–82), 2:124.

45. David R. Goldfield, "Pursuing the American Urban Dream: Cities in the Old South," in *The City in Southern History: The Growth of Urban Civilization in the South*, by Blaine A. Brownell and David R. Goldfield (Port Washington, N.Y., 1977), 52–91. But see esp. J. Mills Thornton III, *Politics and Power in a Slave Society: Alabama, 1800–1860* (Baton Rouge, 1978). [See also Jane H. Pease and William H. Pease, *The Web of Progress: Private Values and Public Styles in Boston and Charleston, 1828–1843* (New York, 1985); O'Brien and Moltke-Hansen, *Intellectual Life in Antebellum Charleston;* Frederick Cople Jaher, *The Urban Establishment: Upper Strata in Boston, New York, Charleston, Chicago, and Los Angeles* (Urbana, Ill., 1982); and David R. Goldfield, *Cotton Fields and Skyscrapers: Southern City and Region, 1607–1980* (Baton Rouge, 1982).]

46. Figures such as these are necessarily crude. I have erred on the side of generosity, however, and they are more likely to be too high than too low. Politics and slavery are scarcely identical, even in the South. And I have included tangential articles, such as a travel sketch of Cuba that barely mentions slavery.

47. Holifield, *Gentlemen Theologians*, esp. 5–49.

48. [These disputes, though sometimes explicit, were often decorously anonymous. This was partly the ethic that gentlemen should not stricture other gentlemen by name, partly that the convention of anonymity required contributors to feign ignorance of their opponents. It is possible that this weakened discourse. On the other hand, it brought about a situation for which many today pine, a discourse of ideas relatively unpolluted by personalities and the settling of scores.]

49. Trent, *Simms*, 45.

50. Taylor, *Cavalier and Yankee*, 37, 38–45, 56–57.
51. Minnie Clare Yarborough, ed., *The Reminiscences of William C. Preston* (Chapel Hill, 1933). They break off, for instance, before Preston began his studies in Edinburgh.
52. Preston to Ticknor, 8 May 1824, Preston Papers, South Caroliniana Library, University of South Carolina, Columbia; *Life, Letters and Journals of George Ticknor,* ed. George S. Hillard, 2 vols. (Boston, 1876), 1:278. I strongly suspect that if we expand the study of the Southern mind away from matters of sectional passion, we shall find many such intersectional friendships and alliances. Cf. John Hope Franklin, *A Southern Odyssey: Travelers in the Antebellum North* (Baton Rouge, 1976).
53. Carl Diehl, *Americans and German Scholarship, 1770–1870* (New Haven, 1978), 148–49.
54. *Catalogue of the Library of the Hon. Hugh S. Legaré* (Washington, D.C., 1843); *Catalogue of the Rare and Valuable Private Library of the Late Hon. H. S. Legaré* (Washington, D.C., 1848). Both can be found in the Legaré Papers, South Caroliniana Library, box 2, folder 62.
55. Diehl, *Americans and German Scholarship,* 145–53. Diehl's book is a good example of intelligent intellectual history that is flawed by an indifference to the Southern dimension, despite his complaints of having to use yet again the dog-eared manuscripts of Bancroft and a paucity of contemporary American sources. He does not seem to know of Jesse Burton Harrison's German diary, now in Charlottesville, or of Legaré's published German journals. Nor is he aware of the admittedly scrappy *Southern Scholars in Goethe's Germany,* by John T. Krumpelmann (Chapel Hill, 1965), and so he misses the Southern appreciation of German scholarship so important to Basil Gildersleeve.

CHAPTER 2

The Lineaments of Antebellum Southern Romanticism

1. Rollin G. Osterweis, *Romanticism and Nationalism in the Old South* (New Haven, 1949), esp. "Appendix: Romanticism Defined," 235–39; Irving Babbitt, *Rousseau and Romanticism* (Boston, 1919); Ernst Cassirer, *The Myth of the State* (New Haven, 1946); Jacques Barzun, *Romanticism and the Modern Ego* (Boston, 1943), revised as *Classic, Romantic, and Modern* (Garden City, N.Y., 1961); Arthur Lovejoy, "On the Discrimination of Romanticisms," in *Essays in the History of Ideas* (Baltimore, 1948), 228–53.
2. Ulrich B. Phillips, *Life and Labor in the Old South* (Boston, 1931); idem, *American Negro Slavery* (New York, 1918). In adopting the notion of a "Great Reaction," Osterweis was much influenced by Clement Eaton, *Freedom of Thought in the Old South* (Durham, 1940); the Jacobite theme is elaborated in Rollin G. Osterweis, *The Myth of the Lost Cause, 1865–1900* (Hamden, Conn., 1973).
3. August Wilhelm von Schlegel, *A Course of Lectures on Dramatic Art and Literature,* trans. John Black (London, 1846); Friedrich von Schlegel, in *Athenaeums-Fragment 116* [1798]. See also Hans Eichner, ed., *'Romantic' and Its Cognates / The European History of a Word* (Toronto, 1972), esp. 98–156.
4. René Wellek, "The Concept of Romanticism in Literary History," in *Concepts of Criticism* (New Haven, 1963), 128–98; Morse Peckham, *The Tri-*

umph of Romanticism: Collected Essays (Columbia, S.C., 1970), esp. 3–83; idem, "Romanticism and Behavior," in *Romanticism and Behavior: Collected Essays II* (Columbia, S.C., 1976), 3–31. A typical account that takes "pre-romanticism" seriously is Lilian R. Furst, *Romanticism in Perspective* (London, 1969); but see also James R. Foster, *History of the Pre-Romantic Novel in England* (New York, 1949). Quentin Skinner, "Meaning and Understanding in the History of Ideas," *History and Theory* 8 (1969): 3–53.

5. For example, Eric Newton, *The Romantic Rebellion* (New York, 1962).

6. M. H. Abrams, *The Mirror and the Lamp: Romantic Theory and the Critical Tradition* (Oxford, 1953); idem, *Natural Supernaturalism: Tradition and Revolution in Romantic Literature* (New York, 1971); Frank Kermode, *Romantic Image* (London, 1957).

7. Victor Brombert, "Going to Extremes," *Times Literary Supplement*, 4 January 1985, 15.

8. Lawrence Lipking, ed., *High Romantic Argument: Essays for M. H. Abrams* (Ithaca, 1981), esp. Jonathan Culler, "The Mirror Stage," 149–63.

9. Henri Brunschwig, *Enlightenment and Romanticism in Eighteenth-Century Prussia*, trans. Frank Jellinek (Chicago, 1974), originally *La Crise de l'état prussien à la fin du XVIIIe siècle et la genèse de la mentalité romantique* [1947].

10. Raymond Williams, "The Romantic Artist," in *Culture and Society, 1780–1950* (London, 1958), 48–64. This premise is used in Drew Gilpin Faust, *A Sacred Circle: The Dilemma of the Intellectual in the Old South, 1840–1860* (Baltimore, 1977), 21–22.

11. *The Autobiography of Johann Wolfgang von Goethe*, trans. John Oxenford, 2 vols. (Chicago, 1974), 1:419–23; Alexander Gillies, *Herder* (Oxford, 1945); Peter Hans Reill, *The German Enlightenment and the Rise of Historicism* (Berkeley and Los Angeles, 1975); W. H. Bruford, *Germany in the Eighteenth Century: The Social Background of the Literary Revival* (Cambridge, 1935).

12. Immanuel Wallerstein, "American Slavery and the Capitalist World-Economy," *American Journal of Sociology* 81 (March 1976): 1199–1213; Elizabeth Fox-Genovese and Eugene D. Genovese, *Fruits of Merchant Capital: Slavery and Bourgeois Property in the Rise and Expansion of Capitalism* (New York, 1983).

13. By this distinction it might be posible to link Romanticism with the "antimodernism" of which Jackson Lears has written, an antimodernism that, to my eye, is much older than the contemporaries of Henry Adams. See T. J. Jackson Lears, *No Place of Grace: Antimodernism and the Transformation of American Culture, 1880–1920* (New York, 1981). The reactions to Antwerp of Hugh Legaré and of Henry Adams, forty years apart, are strikingly similar, which might seem to support William Taylor's suggestion that antebellum Southern intellectuals should be seen as mugwumps.

14. J. Mills Thornton III, *Politics and Power in a Slave Society: Alabama, 1800–1860* (Baton Rouge, 1978); Blaine A. Brownell and David R. Goldfield, *The City in Southern History: The Growth of Urban Civilization in the South* (Port Washington, N.Y., 1977); Lacy K. Ford, "Social Origins of a New South Carolina: The Upcountry in the Nineteenth Century" (Ph.D. diss., University of South Carolina, 1983); idem, "Rednecks and Merchants: Economic Developments and Social Tensions in the South Carolina Upcountry, 1865–1900," *Journal of American History* 71 (June 1984): 294–318; Laylon W. Jordan, "Schemes of Usefulness: Christopher G. Memminger," in *Intellectual Life*

in Antebellum Charleston, ed. Michael O'Brien and David Moltke-Hansen (Knoxville, 1986), 211–29; Gavin Wright, *The Political Economy of the Cotton South: Households, Markets, and Wealth in the Nineteenth Century* (New York, 1978). See also David L. Carlton, *Mill and Town in South Carolina, 1880–1920* (Baton Rouge, 1982).

15. Jan Lewis, *The Pursuit of Happiness: Family and Values in Jefferson's Virginia* (Cambridge, 1983).

16. James Anthony Froude, *Thomas Carlyle: A History of the First Forty Years of His Life, 1795–1835*, 4 vols. (New York, 1882), 2:15.

17. See Joseph J. Ellis, *After the Revolution: Profiles of Early American Culture* (New York, 1979); Lawrence Friedman, *Inventors of the Promised Land* (New York, 1975); Michael Kammen, *A Season of Youth: The American Revolution and the Historical Imagination* (New York, 1978); and William R. Taylor, *Cavalier and Yankee: The Old South and American National Character* (New York, 1961), 67–94.

18. Abrams, *Natural Supernaturalism*, esp. 17–70.

19. *State Papers on Nullification: Including the Public Acts of the Convention of the People of South Carolina, Assembled at Columbia, November 19, 1832 and March 11, 1833* (Boston, 1834), 66.

20. Louis Hartz, *The Liberal Tradition in America: An Interpretation of American Political Thought since the Revolution* (New York, 1955), 145–200; J. W. Burrow, *A Liberal Descent: Victorian Historians and the English Past* (Cambridge, 1981), 11–93.

21. Beverley Tucker, for example, wished to create in Missouri "a true Virginia settlement," or, in the words of his biographer, "a slaveholders' Camelot," a venture as successful as Brook Farm. Robert J. Brugger, *Beverley Tucker: Heart over Head in the Old South* (Baltimore, 1978), 57–71. For a modern British account of the Old South that evidently mistrusts Jacksonianism, see Bruce Collins, *White Society in the Antebellum South* (London, 1985).

22. Eloise M. Behnken, *Thomas Carlyle: "Calvinist without the Theology"* (Columbia, Mo., 1978); Gillies, *Herder*, 6; Thomas Carlyle, *Sartor Resartus: The Life and Opinions of Herr Teufelsdröckh*, in *Complete Works of Thomas Carlyle*, 10 vols. (New York, 1902), 1:3–321, esp. 122–49.

23. E. Brooks Holifield, *The Gentlemen Theologians: American Theology in Southern Culture, 1795–1860* (Durham, 1978); Ralph E. Luker, *A Southern Tradition in Theology and Social Criticism, 1830–1930* (New York, 1984), 15–184; John Adger, ed., *The Collected Writings of James Henley Thornwell*, 4 vols. (Richmond, 1871); James Oscar Farmer, Jr., *The Metaphysical Confederacy: James Henley Thornwell and the Synthesis of Southern Values* (Macon, Ga., 1986).

24. Drew Gilpin Faust, "A Southern Stewardship: The Intellectual and the Proslavery Argument," *American Quarterly* 31 (Spring 1979): 63–80; Jack P. Maddex, Jr., "Proslavery Millennialism: Social Eschatology in Antebellum Southern Calvinism," *American Quarterly* 31 (Spring 1979): 46–62; William B. McCash, *Thomas R. R. Cobb (1823–1862): The Making of a Southern Nationalist* (Macon, Ga., 1983), 217; Brugger, *Beverley Tucker*, 204; Charles Reagan Wilson, *Baptized in Blood: The Religion of the Lost Cause, 1865–1920* (Athens, Ga., 1980).

25. For example, John F. Randolph to Charles Campbell, 16 April 1848, Campbell Papers, College of William and Mary, written from Yazoo City, Mississippi, reads: "Altho' I like the South better than Virginia as a place of residence, it will be a long time before I can become entirely weaned from my

early associations." This was the usage of George Washington's generation in speaking of the Carolinas and Georgia. See John R. Alden, *The First South* (Baton Rouge, 1961), 9–10; Alison Goodyear Freehling, *Drift toward Dissolution: The Virginia Slavery Debate of 1831–1832* (Baton Rouge, 1982); and Dickson D. Bruce, Jr., *The Rhetoric of Conservatism: The Virginia Convention of 1829–30 and the Conservative Tradition in the South* (San Marino, 1982).

26. Alexander Beaufort Meek, *Romantic Passages in Southwestern History* (New York, 1857); Albert Pike, *Prose Sketches and Poems Written in the Western Country* (Boston, 1834). On Pike and Byron see Susan B. Riley, "Albert Pike as an American Don Juan," *Arkansas Historical Quarterly* 19 (Autumn 1960): 207–24.

27. David A. Hollinger, "Historians and the Discourse of Intellectuals," in *New Directions in American Intellectual History,* ed. John Higham and Paul K. Conkin (Baltimore, 1979), 42–63.

28. George M. Fredrickson, *The Black Image in the White Mind: The Debate on Afro-American Character and Destiny, 1817–1914* (New York, 1971), 43–96; Drew Gilpin Faust, ed., *The Ideology of Slavery: Proslavery Thought in the Antebellum South, 1830–1860* (Baton Rouge, 1981), 17; Mark D. Kaplanoff, "Charles Pinckney and the American Republican Tradition," in O'Brien and Moltke-Hansen, *Intellectual Life in Antebellum Charleston,* 85–122.

29. Simms comes closest to the Virginian tone, although South Carolina produced no one quite like William Alexander Caruthers and Philip Pendleton Cooke. But it is justice to add that in Hugh Blair Grigsby and Charles Campbell, Virginia also produced the most severe historical critics of that Cavalier myth, long before T. J. Wertenbaker. See Charles Campbell to Thomas H. Williamson, n.d. [1848], Campbell Papers, William and Mary: "In regard to the Cavaliers & Puritans in Va. Mr. Grigsby's view appears to be just. There were families in the colony of good descent—but the bulk of them were plain people. There was some infusion of Cavalier blood but hardly enough to produce any sensible effect upon the people." See also Frank W. Klingberg and Frank J. Klingberg, eds., *The Correspondence between Henry Stephens Randall and Hugh Blair Grigsby, 1856–1861* (Berkeley, 1952).

30. Randall M. Miller and Jon L. Wakelyn, eds., *Catholics in the Old South: Essays on Church and Culture* (Macon, Ga., 1983); I. A. Reynolds, ed., *The Works of the Right Rev. John England, First Bishop of Charleston,* 5 vols. (Baltimore, 1849); Peter Clarke, *A Free Church in a Free Society: The Ecclesiology of John England, Bishop of Charleston, 1820–1842* (Hartsville, S.C., 1982); Patrick Carey, *An Immigrant Bishop: John England's Adaptation of Irish-Catholicism to American Republicanism* (Yonkers, 1982). An unjustly neglected book that is good on intellectual life is Robert C. Reinders, *End of an Era: New Orleans, 1850–1860* (New Orleans, 1964).

31. Nicholas T. Phillipson, "Culture and Society in the 18th Century Province: The Case of Edinburgh and the Scottish Enlightenment," in *The University in Society,* ed. Lawrence Stone, 2 vols. (Princeton, 1974), 2:407–48; Thomas Bender, "The Cultures of Intellectual Life: The City and the Professions," in Higham and Conkin, *New Directions in American Intellectual History,* 181–95; David Moltke-Hansen, "The Expansion of Intellectual Life: A Prospectus," in O'Brien and Moltke-Hansen, *Intellectual Life in Antebellum Charleston,* 3–44.

32. Ernst Cassirer, *Rousseau, Kant, Goethe: Two Essays* (Princton, 1945);

Isaiah Berlin, *Against the Current: Essays in the History of Ideas* (London, 1979). René Wellek is firmly within this tradition.

33. David Kettler, *The Social and Political Thought of Adam Ferguson* (Columbus, Ohio, 1965); Isaiah Berlin, *Vico and Herder: Two Studies in the History of Ideas* (London, 1976), 150; Roy Pascal, "Herder and the Scottish Historical School," *English Goethe Society Publications*, n.s., 14 (1938–39): 23–42; Alexander Gillies, *A Hebridean in Goethe's Weimar: The Reverend James Macdonald and the Cultural Relations between Scotland and Germany* (Oxford, 1969); John Clive, "The Social Background of the Scottish Renaissance," in *Scotland in the Age of Improvement,* ed. Nicholas T. Phillipson and Rosalind Mitchison (Edinburgh, 1970), 225–44; Jane Rendall, *The Origins of the Scottish Enlightenment* (New York, 1978); R. H. Campbell and Andrew S. Skinner, eds., *The Origins and Nature of the Scottish Enlightenment* (Edinburgh, 1982); Istvan Hont and Michael Ignatieff, eds., *Wealth and Virtue: The Shaping of Political Economy in the Scottish Enlightenment* (Cambridge, 1983); Andrew Hook, *Scotland and America: A Study in Cultural Relations, 1750–1835* (Glasgow, 1975); William R. Brock, *Scotus Americanus* (Edinburgh, 1982); Douglas Sloan, *The Scottish Enlightenment and the American College Ideal* (New York, 1971). *The Glasgow Edition of the Works and Correspondence of Adam Smith,* 6 vols. (Oxford, 1976–83), with its invaluable annotations and intelligent introductions, should not be neglected and is useful for more than Smith. Richard B. Sher, *Church and University in the Scottish Enlightenment: The Moderate Literati of Edinburgh* (Princeton, 1985), has a full bibliography. Gladys Bryson, *Man and Society: The Scottish Inquiry of the Eighteenth Century* (Princeton, 1945), has not yet been supplanted as a synthesis, though the various essays of Nicholas T. Phillipson suggest the natural candidate as this generation's historian of the Scottish Enlightenment.

34. John T. Krumpelmann, *Southern Scholars in Goethe's Germany* (Chapel Hill, 1965), 6–7; Gian N. G. Orsini, *Coleridge and German Idealism: A Study in the History of Philosophy* (Carbondale, 1969), 3–56; Hugh S. Legaré, "Lord Byron's Character and Writings," *Southern Review* 5 (May 1830): 463–522.

35. Preliminary evidence for this can be found in Michael O'Brien, ed., *All Clever Men, Who Make Their Way: Critical Discourse in the Old South* (Fayetteville, Ark., 1982).

36. René Wellek, *Immanuel Kant in England, 1793–1838* (Princeton, 1931); George Whalley, "England/Romantic-Romanticism," in Eichner, *'Romantic' and Its Cognates,* 157–262; F. W. Stokoe, *German Influence in the English Romantic Period* (Cambridge, 1926).

37. Here I differ from Faust, *A Sacred Circle,* 19, which remarks, "These Southerners were cultural provincials who lacked the sophistication of modern or even of the most prominent nineteenth-century critics." I do not see Southerners as any more provincial than Englishmen; nor do I see any marked superiority in modern thought. Hence I doubt that intellectual Southerners gathered allusions "to enhance the significance of their own situation, imparting to it a degree of transcendence," or at least any more so than any group of intellectuals. I find puzzling the implication that for a Southerner to quote Vico was pretentious, while for an Englishman it was not. None of this, of course, challenges the assumption that older intellectual cultures produced more and greater intellectual accomplishments.

38. Johann Wolfgang von Goethe, *Conversations with Eckerman* (New York, 1901), 302; the observation was made on 2 April 1829.

39. "It is noticeable that the word *curiosity,* which in other languages is used in a good sense . . . has in our language no sense of the kind, no sense but a rather bad and disparaging one." Matthew Arnold, "The Function of Criticism at the Present Time" [1864], in *Essays Literary and Critical* (London, 1906), 10.

40. There has been some interesting comparative work lately on Southern slavery and Russian serfdom, with some note of the proslavery and proserfdom arguments. Anyone who knows the Southern antebellum intellectual scene and reads Isaiah Berlin, "A Remarkable Decade," in *Russian Thinkers* (London, 1978), 114–209, will suspect that the project of a more systematic comparison between the life of the mind in the Old South and in Russia would be worthwhile. See Peter Kolchin, "In Defense of Servitude: American Proslavery and Russian Proserfdom Arguments, 1760–1860," *American Historical Review* 85 (October 1980): 809–27.

41. See Hugh Trevor-Roper, "The Invention of Tradition: The Highland Tradition of Scotland," and, especially good, Prys Morgan, "From a Death to a View: The Hunt for the Welsh Past in the Romantic Period," in *The Invention of Tradition,* ed. Eric Hobsbawm and Terence Ranger (Cambridge, 1983), 15–41 and 43–100.

42. Marilyn Butler, *Romantics, Rebels, and Reactionaries: English Literature and Its Background, 1760–1830* (Oxford, 1982). It is worth reiterating that in standing for and appealing to the French provinces Rousseau had been preeminent. See Robert Darnton, "Readers Respond to Rousseau: The Fabrication of Romantic Sensitivity," in *The Great Cat Massacre and Other Episodes in French Cultural History* (New York, 1984), 215–56.

43. Not, it is worth observing, a clubable man.

44. Taylor, *Cavalier and Yankee,* 145–201; Charles H. Bohner, *John Pendleton Kennedy: Gentleman from Baltimore* (Baltimore, 1961); John McCardell, "Poetry and the Practical: William Gilmore Simms," in O'Brien and Moltke-Hansen, *Intellectual Life in Antebellum Charleston,* 186–210; Neal C. Gillespie, *The Collapse of Orthodoxy: The Ordeal of George Frederick Holmes* (Charlottesville, 1972); Curtis Carroll Davis, *Chronicler of the Cavaliers: A Life of the Virginia Novelist, Dr. William A. Caruthers* (Richmond, 1953); Charles Henry Watts II, *Thomas Holley Chivers: His Literary Career and His Poetry* (Athens, Ga., 1956); Edward L. Tucker, *Richard Henry Wilde: His Life and Selected Poems* (Athens, Ga., 1966); Jay B. Hubbell, *The Last Years of Henry Timrod* (Durham, 1941); Drew Gilpin Faust, *James Henry Hammond and the Old South: A Design for Mastery* (Baton Rouge, 1982); Michael O'Brien, *A Character of Hugh Legaré* (Knoxville, 1985); Arthur Hobson Quinn, *Edgar Allan Poe: A Critical Biography* (New York, 1941).

45. Charles Baudelaire, "Edgar Allan Poe: His Life and Works," in *Baudelaire: Selected Writings on Art and Artists* (Harmondsworth, 1972), 165; Patrick F. Quinn, *The French Face of Edgar Poe* (Carbondale, 1957).

46. *Mary Chesnut's Civil War,* ed. C. Vann Woodward (New Haven, 1981).

47. George Fitzhugh, *Cannibals All! or, Slaves Without Masters,* ed. C. Vann Woodward (Cambridge, Mass., 1960). Two useful recent anthologies are Faust, *The Ideology of Slavery;* and, less scholarly, Paul F. Paskoff and Daniel J.

Wilson, eds., *The Cause of the South: Selections from De Bow's Review, 1846–1867* (Baton Rouge, 1982).

48. For an implausible vision of an imperial Van Buren, see Beverley Tucker's novel *The Partisan Leader: A Tale of the Future* (Washington, D.C., 1836).

49. James T. Hillhouse, *The Waverley Novels and Their Critics* (Minneapolis, 1936), is still the best guide to pre-1914 critical appreciation of Scott.

50. David Daiches, "Scott's Achievement as a Novelist," reprinted in *Walter Scott: Modern Judgements,* ed. D. D. Devlin (London, 1969), 33–62; Georg Lukacs, *The Historical Novel,* trans. H. Mitchell and S. Mitchell (London, 1962); Duncan Forbes, "The Rationalism of Sir Walter Scott," *Cambridge Journal* 7 (October 1953): 20–35; Avrom Fleishman, *The English Historical Novel: Walter Scott to Virginia Woolf* (Baltimore, 1971); A. O. J. Cockshut, *The Achievement of Walter Scott* (London, 1969); Alexander Welsh, *The Hero of the Waverley Novels* (New Haven, 1963); David Brown, *Walter Scott and the Historical Imagination* (London, 1979); Graham McMaster, *Scott and Society* (Cambridge, 1981). See also A. Norman Jeffares, ed., *Scott's Mind and Art* (New York, 1970).

51. Daiches, "Scott's Achievement," 33.

52. Though Lukacs thought Scott was not Romantic, largely because he thought of Romanticism as naïve hero-worshiping, hence outside the social realist tradition to which Scott and Marx belonged. Lukacs, *Historical Novel,* 30–88.

53. "Sir Walter Scott," in *Complete Works of Thomas Carlyle,* 3:415.

54. We still have what Osterweis had, that is, Grace Warren Landrum, "Sir Walter Scott and His Literary Rivals in the Old South," *American Literature* 2 (November 1930): 256–76; idem, "Notes on the Reading of the Old South," ibid. 2 (March 1931): 60–71; and G. Harrison Orians, "Walter Scott, Mark Twain, and the Civil War," *South Atlantic Quarterly* 40 (October 1941): 342–59.

55. For example, Hugh S. Legaré, "The Fair Maid of Perth," *Southern Review* 2 (August 1828): 216–63; and William Elliott, "Anne of Geierstein," ibid. 4 (November 1829): 498–522.

56. Hugh S. Legaré, "Classical Learning" [1828], in *Writings of Hugh Swinton Legaré,* ed. Mary Legaré, 2 vols. (Charleston, 1845–46), 2:25, 32; Jesse Burton Harrison, "English Civilization," *Southern Review* 8 (February 1832): 462–91; "Samuel Taylor Coleridge," in *Edgar Allan Poe: Essays and Reviews,* ed. G. R. Thompson (New York, 1984), 181; *The Letters of William Gilmore Simms,* ed. Mary C. Simms Oliphant et al., 6 vols. (Columbia, S.C., 1952–82), 1:216. One of the more interesting recent works on Coleridge, and much else, is E. S. Schaffer, *'Kubla Khan' and the Fall of Jerusalem: The Mythological School in Biblical Criticism and Secular Literature, 1770–1880* (Cambridge, 1975).

57. John Holmes Bocock, "Ralph Waldo Emerson—History," *Southern Literary Messenger* 18 (April 1852): 247–55.

58. Richmond L. Hawkins, *Madame de Staël and the United States* (Cambridge, Mass., 1930); J. Christopher Herold, *Mistress to an Age: A Life of Madame de Staël* (Indianapolis, 1958); Madame de Staël, *Ten Years of Exile,* trans. D. Beik (New York, 1972). Lillian R. Furst, "Mme. de Staël's *De L'Allemagne:* A Misleading Intermediary," *Orbis Litterarum* 31 (1976): 43–58, however, censures even her literary criticism, which was more sensitive to the Sturm und

Drang school than to the later Romantics, such as Novalis. See Robert de Luppé, *Les Idées litteraires de Madame de Staël et l'héritage des lumières* (Paris, 1969).

59. Thomas R. Dew, "On the Influence of the Federative Republican System of Government upon Literature and the Development of Character," *Southern Literary Messenger* 2 (December 1836): 261–82, which draws largely on Madame de Staël's *Influence of Literature upon Society*. There is a good book to be written on Southerners in Italy in the nineteenth century, as a companion piece to C. P. Brand, *Italy and the English Romantics: The Italianate Fashion in Nineteenth-Century England* (Cambridge, 1957).

60. Richard Beale Davis, *Intellectual Life in the Colonial South, 1585–1763*, 3 vols. (Knoxville, 1978); Alden, *The First South.*

CHAPTER 3
Politics, Romanticism, and Hugh Legaré

1. So he is described in John D. Hart, *The Oxford Companion to American Literature*, 4th ed. (New York, 1965), 466–67. Parallel is John R. Welsh's remark, "If Elliott was the city's Franklin, Legaré was its Samuel Johnson," in "An Early Pioneer: Legaré's *Southern Review*," *Southern Literary Journal* 3 (1971): 83, especially inapposite in view of Legaré's harsh opinion of Johnson in *Writings of Hugh Swinton Legaré*, ed. Mary Legaré, 2 vols. (Charleston, 1845–46), 1:130.

2. William Campbell Preston, *Eulogy on Hugh Swinton Legaré* (Charleston, 1843), 31.

3. Legaré to Isaac E. Holmes, 8 April 1833, in *Writings*, 1:215.

4. Paul Hamilton Hayne, "Hugh Swinton Legaré," *Southern Review* 7 (January 1870): 133; William Peterfield Trent, *William Gilmore Simms* (Boston, 1892), 51. It is worth noting that the first biography of Legaré was written as a dissertation at Vanderbilt University under John Donald Wade, who had studied with Trent at Columbia, and the book bears Trent's imprint: see Linda Rhea, *Hugh Swinton Legaré: A Charleston Intellectual* (Chapel Hill, 1934).

5. Hayne, "Legaré," 134; cf. Hayne to James Russell Lowell, 11 August 1860, in *A Collection of Hayne Letters*, ed. Daniel M. McKeithan (Austin, 1944), 101: "But often—, how often! I think of the dear friends I have in Boston & contrasting the society there, with the society of Charleston, (I mean of a *literary* kind),—it is impossible for me to feel otherwise than '*sad*.'"

6. Donald Davidson, "Introduction," in *The Letters of William Gilmore Simms*, ed. Mary Simms Oliphant et al., 6 vols. (Columbia, S.C., 1952–82), 1:xxxiv–xxxvi.

7. It is proper to observe that William R. Taylor, *Cavalier and Yankee: The Old South and American National Character* (New York, 1961), 53–57, has an interesting discussion of Legaré's alienation, though Taylor is sometimes mistaken.

8. Biographical information on Legaré can be found in Rhea, *Legaré*, though the book is very often in error and should probably be avoided; [E. W. Johnston,] "Biographical Notice," in *Writings*, 1:v–lxxii; and, in many ways superior to Rhea, Merrill G. Christophersen, "A Rhetorical Study of Hugh Swinton Legaré: South Carolina Unionist" (Ph.D. diss., University of Flor-

ida, 1954), which has more than its title implies. See also Michael O'Brien, *A Character of Hugh Legaré* (Knoxville, 1985), from which part of this essay is drawn.

9. I use the distinction derived from E. Digby Baltzell, *Philadelphia Gentlemen: The Making of a National Upper Class* (Glencoe, Ill., 1958), cited by Jane H. Pease and William H. Pease, "The Economics and Politics of Charleston's Nullification Crisis," *Journal of Southern History* 47 (August 1981); 348–49, which has influenced my understanding of both Nullification and Legaré. As the Peases have it, "The elite are those with the power and skills to establish and carry out a community's values and goals; the upper class derives its influence from family, church, and club membership as well as form of wealth."

10. Legaré to Francis Walker Gilmer, 1 October 1816, Gilmer Papers, Alderman Library, University of Virginia, Charlottesville.

11. Benjamin Perry, *Reminiscences of Public Men*, in *The Writings of Benjamin F. Perry*, ed. Stephen Meats and Edwin T. Arnold, 3 vols. (Spartanburg, S.C., 1980), 3:38.

12. Legaré to Mary Swinton Legaré (mother), 4 November 1832, Legaré Papers, South Caroliniana Library, University of South Carolina, Columbia; all manuscripts not otherwise cited may be assumed to be in this collection.

13. For example, Legaré to Mary Legaré (sister), 4 August 1833 and 19 August 1835; Legaré to Mary Swinton Legaré, 16 March 1835.

14. Legaré to Judith Rives, 19 October 1838, and Legaré to William Cabell Rives, 3 December 1840 and 5 June 1840, Rives Papers, Library of Congress.

15. James Louis Petigru to Legaré, 17 February 1836, in James Petigru Carson, *Life, Letters, and Speeches of James Louis Petigru: The Union Man of South Carolina* (Washington, D.C., 1920), 181; Legaré to Mary Swinton Legaré, 24/25 November 1835; Stephen Elliott, Jr., to Legaré, 4 December 1839.

16. Legaré to Mary Legaré, 4 August 1833.

17. Legaré to Alfred Huger, 23 September 1838.

18. Legaré to Mary Swinton Legaré, 13 September 1841.

19. Legaré to Thomas White, 10 May 1838; Legaré to George Frederick Holmes, 10 December 1842, Holmes Papers, Library of Congress.

20. Legaré to Mary Swinton Legaré, 24 January 1829.

21. Legaré, "Hall's Travels in North America" [1829], in *Writings*, 2:264, 288.

22. Legaré to Judith Rives, 5 April 1841, Rives Papers.

23. Note Legaré's sorrowful condemnation of the insecurity of American judges in "Kent's Commentaries" [1828], in *Writings*, 2:141.

24. Legaré to Mary Legaré, 19 October 1835; Legaré to Mary Swinton Legaré, 2 September 1841.

25. Legaré to Mary Swinton Legaré, n.d. [1819] and 13 August 1832.

26. *Writings*, 1:123, 126; Legaré to Mary Swinton Legaré, 14 September 1840; Legaré, "Spirit of the Sub-Treasury" [1837], in *Writings*, 1:284–85.

27. Legaré, "Stephen Elliott," *Charleston Courier*, 30 March 1840; Samuel Prioleau, "Dyspepsia," *Southern Review* 4 (August 1829): 208–41; Legaré to Mary Legaré, 25 January 1836; Legaré, "Classical Learning" [1828], in *Writings*, 2:7; Legaré to Jesse Burton Harrison, 3 November 1828.

28. Legaré to Mary Swinton Legaré, 25 September 1838; Legaré to W. C. Rives, 5 October 1838, Rives Papers; Legaré to Alfred Huger, 15 December 1834, in *Writings*, 1:216–19; Legaré to Mary Swinton Legaré, 4 November

1832; Legaré to Mary Legaré, 10 October 1839; Legaré to Mary Swinton Legaré, 27 September 1840.

29. Mitchell King to Legaré, 5 May 1833; Legaré to W. C. Rives, 5 October 1838, Rives Papers; Mary Legaré to Paul H. Hayne, 27 July 1878, Paul Hamilton Hayne Papers, Perkins Library, Duke University, Durham, N.C.: "I am gratified & well pleased with your own original remarks on my brother's career & character but deeply regret that so eloquent & beautiful a pen should have been betrayed by the *misrepresentations* of Wm. C. Preston & his creature Wm. Johnson (a little grammar master) whom the Hon Senator in a manner forced upon me as a proper person to write the Biography of Legaré. . . . Preston the appointed Eulogist of HSL opens his address with the remark that H S Legaré had been overpraised & he meant then and there to prove that he was so."

30. Legaré to W. C. Rives, 5 October 1838, Rives Papers.

31. George Ticknor to Legaré, 29 December 1839 and 9 June 1842, in *Life, Letters and Journals of George Ticknor*, ed. George S. Hillard, 2 vols. (Boston, 1876), 2:191, 207; Legaré, "Classical Learning," 7.

32. Joseph Cogswell to Legaré, 22 December 1838.

33. Nassau Senior to Legaré, 28 January 1840; Legaré to Mary Legaré, 12 October 1838; Legaré to Gouverneur Kemble, 9 June 1839, Charles L. Chandler Papers, Southern Historical Collection, Wilson Library, University of North Carolina, Chapel Hill; Legaré to W. C. Rives, 29 October 1839, Rives Papers.

34. Legaré to Judith Rives, 19 October 1838, Rives Papers; Legaré to Mary Legaré, 10 September 1838 and 12 October 1838.

35. Joseph Cogswell to Legaré, 22 December 1838 and 24 April 1839; Legaré to Thomas C. Reynolds, 6 February 1841, in *Writings*, 1:236.

36. Legaré to Mary Legaré, 15 April 1835; Gouverneur Kemble to Joel Poinsett, 29 June 1843, Gilpin/Poinsett Papers, Historical Society of Pennsylvania, Philadelphia. Richard Lounsbury, on reading this characterization of Legaré the politician, observed that it reminded him of Cicero, Legaré's model. Cf. Ronald Syme, *The Roman Revolution* (Oxford, 1939), 135–48, esp. Syme's remark (p. 11), parallel to Kemble's judgment, "Cicero would have preserved both dignity and peace of mind had not ambition and vanity blinded him to the true causes of his own elevation."

37. Legaré to Stephen Elliott, Jr., 14 April 1839, Legaré Papers, Perkins Library, Duke University, Durham, N.C.

38. Preston, *Eulogy*, 31; Legaré to Mary Swinton Legaré, 3 May 1838.

39. Legaré to Mary Legaré, 25 January 1836; Legaré to Mary Swinton Legaré, 10 May 1833.

40. Drew Gilpin Faust, *A Sacred Circle: The Dilemma of the Intellectual in the Old South, 1840–1860* (Baltimore, 1977).

41. William Campbell Preston to Waddy Thompson, 28 August 1855, Preston Papers, South Caroliniana Library, University of South Carolina, Columbia.

42. Legaré, "Law of Tenures," *Southern Review* 3 (February 1829): 18.

43. Legaré, "Classical Learning," 41–42; cf. Victor Hugo, "En trouvant fort ridicules les Néréides dont Camöeus obsède les compagnons de Gama, on désirerait, dans le célèbre *Passage du Rhin* de Boileau, voir autre chose que des naiades craintives fuir devant Louis, par la grâce de Dieu, roi de France et de

Navarre, accompagné de ses marechaux-des-camps et-armées." Preface to *Nouvelles Odes* [1824], quoted in Basil Gildersleeve, "Necessity of the Classics," *Southern Quarterly Review*, n.s., 10 (July 1854): 155.

44. Legaré, "Classical Learning," 42; Gladys Bryson, *Man and Society: The Scottish Inquiry of the Eighteenth Century* (Princeton, 1945), 85–86, 106; Donald R. Kelley, *Foundations of Modern Historical Scholarship: Language, Law, and History in the French Renaissance* (New York, 1970). Cf. Legaré, "Roman Literature" [1828], in *Writings*, 2:67, with "The Origin, History and Influence of Roman Legislation" [1837], ibid. 1:504–8.

45. Legaré, "Roman Literature," 53–54.

46. Legaré, "The Public Economy of Athens" [1832], in *Writings*, 2:503; idem, "Cicero de Republica" [1829], ibid. 2:242.

47. Legaré, "Law of Tenures," 19.

48. Legaré, "Hoffman's Legal Outlines," *Southern Review* 3 (August 1829): 61–69, has a discussion of the social compact.

49. Legaré, "Hall's Travels in North America," 268.

50. Legaré, "Lord Byron's Character and Writings" [1830], in *Writings*, 2:390–91.

51. Jane Rendall, *The Origins of the Scottish Enlightenment* (New York, 1978), 1–27. Cf. *Boswell in Holland, 1763–1764*, ed. Frederick A. Pottle (New York, 1952), 49; Walter Scott to William Clerk, 6 August 1790, in *The Letters of Sir Walter Scott, 1787–1807*, ed. H. J. C. Grierson (London, 1932), 11: "I read *no* civil law. Heineccius and his fellow worthies have ample time to gather a venerable coat of dust"; and Scott, *Redgauntlet: A Tale of the Eighteenth Century* (1824; reprint, London, 1897), 11–12: "And what ill would the Scottish law do to him, though he had as much of it as either Stair or Bankton, sir? Is not the foundation of our municipal law the ancient code of the Roman Empire, devised at a time when it was so much renowned for its civil polity, sir, and wisdom?" There is a marked lack of writing about Heineccius, but see his *Methodical System of Universal Law*, trans. George Turnbull (London, 1763), and articles in the *Encyclopaedia Brittanica*, 11th ed., and in the *Biographie universelle: ancienne et moderne*, 45 vols. (Paris, 1856), 19:59–60, both of which are based upon his son's memoir, Johann Christian Heineccius, *Memoria Ioh. Gottl. Heineccii*, which prefaces the *Omnia Opera*. See also Duncan Forbes, *Hume's Philosophical Politics* (Cambridge, 1975), 3–5, 27, 31–32, 38n, 43–47, 51–54, 72n.

52. Legaré, "Roman Legislation," 509, 511.

53. Joseph Story, "Sketch of the Character of Hugh S. Legaré," in *The Miscellaneous Writings of Joseph Story*, ed. William W. Story (Boston, 1852), 820–24.

54. Legaré, "Classical Learning," 22, 24, 25.

55. Ibid., 33–34, 8, 30–31; Legaré, "Jeremy Bentham and the Utilitarians" [1831], in *Writings*, 2:469; Legaré to Mary Swinton Legaré, 9 September 1834 (confessing a lack of religious instinct); Alexander Everett to Lucretia Everett, 25 June 1840, Everett Papers, Massachusetts Historical Society, Boston (I am grateful to Jane and William Pease for bringing this letter to my attention).

56. Legaré to Mary Legaré, 5 May 1833, in *Writings*, 1:225; Legaré to Judith Rives, 26 April 1833, Rives Papers; Legaré, "Classical Learning," 25.

57. Legaré to Thomas White, 10 May 1838.

58. Legaré, "D'Aguesseau" [1832], in *Writings*, 2:591; idem, "Cicero de Republica," 253. Cf. David Hume, "Whether the British Government Inclines More to Absolute Monarchy, or to a Republic," in Hume, *Essays Moral, Politi-*

cal, and Literary, ed. Eugene F. Miller (Indianapolis, 1985), 47.

59. August von Schlegel, "Abriss von den europäischen Verhältnissen der deutschen Literatur," quoted in René Wellek, *A History of Modern Criticism, 1750–1950,* 7 vols. (New Haven, 1955–86), 2:38; Legaré, "Travels of the Duke of Saxe-Weimar" [1830] and "Early Spanish Ballads" [1830], in *Writings,* 2:168 and 2:299–300; Bryson, *Man and Society,* 78–113. The final quotation in Legaré's discussion is from *Hamlet.*

60. Legaré, "Classical Learning," 32, 48; idem, "Hoffman's Legal Outlines," 49–58; Bryson, *Man and Society,* 53–77. Cf. Josiah C. Nott, *Two Lectures on the Natural History of the Caucasian and Negro Races* (Mobile, 1844), with Legaré's amusement at Monboddo on the Etruscans in "Roman Literature," 61.

61. Legaré, "Byron's Letters and Journals" [1831], in *Writings,* 2:426–28.

62. Ibid., 428–29.

63. Ibid., 430–31; Wellek, *History of Modern Criticism,* 2:59.

64. Legaré, "Byron's Letters and Journals," 431–32, 432–33, 435, 440.

65. Ibid., 439, 441–42, 443, 437.

66. Legaré, "Lord Byron's Character and Writings," 380; cf. Adam Smith, *The Theory of Moral Sentiments,* ed. D. D. Raphael and A. L. Macfie (Oxford, 1976).

67. Legaré, "Early Spanish Ballads," 2:320–21; M. H. Abrams, *Natural Supernaturalism: Tradition and Revolution in Romantic Literature* (New York, 1971), passim; Avrom Fleishman, *The English Historical Novel: Walter Scott to Virginia Woolf* (Baltimore, 1971), 37–101.

68. Legaré, "Classical Learning," 32, 40, 44–45.

69. Preston, *Eulogy,* 25.

70. Charles Fraser, *Reminiscences of Charleston* (Charleston, 1854), 114–15; Henry Cruger, "Cooper's *Bravo,*" *Southern Review* 9 (February 1832): 398; William Gilmore Simms, *The Social Principle: The True Source of National Permanence* (Tuscaloosa, 1843), 7.

71. Hayne, "Legaré," 133–34; Vernon L. Parrington, *The Romantic Revolution in America, 1800–1860* (New York, 1927), 124; William W. Freehling, *Prelude to Civil War: The Nullification Controversy in South Carolina, 1816–1836* (New York, 1966), 5.

72. Legaré to Holmes, 8 April 1833, in *Writings,* 1:215.

73. Legaré to Harrison, 3 November 1828.

74. For an interesting case for Wordsworth as a transitional figure between the Enlightenment and Romanticism and as a social conservative, see Marilyn Butler, *Romantics, Rebels, and Reactionaries: English Literature and Its Background, 1760–1830* (Oxford, 1982), 157–68. Butler has transferred from art history (pp. 1–10) the term *neoclassical* to describe this sensibility, which itself may be applicable to Legaré. As Abrams has argued that Wordsworth is the quintessential Romantic, Butler here dissents from *Natural Supernaturalism,* which elsewhere she has contended is insufficiently sensitive to the late eighteenth century. See Butler, "Against Tradition: The Case for a Particularized Historical Method," in *Historical Studies and Literary Criticism,* ed. Jerome J. McGann (Madison, 1985), 25–47.

75. Preston to Thompson, 28 August 1855, Preston Papers. For all its apparently artless simplicity, this passage, like much in Preston, is adapted from a literary source. Cf. Fénelon's passage on the grief of Idomeneus in *Adventures*

of Telemachus, trans. John Hawkesworth (New York, 1859), 531: "He withered like a stately tree which covers the earth with its shade, but is gnawed by a worm at the root: the winds in their fury may have attacked it in vain; the earth may have nourished it with delight; and it may have been spared, in reverence, by the axe; but if the latent mischief is not discovered, it will fade; its leaves, which are its honors, will be scattered in the dust; and the trunk and branches only, rifted and sapless, will remain. Such, in appearance, was Idomeneus, the victim of inconsolable grief." A more remote ancestor is Lucan, *Pharsalia,* 1:129–43.

76. *Charleston Courier,* 3 April 1846; Legaré to Alfred Huger, 15 December 1834, in *Writings,* 1:218.

CHAPTER 4
Italy and the Southern Romantics

1. William Douglas Smyth, "The Artistic Experience of South Carolinians Abroad," in *Art in the Lives of South Carolinians: Nineteenth-Century Chapters,* ed. David Moltke-Hansen (Charleston, 1979), WS-9; Anna Wells Rutledge, *Artists in the Life of Charleston: Through Colony and State from Restoration to Reconstruction* (Columbia, S.C., 1980), 116, 173; Francis W. Bilodeau et al., eds., *Art in South Carolina, 1670–1970* (Charleston, 1970), 106.

2. Sarah Lytle, "Thomas Middleton: At Ease with the Arts in Charleston," in Moltke-Hansen, *Art in the Lives,* SL-7; Langdon Cheves, "Middleton of South Carolina," *South Carolina Historical and Genealogical Magazine* 1 (July 1900): 243, 244; Bilodeau et al., *Art in South Carolina,* 115.

3. Charles Eliot Norton, "The First American Classical Archaeologist," *American Journal of Archaeology* 1 (1885): 3–9; John Izard Middleton, *Grecian Remains in Italy, A Description of Cyclopian Walls and of Roman Antiquities. With Topographical and Picturesque Views of Ancient Latium* (London, 1812), 2, 9.

4. Cheves, "Middleton of South Carolina," 247, 248.

5. *The Reminiscences of William C. Preston,* ed. Minnie Clare Yarborough (Chapel Hill, 1933), 70–124; Marion Edmunds, "James Henry Hammond's Art Collecting on His European Tour of May 1836–November 1837," in Moltke-Hansen, *Art in the Lives,* ME-1–16; Robert W. Gibbes, *A Memoir of James De Veaux of Charleston, South Carolina* (Columbia, S.C., 1846); Sylvia E. Crane, *White Silence: Greenough, Powers, and Crawford, American Sculptors in Nineteenth-Century Italy* (Coral Gables, 1972), 183, 190; Martha Severens and Charles L. Wyrick, Jr., eds., *Charles Fraser of Charleston: Essays on the Man, His Art, and His Times* (Charleston, 1983), pl. 19. Pausilippo is the traditional site of the tomb of Vergil.

6. Relatively little has been written on Southern travelers, except John Hope Franklin, *A Southern Odyssey: Travelers in the Antebellum North* (Baton Rouge, 1976), which does not deal with Southerners abroad.

7. Wolfgang Leppmann, *Winckelmann* (New York, 1970); Johann Wolfgang von Goethe, *Italian Journey, 1786–1788,* trans. W. H. Auden and Elizabeth Mayer (New York, 1968); Edward Gibbon, *Memoirs of My Life,* ed. Georges Bonnard (New York, 1966), 133–37; *Boswell on the Grand Tour: Italy, Corsica, and France, 1765–1766,* ed. Frank Brady and Frederick A. Pottle (New York, 1955). On the English see Geoffrey Trease, *The Grand Tour* (New York, 1967); and C. P. Brand, *Italy and the English Romantics: The Italianate Fashion in*

Early Nineteenth-Century England (Cambridge, 1957).

8. Stendhal, *A Roman Journal,* ed. Haakon Chevalier (New York, 1957); *Letters of Charles Eliot Norton,* ed. Sara Norton and M. A. DeWolfe Howe, 2 vols. (Boston, 1913), 1:149.

9. Gibbes, *Memoir of James De Veaux,* 95.

10. Van Wyck Brooks, *The Dream of Arcadia: American Writers and Artists in Italy, 1760–1915* (New York, 1958), 16; Georges Solovieff, ed., *Madame de Staël, ses amis, ses correspondants: choix des lettres (1778–1817)* (Paris, 1970), 376, 397; Edouard Herriott, *Madame Récamier,* 2 vols. (New York, 1926), 1:147; Geneviève Gennari, *Le Premier Voyage de Madame de Staël en Italie et la genèse de "Corinne"* (Paris, 1947), 69–70, 135.

11. Madame de Staël, *Corinne, or Italy,* 2 vols. (London, 1894), 1:38, 44, 24, 45–46.

12. Ibid., 1:65, 143, 144–45, 147, 148, 83, 90, 93, 156, 155.

13. Ibid., 1:66, 67, 173, 179.

14. Ibid., 1:45, 47, 75, 307; 2:77, 45–46; 1:277, 171–72.

15. Ibid., 1:299.

16. Ibid., 2:6, 69, 73, 74, 76, 46; 1:206.

17. Ibid., 2:84, 86.

18. Madelyn Gutwirth, *Madame de Staël, Novelist* (Urbana, 1978), 154–309.

19. Madame de Staël, *The Influence of Literature upon Society,* 2d ed. (1812; reprint, Hartford, Conn., 1850), 46; Gutwirth, *Madame de Staël,* 170.

20. Gutwirth, *Madame de Staël,* 215.

21. See Thomas J. Schlereth, *The Cosmopolitan Ideal in Enlightenment Thought: Its Form and Function in the Ideas of Franklin, Hume, and Voltaire, 1694–1790* (Notre Dame, Ind., 1977).

22. Brantz Mayer, "Italy," *Southern Quarterly Review* 10 (July 1846): 92. On American visitors generally see Paul R. Baker, *Fortunate Pilgrims: Americans in Italy, 1800–1860* (Cambridge, Mass., 1964).

23. Gibbes, *Memoir of James De Veaux,* 59–60, 164; William B. Crawford Journal, Gorgas Family Papers, University of Alabama, Tuscaloosa; Richard G. Haynesworth Diary, ibid.

24. Henry H. Cumming to Thomas Cumming, n.d. [1819], Hammond-Bryan-Cumming Papers, South Caroliniana Library, University of South Carolina, Columbia.

25. Crawford Journal; William Campbell Preston to Washington Irving, 16 March 1818, Preston Family Papers, Virginia Historical Society, Richmond; Charles P. Pelham to James Henley Thornwell, 20 February 1845, Thornwell Papers, South Caroliniana Library. See also D. D. Saunders to Victoria Martin, 15 June 1857, Alabama Department of Archives and History, Montgomery.

26. Preston, *Reminiscences,* 78–79.

27. Gibbes, *Memoir of James De Veaux,* 111–12; "Letters to Forsyth on Domestic Slavery" and "Letters from Rome," in *The Works of the Right Rev. John England, First Bishop of Charleston,* ed. I. A. Reynolds, 5 vols. (Baltimore, 1849), 3:106–91, 4:122–49.

28. Gibbes, *Memoir of James De Veaux,* 94–95; Preston to Irving, 16 March 1818; Crawford Journal.

29. Preston, *Reminiscences,* 78; Henry James, *Italian Hours* (1910; reprint, New York, 1968), 3.

30. E. P. Richardson, *Washington Allston: A Study of the Romantic Artist in*

America (New York, 1948), 10–11; Joy S. Kasson, *Artistic Voyagers: Europe and the American Imagination in the Works of Irving, Allston, Cole, Cooper, and Hawthorne* (Westport, Conn., 1982), 45–46, 51–76.

31. Jared B. Flagg, *The Life and Letters of Washington Allston* (New York, 1892), 172.

32. Kasson, *Artistic Voyagers,* 53–54; Flagg, *Allston,* 397, 47; Richardson, *Allston,* 39; Gibbes, *Memoir of James De Veaux,* 139–40.

33. Flagg, *Allston,* 365, 69, 292; Richardson, *Allston,* 59–60.

34. Flagg, *Allston,* 65–66, 71. Allston's portrait of Coleridge, now in the National Portrait Gallery in London, has as its background a fine set of Gothic church windows.

35. Cf. William L. Vance, "The Sidelong Glance: Victorian Americans and Baroque Rome," *New England Quarterly* 58 (December 1985): 501–32.

36. Flagg, *Allston,* 64; Washington Allston, *Lectures on Art, and Poems,* ed. Richard Henry Dana, Jr. (New York, 1850), 158.

37. Goethe, *Italian Journey,* 137–38. Flagg, *Allston,* 60, quotes John Vanderlyn to the effect that Allston shared the city with Byron, Keats, and Shelley. In fact, Byron did not see Rome until 1817, Shelley not until 1819, Keats not until 1820.

38. William H. Gerdts and Theodore E. Stebbins, Jr., *"A Man of Genius": The Art of Washington Allston (1779–1843)* (Charlottesville, 1979), 39–43; Flagg, *Allston,* 77; Regina Soria, "Washington Allston's Lectures on Art: The First American Art Treatise," *Journal of Aesthetics and Art Criticism* 18 (March 1960): 329–44; Gibbes, *Memoir of James De Veaux,* 55; Nathalia Wright, *American Novelists in Italy: The Discoverers, Allston to James* (Philadelphia, 1965).

39. Flagg, *Allston,* 59–60, 198–99.

40. Gerdts and Stebbins, *"A Man of Genius,"* 9.

41. Flagg, *Allston,* 230–34. He did have some interest in painting a scene of Columbus returning to proclaim the discovery of the New World to Ferdinand and Isabella.

42. Cf. Neil Harris, *The Artist in American Society: The Formative Years, 1790–1860* (Chicago, 1966), 56–88, on the "burden of portraiture" for American artists.

43. Kasson, *Artistic Voyagers,* 45–46, 68; Flagg, *Allston,* 326, 265–67.

44. Here I dissent from John R. Welsh, "Washington Allston: Expatriate South Carolinian," *South Carolina Historical Magazine* 67 (April 1966): 84–98, which remarks that Allston "became a New Englander."

45. Edward L. Tucker, *Richard Henry Wilde: His Life and Selected Poems* (Athens, Ga., 1966), 1–42.

46. Ibid., 42; Richard Henry Wilde, *Hesperia: A Poem,* ed. W. C. Wilde (Boston, 1867), 93.

47. Tucker, *Wilde,* 43, 45; cf. Wilde, "Sonnet to Lord Byron," in ibid., 133.

48. Crane, *White Silence,* 273–320, passim; Nathalia Wright, ed., *Letters of Horatio Greenough, American Sculptor* (Madison, 1972), 111, 156, 287–88, 192; Tucker, *Wilde,* 47–50; Nathalia Wright, "The Italian Son of Richard Henry Wilde," *Georgia Historical Quarterly* 43 (December 1959): 419–27.

49. Richard Henry Wilde, *Conjectures and Researches Concerning the Love, Madness, and Imprisonment of Torquato Tasso,* 2 vols. (New York, 1842), 1:141, 209, 53, 39; 2:74. Tucker, *Wilde,* 52–59. Meryle Secrest, *Being Bernard Berenson* (New York, 1979).

50. Ralph S. Graber, "New Light on the Dedication of Richard Henry Wilde's *Hesperia*," *Georgia Historical Quarterly* 44 (March 1960): 97–99; Wilde, *Hesperia*, 67, 230, 138, 295; de Staël, *Corinne*, 1:233.

51. Wilde, *Hesperia*, 66, 24, 73, 72.

52. Ibid., 167–95.

53. Nathalia Wright, ed., "The Letters of Richard Henry Wilde to Hiram Powers," *Georgia Historical Quarterly* 46 (December 1962): 430–31.

54. Paul Hamilton Hayne to Richard Stoddard, 23 July 1855, Paul Hamilton Hayne Papers, Perkins Library, Duke University, Durham, N.C.; Gibbes, *Memoir of James De Veaux*, 58–59.

55. Charles Eliot Norton to Francis Child, 15 March 1855, quoted in Kermit Vanderbilt, *Charles Eliot Norton: Apostle of Culture in a Democracy* (Cambridge, Mass., 1959), 76.

56. This antislavery analysis, which draws upon European sources, can, unsurprisingly, be found in European analyses of the United States. The passages in Alexis de Tocqueville's *Democracy in America* in which he discusses the contrary social condition of North and South are squarely in the Romantic tradition of contrasting northern Europe and Italy, except that the institution of slavery does service for the enervations of the Catholic church, and the Ohio River supplants the Alps. See Alexis de Tocqueville, *Democracy in America*, ed. J. P. Mayer (New York, 1969), 347–48.

57. Mayer, "Italy," 99.

CHAPTER 5

Modernization and the Nineteenth-Century South

1. For example, Seymour Martin Lipset, *The First New Nation: The United States in Historical and Comparative Perspective* (New York, 1963).

2. David M. Potter, "Civil War," in *The Comparative Approach to American History*, ed. C. Vann Woodward (New York, 1968), 135.

3. John McCardell, *The Idea of a Southern Nation: Southern Nationalists and Southern Nationalism, 1830–1860* (New York, 1979), 8, 3.

4. William R. Taylor, *Cavalier and Yankee: The Old South and American National Character* (New York, 1961); Donald G. Mathews, *Slavery and Methodism: A Chapter in American Morality, 1780–1845* (Princeton, 1965); William Sumner Jenkins, *Pro-Slavery Thought in the Old South* (Chapel Hill, 1935); William W. Freehling, *Prelude to Civil War: The Nullification Controversy in South Carolina, 1816–1836* (New York, 1966).

5. John Higham, Introduction to *New Directions in American Intellectual History*, ed. John Higham and Paul K. Conkin (Baltimore, 1979), xvi–xvii.

6. Joyce Appleby, "Modernization Theory and the Formation of Modern Social Theories in England and America," *Comparative Studies in Society and History* 20 (April 1978): 261.

7. J. Mills Thornton III, *Politics and Power in a Slave Society: Alabama, 1800–1860* (Baton Rouge, 1978), xvii.

8. William J. Cooper, Jr., *The South and the Politics of Slavery, 1828–1856* (Baton Rouge, 1978), is prey to a circular logic, however; it assumes that Southern politics are centrally about slavery, proceeds to document what politicians said on the matter of slavery (with, it must be said, great skill and thor-

oughness), and then triumphantly concludes that this demonstrates the centrality of slavery.

9. Fletcher M. Green, *Constitutional Development in the South Atlantic States, 1776–1860* (Chapel Hill, 1930); Frank L. Owsley, *Plain Folk of the Old South* (Baton Rouge, 1950); Eugene D. Genovese, *The World the Slaveholders Made: Two Essays in the Interpretation* (New York, 1969); Otto H. Olsen, "Historians and the Extent of Slave Ownership in the Southern United States," *Civil War History* 17 (June 1972): 101–16; George M. Fredrickson, *The Black Image in the White Mind: The Debate on Afro-American Character and Destiny, 1817–1914* (New York, 1971).

10. [Since 1981 this mining has gone on apace, such that Genovese has now felt moved to exclaim, when reviewing Kenneth S. Greenberg, *Masters and Statesmen: The Political Culture of American Slavery* (Baltimore, 1985), in the *Journal of Southern History* 53 (February 1987): 111–12: "In keeping with current fashion, Mr. Greenberg cannot resist casting too much of his argument within the framework of that 'republicanism' that has become the hobbyhorse of those who seek to subsume contradictory and even mutually antagonistic political ideas under a single rubric. 'Republicanism' has its uses but is now so widely stretched and abused as to justify a sharp reaction. Personally, I cannot even bring myself to paraphrase that fabled Nazi and exclaim, 'When I hear the word "republicanism" I reach for my revolver.'"]

11. Thornton, *Politics and Power*, xix.

12. [See, now, J. Mills Thornton III, "Fiscal Policy and the Failure of Radical Reconstruction in the Lower South," in *Region, Race, and Reconstruction: Essays in Honor of C. Vann Woodward*, ed. J. Morgan Kousser and James M. McPherson (New York, 1982), 349–94.]

13. David Donald, "An Excess of Democracy: The American Civil War and the Social Process," in *Lincoln Reconsidered: Essays on the Civil War Era* (New York, 1956), 209–35; this was Donald's inaugural address as Harmsworth Professor at Oxford, which may help to explain its Tory tone and willingness to use Henry James as an expositor of American social history.

14. Richard D. Brown, *Modernization: The Transformation of American Life, 1600–1865* (New York, 1976), 183; Raimondo Luraghi, "The Civil War and the Modernization of American Society: Social Structure and Industrial Revolution in the Old South Before and During the War," *Civil War History* 18 (September 1972): 230–50; Emory M. Thomas, *The Confederate Nation, 1861–1865* (New York, 1979).

15. [Now, however, powerful support for Thornton has been supplied in the most unlikely state, South Carolina. See Lacy K. Ford, "Social Origins of a New South Carolina: The Upcountry in the Nineteenth Century" (Ph.D. diss., University of South Carolina, 1983).]

16. Kenneth M. Stampp, *The Imperiled Union: Essays on the Background of the Civil War* (New York, 1980), 107, 235.

17. Eric Foner, *Politics and Ideology in the Age of the Civil War* (New York, 1980), 32, 33.

18. Gavin Wright, *The Political Economy of the Cotton South: Households, Markets, and Wealth in the Nineteenth Century* (New York, 1978). But it is important to remember, here as elsewhere, that Wright's analysis applies only to those parts of the South identical with the cotton economy, which are not interchangeable with the whole region.

19. Immanuel Wallerstein, "American Slavery and the Capitalist World-Economy," *American Journal of Sociology* 81 (March 1976): 1199–1213; "The Memoirs of Frederick Adolphus Porcher," ed. Samuel Gaillard Stoney, *South Carolina Historical and Genealogical Magazine* 47 (April 1946): 95.

20. [Though Burger has given way to Rehnquist, Thurmond is relegated to the minority, and the Voting Rights Act survives though diffidently enforced, the times are still Thermidorean.]

21. William Gillette, *Retreat from Reconstruction, 1869–1879* (Baton Rouge, 1979), 450.

22. *The Works and Life of Walter Bagehot,* ed. Mrs. Russell Barrington, 10 vols. (London, 1915), 2:323, quoted in W. L. Burn, *The Age of Equipoise: A Study of the Mid-Victorian Generation* (London, 1964), 55.

23. [On this see, now, George C. Rable, *But There Was No Peace: The Role of Violence in the Politics of Reconstruction* (Athens, Ga., 1984).]

24. Jonathan M. Wiener, *Social Origins of the New South: Alabama, 1860–1885* (Baton Rouge, 1978), 3.

25. Ibid., 219.

26. Thornton, *Politics and Power,* 444.

27. Dwight B. Billings, Jr., *Planters and the Making of a "New South": Class, Politics, and Development in North Carolina, 1865–1900* (Chapel Hill, 1979), 34.

28. Cf. Jonathan M. Wiener, "Class Structure and Economic Development in the American South, 1865–1955," *American Historical Review* 84 (October 1979): 970–92, and the indignant comment by Robert Higgs, 993–97.

CHAPTER 6
The Middle Years: Edwin Mims

1. Paul M. Gaston, *The New South Creed: A Study in Southern Mythmaking* (New York, 1970); Thomas L. Connelly, *The Marble Man: Robert E. Lee and His Image in American Society* (Baton Rouge, 1977); Charles Reagan Wilson, *Baptized in Blood: The Religion of the Lost Cause, 1865–1920* (Athens, Ga., 1980); Lawrence Goodwyn, *Democratic Promise* (New York, 1976); Joel Williamson, *The Crucible of Race: Black-White Relations in the American South since Emancipation* (New York, 1984).

2. For example, Robert Wohl, *The Generation of 1914* (Cambridge, Mass., 1979).

3. Interview with Catherine and Ella Puryear Mims, Nashville, 1971.

4. The manuscript of Mims's autobiography is in the Edwin Mims Papers, Special Collections Department, Joint University Libraries, Nashville. All manuscripts not otherwise cited may be assumed to be in this collection.

5. See Laurence McMillin, *The Schoolmaker: Sawney Webb and the Bell Buckle Story* (Chapel Hill, 1971); Mims, *John Maurice Webb (1847–1916)* (Nashville, 1946); idem, *History of Vanderbilt University* (Nashville, 1946); and Earl W. Porter, *Trinity and Duke, 1892–1924: Foundations of Duke University* (Durham, 1964).

6. Mims to Clara Puryear, 23 February 1896; Paul K. Conkin, *Gone with the Ivy: A Biography of Vanderbilt University* (Knoxville, 1985), 222.

7. Hunter D. Farish, *The Circuit Rider Dismounts: A Social History of Southern Methodism* (Richmond, 1938).

8. Richard B. Sher, *Church and the University in the Scottish Enlightenment:*

The Moderate Literati of Edinburgh (Princeton, 1985), 151–212.

9. Henry F. May, *Protestant Churches and Industrial America* (New York, 1949); McMillin, *Schoolmaker,* 130–40; Mims, *Webb.*

10. Mims to Clara Puryear, 2 August 1894, 10 September 1893.

11. Paul N. Garber, *John Carlisle Kilgo: President of Trinity College, 1894–1910* (Durham, 1937); Mims to Clara Puryear, 8 September 1894.

12. Louis R. Harlan, *Separate and Unequal: Public School Campaigns and Racism in the Southern Seaboard States, 1901–1915* (Chapel Hill, 1958), 60.

13. Mims to Clara Puryear, 1 March 1897; William Peterfield Trent, *"The Authority of Criticism" and Other Essays* (New York, 1899), 103–4, 113.

14. Thomas Carlyle, *Essay on Burns,* ed. Edwin Mims (New York, 1903), 7–53.

15. Mims to Clara Puryear, 1 February 1897.

16. Ibid., 18 June 1898, 3 February 1895.

17. Ibid., 6 January 1895, does mention, however, that Mims spent his Christmas vacation with grandparents who lived "out on a large plantation— a typical old ante-bellum Southern mansion." But he never speaks with a sense of intimacy about such a way of life.

18. Mims, "Thomas Nelson Page," *Atlantic Monthly* 100 (July 1907): 114.

19. Mims, "University Extension," *Vanderbilt Observer* 14 (1892): 170–73; Curt Porter, "Chautauqua and Tennessee: A Study of the Chautauqua Movement in Tennessee" (Honors thesis, Vanderbilt University, 1963).

20. William K. Boyd, *The Story of Durham: City of the New South* (Durham, 1927), 262; Mims to Clara Puryear, 19 September 1894.

21. Mims, autobiography, chap. 6; ibid., 14. On Aycock see Oliver H. Orr, Jr., *Charles Brantley Aycock* (Chapel Hill, 1961). The best account of the Southern Education Board is Harlan, *Separate and Unequal,* 75–101.

22. Mims to William Preston Few, 3 September 1896; Mims to Walter Hines Page, 27 December 1910, Walter Hines Page Papers, Houghton Library, Harvard University, Cambridge, Mass.

23. Mims to Clara Puryear, 11 February 1897.

24. Mims, "The Function of Criticism in the South," *South Atlantic Quarterly* 2 (October 1903): 342, quoted in Mims, *The Advancing South: Stories of Progress and Reaction* (Garden City, N.Y., 1926), 49; John Spencer Bassett to Mims, 4 September 1910.

25. Mims, *Advancing South,* ix.

26. Mims, "Masters of Modern French Criticism," *South Atlantic Quarterly* 13 (January 1914): 75–80.

27. Mims, Introduction to *History of Southern Fiction,* ed. Edwin Mims (Richmond, 1909), xi–xlvii (quotation on xlvii); idem, "European Influences in the South," in *History of the Social Life of the Southern States,* ed. Samuel C. Mitchell (Richmond, 1909), 44–63.

28. Mims, "Southern Magazines," in *History of the Literary and Intellectual Life of the Southern States,* ed. John Bell Henneman (Richmond, 1909), 437–69 (quotation on 454); William Gilmore Simms, "Literary Prospects of the South," *Russell's Magazine* 3 (June 1858): 193–206.

29. Cf. John Holmes Bocock, "Ralph Waldo Emerson—History," *Southern Literary Messenger* 18 (April 1852): 247–55.

30. The best brief account is Richard Hofstadter and Walter P. Metzger, *The Development of Academic Freedom in the South* (New York, 1955), 445–50.

31. Mims to Walter Hines Page, 30 December 1907, Page Papers. Louis Round Wilson, explaining in 1932 why he had reluctantly decided to leave Chapel Hill for the University of Chicago, was to observe that he and Mims had their "beginnings too close to the Civil War and Reconstruction, and the surroundings were such that we probably have never found ourselves quite willing to act in matters of this sort as people in other sections of the country do." Wilson to Mims, 14 January 1932. In contrast, despite an ideology confessedly "rooted," five of the Agrarians (Allen Tate, John Crowe Ransom, Lyle Lanier, Robert Penn Warren, and Stark Young) were to leave the South.

32. On Corson see the sketch in Allen Johnson and Dumas Malone, eds., *Dictionary of American Biography*, 22 vols. (New York, 1928–40), 4:453–54; Corson, *The Aims of Literary Study* (New York, 1894), 82; and Mims to Clara Puryear, 1 January 1897, 29 November 1896.

33. Burr J. Ramage, "Notes," *Sewanee Review* 9 (July 1901); 379.

34. William Peterfield Trent, *"Greatness in Literature," and Other Papers* (New York, 1905), 61; Mims to Clara Puryear, 30 June 1897; Robert H. Woody, ed., *The Papers and Addresses of William Preston Few, Late President of Duke University* (Durham, 1951), 15.

35. Mims to Clara Puryear, 11 July 1896. Herbert Baxter Adams, the historical mentor of Trent and a prime exponent of German ideas at Johns Hopkins, moved towards causes such as university extension, Chautauqua, public libraries, and labor reform in the 1880s at the peril of his allegiance to his academic training. See Jurgen Herbst, *The German Historical School in American Scholarship: A Study in the Transfer of Culture* (Ithaca, 1965), 178–79.

36. Cf. "From Anglophobia to New Anglophobia," in Kenneth S. Greenberg, *Masters and Statesmen: The Political Culture of American Slavery* (Baltimore, 1985), 107–25.

37. John Henry Raleigh, *Matthew Arnold and American Culture* (Berkeley and Los Angeles, 1961), 132–33; Mims, autobiography, 3; Rhodes Scholarship Trust to Frank P. Venable, 4 May 1906, University of North Carolina Papers, University Archives, Chapel Hill.

38. Charles B. Aycock to Mims, 6 November 1903, observes: "Probably if Dr. Bassett would read King Edward's speech to Parliament he would not regard his own folks so lightly and hold their views in such contempt. In substance King Edward says in reference to South Africa 'My policy toward South Africa shall be one of equality for whites and justice to the blacks.' A superior race can occupy no other attitude."

39. Mims, "President Theodore Roosevelt," *South Atlantic Quarterly* 4 (January 1905): 48–62.

40. Mims, autobiography, "The Advancing South and Aftermath," 21.

41. Mims to Clara Puryear, 4 October 1896.

42. On this Anglo-American tradition see Robert Kelley, *The Transatlantic Persuasion: The Liberal-Democratic Mind in the Age of Gladstone* (New York, 1969); Joseph L. Morrison, *Josephus Daniels Says. . . : An Editor's Political Odyssey from Bryan to Wilson and F.D.R., 1894–1913* (Chapel Hill, 1962), 160–61.

43. Harlan, *Separate and Unequal*, 82; W. H. Page to Mims, 5 January 1911.

44. Mims, "The International Mind," draft of a speech to Edinburgh University, 1935.

45. H. L. Mencken, "The South Looks Ahead," *American Mercury* 8 (August 1926): 506; Mims, autobiography, chap. 8, 7.

46. On the origins of the Fugitives see Louise Cowan, *The Fugitive Group: A Literary History* (Baton Rouge, 1959).

47. Interview with Jesse Wills, Nashville, January 1971.

48. See esp. Robert Penn Warren to Allen Tate, letter headed "The Unstilled Cyclades, Night of Black Friday" [early spring 1924], Allen Tate Papers, Firestone Library, Princeton University.

49. Allen Tate, "Letter to the Editor," *Vanderbilt Alumnus* 26 (March 1941): 15, quoted in Cowan, *Fugitive Group*, 47; see also Tate, *Memoirs and Opinions, 1926–1974* (Chicago, 1975), 28.

50. Mims, *Advancing South*, 201.

51. Tate to Davidson, 27 August, 7 September 1923; 28 June 1927, Donald Davidson Papers, Joint University Libraries, Nashville.

52. Ridley Wills to Davidson, 16 November 1924, Davidson Papers; interview with Jesse Wills.

53. Stanley Johnson, *Professor* (New York, 1925); Tate to Davidson, 26 January 1925, Davidson Papers; interview with Will Ella Tatum Smith, Nashville, May 1971 [Mrs. Smith was Johnson's first wife].

54. John Ransom to Ellen Ransom, 5 March 1939, Ransom Family Papers, Tennessee State Archives, Nashville.

55. Davidson to John Gould Fletcher, 14 June 1930, Davidson Papers.

56. For a brief amplification of this see Michael O'Brien, ed., "Edwin Mims and Donald Davidson: A Correspondence, 1923–1958," *Southern Review* 10 (October 1974): 904–22.

57. Mims, *Advancing South*, 201.

58. Allen Tate, "Last Days of the Charming Lady," *Nation* 121 (28 October 1925): 486; Tate to Davidson, 29 July 1926, Davidson Papers. See also Tate's observation in ibid., 28 May 1924: "Mims is one of the hero-worshippers of literature that think literature is very godly and hence must always be written elsewhere."

59. Davidson to Louis D. Rubin, Jr., 24 January 1954, Davidson Papers.

60. Allen Tate, "A Southern Romantic," *New Republic* 76 (30 August 1933): 67–70; Robert Penn Warren, "The Blind Poet: Sidney Lanier," *American Review* 2 (November 1933): 27–45; John Crowe Ransom, "Hearts and Heads," *American Review* 2 (March 1934): 554–71.

61. Mims seems to have written it with no great confidence; Davidson to Tate, 26 October 1929, Tate Papers, speaks of Mims as "quite humble & apprehensive about his book."

62. Tate to Davidson, 11 December 1929, Davidson Papers.

63. Mims, autobiography, chap. 8, 15a; idem, draft of an address, "Bright Intervals and Inner Resources."

64. Mims to Kirkland, 10 April 1925, Chancellor's Archives, Joint University Libraries, Nashville; see also ibid., 2 March 1927.

65. See Davidson to Richard Weaver, 25 March 1949, Davidson Papers, for an account of this.

66. Thomas Daniel Young, *Gentleman in a Dustcoat: A Biography of John Crowe Ransom* (Baton Rouge, 1976), 270–90, has a good summary of this *affaire*, as has Conkin, *Gone with the Ivy*, 398–400.

67. H. L. Mencken, *Prejudices: Second Series* (New York, 1921), 92.

68. Mims, *Chancellor Kirkland of Vanderbilt* (Nashville, 1940); *Great Writ-*

ers as Interpreters of Religion (New York, 1945); *The Christ of the Poets* (Nashville, 1948).

69. Mims, autobiography.

CHAPTER 7
A Heterodox Note on the Southern Renaissance

1. Allen Tate, "The New Provincialism" (1940), in *Essays of Four Decades* (New York, 1970), 545–46 (quoting Tate, "The Profession of Letters in the South" [1935], in ibid., 533).

2. See Louis D. Rubin, Jr., and C. Hugh Holman, eds., *Southern Literary Study: Problems and Possibilities* (Chapel Hill, 1975).

3. Robert Penn Warren, "A Conversation with Cleanth Brooks," in *The Possibilities of Order: Cleanth Brooks and His Work,* ed. Lewis P. Simpson (Baton Rouge, 1976), 61.

4. Lewis P. Simpson, *The Dispossessed Garden: Pastoral and History in Southern Literature* (Athens, Ga., 1975), 37–38.

5. Lewis P. Simpson, *The Man of Letters in New England and the South: Essays on the History of the Literary Vocation in America* (Baton Rouge, 1973), 235–36; Louis D. Rubin, Jr., *William Elliott Shoots a Bear: Essays on the Southern Literary Imagination* (Baton Rouge, 1975), 28–60, 107–44, 195–212. Cf. Richard Gray, *Writing the South: Ideas of an American Region* (Cambridge, 1986), 102–21, which makes an unusually persuasive case for Twain as a Southerner.

6. Louis D. Rubin, Jr., *The Writer in the South: Studies in a Literary Community* (Athens, Ga., 1972), 82–116; Simpson, *Man of Letters,* 248.

7. Walter Sullivan, *A Requiem for the Renascence: The State of Fiction in the Modern South* (Athens, Ga., 1976), xv, xxii–xxiii, 63–73.

8. Rubin, *William Elliott,* 253–54, 256–57; Sullivan, *Requiem,* xvi, xi; C. Hugh Holman, *The Roots of Southern Writing: Essays on the Literature of the American South* (Athens, Ga., 1972), 176.

9. "Memorandum" [April 1933], Donald Davidson Papers, Joint University Libraries, Nashville.

10. Rubin, *William Elliott,* 257.

11. Warren, "Conversation with Cleanth Brooks," 72.

12. Sullivan, *Requiem,* 73.

13. Edmund Wilson, *Letters on Literature and Politics, 1912–1972,* ed. Elena Wilson (New York, 1977), 212.

14. C. Vann Woodward, "Why the Southern Renaissance?" *Virginia Quarterly Review* 51 (Spring 1975): 222–29; Daniel Joseph Singal, *The War Within: From Victorian to Modernist Thought in the South, 1919–1945* (Chapel Hill, 1982), xii–xiii; Richard H. King, "Victorian to Modernist Thought," *Southern Literary Journal* 15 (Spring 1983): 127. King claims that Tate's analysis emphasized, not real social changes, but subjective changes, which I doubt a reading of Tate substantiates.

15. John Pendleton Kennedy, *Swallow Barn; or, A Sojourn in the Old Dominion,* 2d ed. (1853; reprint, New York, 1962), 8–9; Raymond Williams, *The Country and the City* (London, 1973), 9–22.

16. Lewis P. Simpson, *The Brazen Face of History: Studies in the Literary Consciousness in America* (Baton Rouge, 1980), 77.

17. Ibid., 91.

18. Ibid., vii, 275–76.

19. Simpson, *Dispossessed Garden,* 34.

20. Especially those debates recorded in Rubin and Holman, *Southern Literary Study.*

21. Fred C. Hobson, Jr., *Serpent in Eden: H. L. Mencken and the South* (Chapel Hill, 1974).

22. John M. Bradbury, *Renaissance in the South: A Critical History of the Literature, 1920–1960* (Chapel Hill, 1963), 3–4, reproved by Woodward, "Why the Southern Renaissance?" 223–24.

23. Allen Tate, "Literature as Knowledge" and "The Function of the Critical Quarterly," in *Essays,* 92ff, and 48, 55, respectively. On the issue of canons see Robert von Hallberg, ed., *Canons* (Chicago, 1984), esp. John Guillory, "The Ideology of Canon-Formation: T. S. Eliot and Cleanth Brooks," 337–62.

24. Frank Kermode, *The Sense of an Ending* (London, 1966).

25. Morton Sosna, *In Search of the Silent South: Southern Liberals and the Race Issue* (New York, 1977), ix; Richard H. King, *A Southern Renaissance: The Cultural Awakening of the American South, 1930–1955* (New York, 1980), vii.

26. Louis D. Rubin, Jr., and Robert D. Jacobs, eds., *Southern Renascence: The Literature of the Modern South* (Baltimore, 1953); idem, *South: Modern Southern Literature in Its Cultural Setting* (New York, 1961).

27. King, *A Southern Renaissance;* Singal, *The War Within;* John Shelton Reed and Daniel Joseph Singal, eds., *Regionalism and the South: Selected Papers of Rupert Vance* (Chapel Hill, 1982); Fred Hobson, ed., *South-Watching: Selected Essays by Gerald W. Johnson* (Chapel Hill, 1983); Sosna, *In Search of the Silent South;* Michael O'Brien, *The Idea of the American South, 1920–1941* (Baltimore, 1979); Charles W. Eagles, *Jonathan Daniels and Race Relations: The Evolution of a Southern Liberal* (Knoxville, 1982); Lewis Baker, *The Percys of Mississippi: Politics and Literature in the New South* (Baton Rouge, 1983); Darden Asbury Pyron, ed., *Recasting: "Gone With the Wind" in American Culture* (Miami, 1983); John T. Kneebone, *Southern Liberals and the Issue of Race, 1920–1944* (Chapel Hill, 1985).

28. For secondary discussions, see Murray Krieger, *The New Apologists for Poetry* (Minneapolis, 1956); Walter Sutton, *Modern American Criticism* (Princeton, 1963), 98–151; Walter J. Ong, "From Rhetorical Culture to New Criticism: The Poem as a Closed Field," in Simpson, *Possibilities of Order,* 150–67; and Richard Foster, *The New Romantics: A Reappraisal of the New Criticism* (Bloomington, 1962).

29. Louis D. Rubin, Jr., Introduction to Twelve Southerners, *I'll Take My Stand: The South and the Agrarian Tradition* (1930; reprint, Baton Rouge, 1977), xvi–xvii; John Crowe Ransom, "Reconstructed but Unregenerate," in ibid., 24–25; Allen Tate, "Remarks on the Southern Religion," in ibid., 174. Cf. Tate to Donald Davidson, 10 August 1929, in *The Literary Correspondence of Donald Davidson and Allen Tate,* ed. John Tyree Fain and Thomas Daniel Young (Athens, Ga., 1974), 229–33; and Tate to Ransom, 27 July 1929, Davidson Papers.

30. Singal, *The War Within,* 115–97; King, *A Southern Renaissance,* 242–86; Fred Hobson, *Tell about the South: The Southern Rage to Explain* (Baton Rouge, 1983).

31. King, *A Southern Renaissance,* 8; Singal, *The War Within,* xiv.

32. Lucinda McKethan, however, though otherwise orthodox, does discuss Charles Chesnutt and Jean Toomer in *The Dream of Arcady: Place and Time in Southern Literature* (Baton Rouge, 1980), 86–127.

33. Woodward, "Why the Southern Renaissance?" 222–23.

34. It should be said, however, that the conventions of a jazz group, whether small or big-band, with the ordered sequences of chorus, riff, and solo, are rigorously social.

35. It is heartening that the Center for the Study of Southern Culture at the University of Mississippi encourages such exploration of jazz and, perhaps less important for the interwar years, country music.

36. King, "Victorian to Modernist Thought," 123; idem, *A Southern Renaissance,* 53, 112, 292–93. Woodward, "Why the Southern Renaissance?" 238–39, does offer a list of Southern "necessary conditions," culled from Cleanth Brooks, but then evasively dismisses them as only conditions, not causes.

37. This may be an idiosyncratic judgment, but I doubt that the intellectual culture of the South recovers to the level of 1850 until about 1925, and it moves decisively beyond it only during the 1930s. There is not significantly more sophistication of argument in *I'll Take My Stand* than in the *Proslavery Arguments* of 1860.

38. Singal, *The War Within,* 3–10. O'Brien, *Idea of the American South,* xiv, hints sloppily at Victorianism as a "formal intellectual structure" but does little with it.

39. Singal, *The War Within,* 4–5, cites Peter Gay, *Freud, Jews, and Other Germans: Masters and Victims in Modernist Culture* (New York, 1978), 21–26, 70–71, in support of seeing modernism as distinctive, although Gay seems to see modernism as the intellectual culture of the post-Enlightenment period, not just of the twentieth century. Singal quotes Gay on modernism as "a pervasive cultural revolution, a second Renaissance," which has "transformed culture in all its branches," but neglects to quote the clauses that intervene: "Whether it had its inception with the German Romantics, with the intense artistic and literary atmosphere of Paris in the days of Baudelaire and Daumier, or with the informal alliance of French impressionists."

40. Singal, *The War Within,* 3, 212, 200, 222, 368, 7; King, "Victorian to Modernist Thought," 124.

41. Singal, *The War Within,* 3, 29, 374.

42. Ibid., 6, 25.

43. Ibid., 28, 355; Robert Louis Stevenson, *The Strange Case of Dr. Jekyll and Mr. Hyde* (1886; reprint, London, 1924), 57–59.

44. Singal, *The War Within,* 242.

45. Malcolm Bradbury and James McFarlane, "The Nature and Name of Modernism," in *Modernism, 1890–1930,* ed. Bradbury and McFarlane (Harmondsworth, 1976), 25.

46. Singal, *The War Within,* 300, 33, 261, 149, 197, 258–59, 206, 257, 270, 341. It is puzzling why cultural relativism predisposes to reform; to the contrary, anthropology is a profoundly conservative intellectual discipline, since it is committed only to observation. Anthropologists are much put out when their tribes change.

47. William Gilmore Simms, *Views and Reviews in American Literature, History, and Fiction: First Series,* ed. C. Hugh Holman (Cambridge, Mass., 1962), 29; George Fitzhugh, "Southern Thought" (1857), reprinted in Drew Gilpin Faust, ed., *The Ideology of Slavery: Proslavery Thought in the Antebellum South, 1830–1860* (Baton Rouge, 1981), 274–99; William Peterfield Trent, Introduction to *History of the Literary and Intellectual Life of the Southern States,* ed. J. B. Henneman (Richmond, 1909), xv–xxxi; Edwin Mims, "The Renaissance in New England," *South Atlantic Quarterly* 1 (July 1902): 224.

48. Wallace K. Ferguson, *The Renaissance in Historical Thought: Five Centuries of Interpretation* (Cambridge, Mass., 1948), is a useful guide.

49. William Preston Few, "Some Educational Needs of the South," in *The Papers and Addresses of William Preston Few, Late President of Duke University,* ed. Robert H. Woody (Durham, 1951), 173; Tate, "The Profession of Letters in the South," 533.

50. Ferguson, *The Renaissance in Historical Thought,* 229–38, 290–385, esp. 381ff.

51. Tate, "The Profession of Letters in the South," 519, 521, 524–29.

52. Ibid., 531, 521.

CHAPTER 8
A Private Passion: W. J. Cash

1. I draw the sharpest barbs from C. Vann Woodward, *American Counterpoint: Slavery and Racism in the North-South Dialogue* (Boston, 1971), 261–83; Eugene D. Genovese, *The World the Slaveholders Made: Two Essays in Interpretation* (New York, 1969), 137–50; and Joel Williamson, *The Crucible of Race: Black-White Relations in the American South since Emancipation* (New York, 1984), 3, and have added a few of my own.

2. See esp. Dwight B. Billings, Jr., *Planters and the Making of a "New South": Class, Politics, and Development in North Carolina, 1865–1900* (Chapel Hill, 1979).

3. Bertram Wyatt-Brown, "W. J. Cash and Southern Culture," in *Yankee Saints and Southern Sinners* (Baton Rouge, 1985), 131–54.

4. W. J. Cash, *The Mind of the South* (New York, 1941), 48, 32, 33, 34, 36. All references are to the Vintage paperback edition.

5. Ibid., 68, 82–84, 93–94, 75, 70, 115.

6. It must be said that Woodward, *American Counterpoint,* 273, is careful to avoid denying to Cash all sense of historical change. If the reader is interested in the sources, upon which my understanding of Hegel is based, he is referred to the footnotes of my "W. J. Cash, Hegel, and the South." I have been most influenced by *The Philosophy of History, The Phenomenology of Spirit,* and, less so, *The Philosophy of Right.* Among commentaries, I have found most illuminating John N. Findlay, *Hegel: A Re-examination* (London, 1958); Walter Kaufmann, *Hegel: Reinterpretation, Texts, and Commentary* (Garden City, N.Y., 1965); Duncan Forbes, Introduction to G. W. F. Hegel, *Lectures on the Philosophy of World History: Introduction* (Cambridge, 1975), vii–xxxv; Herbert Marcuse, *Reason and Revolution: Hegel and the Rise of Social Theory* (London, 1941); and Alasdair C. MacIntyre, ed., *Hegel: A Collection of Critical Essays* (Garden City, N.Y., 1972).

7. Cash, *Mind of the South*, 290, 362.

8. Ibid., 64, 85, 387–88.

9. Ibid., 106, 165, 250, 197.

10. John Crowe Ransom, *God without Thunder: An Unorthodox Defense of Orthodoxy* (New York, 1930); idem, "The Aesthetic of Regionalism," *American Review* 2 (January 1934): 290–310; Howard W. Odum, *An American Epoch: Southern Portraiture in the National Picture* (New York, 1930), 66–116; John Donald Wade to Donald Davidson, 8 August 1954, Donald Davidson Papers, Joint University Libraries, Nashville; Frank E. Vandiver, ed., *The Idea of the South: Pursuit of a Central Theme* (Chicago, 1964).

11. Cash, *Mind of the South*, 48; Joseph L. Morrison, *W. J. Cash, Southern Prophet: A Biography and a Reader* (New York, 1967), 60.

12. Morrison, *Cash*, 429, 47.

13. Ibid., 5, 4.

14. Richard H. King, *A Southern Renaissance: The Cultural Awakening of the American South, 1930–1955* (New York, 1980), 151.

15. Michael P. Dean, "W. J. Cash's *The Mind of the South*: Southern History, Southern Style," *Southern Studies* 20 (Fall 1981): 297–302.

16. Cash, *Mind of the South*, 311.

17. Clarence Cason, *90° in the Shade* (Chapel Hill, 1935), vii; Carl Carmer, *Stars Fell on Alabama* (New York, 1934), 3; Jonathan Daniels, *A Southerner Discovers the South* (New York, 1938), 1, 2; Cash, *Mind of the South*, 334, 339–40, 389.

18. Cash, *Mind of the South*, 100, 295–96.

19. Morrison, *Cash*, 15, 65, 64, 46, 109, 40, 83, 36, 123.

20. Ibid., 80, 150–55.

21. Ibid., 42–44, 76, 52; Cash, *Mind of the South*, 336, 100, 301, 144, 385, 299–303.

22. Cash, *Mind of the South*, 336, 440, 390–91.

23. Donald Davidson, *"Still Rebels, Still Yankees" and Other Essays* (Baton Rouge, 1972), 191–212.

CHAPTER 9
From a Chase to a View: C. Vann Woodward

1. C. Vann Woodward, *American Counterpoint: Slavery and Racism in the North-South Dialogue* (Boston, 1971), 282; idem, *Thinking Back: The Perils of Writing History* (Baton Rouge, 1986), 5, 4.

2. John H. Roper, "C. Vann Woodward's Early Career—The Historian as Dissident Youth," *Georgia Historical Quarterly* 44 (Spring 1980): 7–9. Religion occupies five pages (448–53) of Woodward's *Origins of the New South, 1877–1913* (Baton Rouge, 1951).

3. Roper, "Woodward's Early Career," 7–8.

4. Woodward, *Tom Watson: Agrarian Rebel* (New York, 1938), 53, 59, 165, 217, 229, 219, 486.

5. Woodward, *Thinking Back*, 86; Roper, "Woodward's Early Career," 13.

6. Woodward, *Thinking Back*, 21–27.

7. Roper, "Woodward's Early Career," 11–12; Rupert Vance, *Human Factors in Cotton Culture* (Chapel Hill, 1929).

8. Woodward, *Thinking Back,* 135–36.

9. Woodward, *Origins of the New South,* 429–36.

10. Woodward, "The Historical Dimension," in *The Burden of Southern History,* enlarged ed. (Baton Rouge, 1968), 27–39; idem, "Why the Southern Renaissance?" *Virginia Quarterly Review* 51 (Spring 1975): 222–39; idem, *Thinking Back,* 23.

11. Woodward, *The South in Search of a Philosophy* (Gainesville, 1938), 15.

12. Ibid., 15–16; Woodward, *Thinking Back,* 18–19.

13. Woodward, *South in Search,* 17–19.

14. Woodward, *Thinking Back,* 17–20.

15. Benjamin B. Kendrick, "Agrarian Discontent in the South: 1880–1900," *Annual Report of the American Historical Association: 1920* (Washington, D.C., 1920), 267–72; Alex Matthews Arnett, *The Populist Movement in Georgia* (New York, 1922); Francis B. Simkins, *The Tillman Movement in South Carolina* (Durham, 1926).

16. Woodward, "Preface to the 1955 Reissue," in *Tom Watson: Agrarian Rebel* (New York, 1955). Hereafter citations will be to the 1955 edition.

17. Woodward, *Tom Watson,* 88.

18. See Robert Saunders, "Southern Populists and the Negro, 1893–1895," *Journal of Negro History* 54 (July 1969): 240–61. Saunders expresses reservations about the "Populist failure to accept the Negro as an intellectual, moral or political equal."

19. Woodward, "The Elusive Mind of the South," in *American Counterpoint,* 275–76.

20. Woodward, "The Question of Loyalty," *American Scholar* 33 (Autumn 1964): 561–67.

21. This is the chapter heading of the first lecture in Woodward's *The Strange Career of Jim Crow* (New York, 1955).

22. Howard N. Rabinowitz, "The Woodward Thesis and More: Three Contributions of *The Strange Career of Jim Crow*" (Paper presented to the American Historical Association, Chicago, 1986), is severe about the accuracy of Woodward on segregation in the late nineteenth century, while arguing that Woodward on the late twentieth century is unusually prescient. (I am obliged to Professor Rabinowitz for showing me his paper.)

23. Woodward, *Origins of the New South,* 142–43; idem, ed., *The Comparative Approach to American History* (New York, 1968); idem, *Thinking Back,* 104–5, 2.

24. Woodward, *Origins of the New South,* 482.

25. I say partial exception because Woodward, ed., *Mary Chesnut's Civil War* (New Haven, 1981), xi–xii, thanks no fewer than twenty-eight people for assistance with transcription, collation, and annotation.

26. George M. Fredrickson, "The Renaissance of Southern History: Or the Life and Work of C. Vann Woodward," *Dissent* 34 (Winter 1987): 68.

27. The nearest to an extended analysis of the Old South is in the group of essays in *American Counterpoint* that deal with slavery.

28. Woodward, review of *Revolt of the Rednecks: Mississippi Politics, 1876–1925* by Albert D. Kirwan, *American Historical Review* 56 (July 1951): 918.

29. Woodward, *Origins of the New South,* 482, 499.

30. See Reinhold Niebuhr, *The Irony of American History* (New York,

1952), and the useful commentary of Richard Reinitz, "Niebuhrian Irony and Historical Interpretation: The Relationship between Consensus and New Left History," in *The Writing of History: Literary Form and Historical Understanding*, ed. Robert H. Canary and Henry Kozicki (Madison, 1978), 93–128.

31. Woodward, *Origins of the New South*, 174, 167, 395.

32. Robert B. Westbrook, "C. Vann Woodward: The Southerner as Liberal Realist," *South Atlantic Quarterly* 77 (Winter 1978): 54–71.

33. Woodward, *Thinking Back*, 22; idem, *Tom Watson*, 95.

34. Woodward, *Thinking Back*, 88–89; idem, *Burden of Southern History*, 69–107; idem, *American Counterpoint*, 163–83.

35. Richard Hofstadter, *The American Political Tradition and the Men Who Made It* (New York, 1948), vii.

36. Woodward, *Burden of Southern History*, 166. This essay was originally published in *American Scholar* 29 (Winter 1959–60): 55–72.

37. Woodward, "The North and the South of It," *American Scholar* 35 (Autumn 1966): 648.

38. Woodward, *Burden of Southern History*, 21. In fact, I am not sure the Old South was "basically pessimistic."

39. Ibid., 230.

40. Ibid., 233; Woodward, *Thinking Back*, 117.

41. Edwin Mims, *The Advancing South: Stories of Progress and Reaction* (Garden City, N.Y., 1926), 315.

42. "George Fitzhugh: *Sui Generis*," in George Fitzhugh, *Cannibals All! or, Slaves Without Masters*, ed. C. Vann Woodward (Cambridge, Mass., 1960), vii–xxxix.

43. All of this criticism is usefully listed in Woodward, *Thinking Back*, 147–51.

44. Ibid., 92.

45. Woodward, "Clio With Soul," *Journal of American History* 56 (June 1969): 20; see also idem, "The Future of the Past," *American Historical Review* 75 (February 1970): 711–26.

46. Both quality and devotion can be measured in J. Morgan Kousser and James M. McPherson, eds., *Region, Race, and Reconstruction: Essays in Honor of C. Vann Woodward* (New York, 1982).

CHAPTER 10

Intellectual History and the Search for Southern Identity

1. C. Vann Woodward, "The Elusive Mind of the South," in *American Counterpoint: Slavery and Racism in the North-South Dialogue* (Boston, 1971), 261–83.

2. Perry Miller, *The New England Mind: The Seventeenth Century* (New York, 1939), vii; Felix Gilbert, "Intellectual History: Its Aims and Methods," in *Historical Studies Today*, ed. Felix Gilbert and Stephen R. Graubard (New York, 1972), 141.

3. Robert Darnton, "Intellectual and Cultural History," in *The Past before Us: Contemporary Historical Writing in the United States*, ed. Michael Kammen (Ithaca, 1980), 330.

4. Fred Hobson, ed., *South-Watching: Selected Essays by Gerald W. Johnson* (Chapel Hill, 1983), 74.

5. Richard H. King, *A Southern Renaissance: The Cultural Awakening of the American South, 1930–1955* (New York, 1980), viii.

6. Daniel Joseph Singal, *The War Within: From Victorian to Modernist Thought in the South, 1919–1945* (Chapel Hill, 1982), xii; Michael O'Brien, *The Idea of the American South, 1920–1941* (Baltimore, 1979), xvi.

7. William J. Bouwsma, "From History of Ideas to History of Meaning," *Journal of Interdisciplinary History* 12 (Autumn 1981): 279–91; Robert Darnton, "In Search of the Enlightenment: Recent Attempts to Create a Social History of Ideas," *Journal of Modern History* 43 (March 1971): 113–32; Ernst Schulin, "German 'Geistesgeschichte,' American 'Intellectual History,' and French 'Histoire des Mentalités' since 1900: A Comparison," *History of European Ideas* 1 (1981): 195–214; John Higham and Paul K. Conkin, eds. *New Directions in American Intellectual History* (Baltimore, 1979).

8. Higham and Conkin, *New Directions,* xvii, in which Higham observes, "Intellectual history, as represented in the present volume, does little to encourage the study of distinctive individuals," although he adds, to compromise his own case: "A qualification may be in order. Two of the original group of Wingspread papers did focus on the ideas of a single intellectual, with the object of demonstrating the historical significance of those ideas. The editors have chosen not to include these papers, since neither seemed altogether to serve the exemplary purposes of the present book. Thus our own criteria are partly responsible for the absence of studies of individuals" (xix).

9. Singal, *The War Within,* xiii.

10. On the grounds that he comes from Knoxville, I am electing Richard King a non-Southerner for the nonce.

11. C. Vann Woodward, "The Future of Southern History," in *The Future of History,* ed. Charles F. Delzell (Nashville, 1977), 135–49 (quotation on 144).

12. For example, Samuel S. Hill, Jr., et al., *Religion and the Solid South* (Nashville, 1972); and Charles Reagan Wilson, *Baptized in Blood: The Religion of the Lost Cause, 1865–1920* (Athens, Ga., 1980). An artifact of the gulf between indigenous Christian and exotic agnostic analysis is Michael O'Brien, "The Last Theologians: Recent Southern Literary Criticism," *Michigan Quarterly Review* 17 (Summer 1978): 404–13.

13. Bertram Wyatt-Brown, *Southern Honor: Ethics and Behavior in the Old South* (New York, 1982).

14. James J. Thompson, Jr., "Does the South Exist?" *Southern Partisan* 2 (Spring 1982): 36.

15. A more subtle reading, which still half misses the point of the analysis by emphasizing the first chapter of the book and neglecting the last, is William C. Havard, "The Intellectual as Southerner or the Southerner as Intellectual?" *Georgia Review* 34 (Spring 1980): 213–21.

16. Clyde N. Wilson, "Introduction: Should the South Survive?" in Fifteen Southerners, *Why the South Will Survive* (Athens, Ga., 1981), 7.

17. James Whitehead, *Joiner* (New York, 1971).

18. Which translates precisely as "populists."

19. The phrase "simpler folk" is from Thompson, "Does the South Exist?" in a sentence that nearly encapsulates the mingled condescension and adulation that *Volk*ishness brings: "Allen Tate, somewhat deracinated and striving for cosmopolitanism in the 1920s, could not grasp what simpler folk readily perceived" (36).

20. Thompson, "Does the South Exist?" 36.

21. Howard W. Odum, *Southern Regions of the United States* (Chapel Hill, 1936), is literally a collection of lists.

22. Ulrich B. Phillips, "The Central Theme of Southern History," in *The Course of the South to Secession,* ed. E. M. Coulter (Washington, D.C., 1939), 151–65; John Crowe Ransom, "Reconstructed but Unregenerate," in Twelve Southerners, *I'll Take My Stand: The South and the Agrarian Tradition* (New York, 1930), 1–27; C. Vann Woodward, "The Search for Southern Identity," in *The Burden of Southern History,* enlarged ed. (Baton Rouge, 1968), 3–25.

23. Cleanth Brooks, "The Enduring Faith," in Fifteen Southerners, *Why the South Will Survive,* 230.

24. Hugh Legaré, "Spirit of the Sub-Treasury," in *Writings of Hugh Swinton Legaré,* ed. Mary Legaré, 2 vols. (Charleston, 1845–46), 1:301.

25. Woodward, "The Search for Southern Identity" and, contra-Woodward, "A Second Look at the Theme of Irony," in *Burden of Southern History,* 230.

26. Hamilton C. Horton, Jr., "The Enduring Soil," in Fifteen Southerners, *Why the South Will Survive,* 57–67; D. F. Sarmiento, *Life in the Argentine Republic in the Days of the Tyrants* [1845] (New York, 1961), 33.

27. Donald Davidson, *"Still Rebels, Still Yankees" and Other Essays* (Baton Rouge, 1972), 231–53.

28. Forrest McDonald and Grady McWhiney, "The South from Self-Sufficiency to Peonage: An Interpretation," *American Historical Review* 85 (December 1980): 1095–1118.

29. Francis Jeffrey, "The Excursion," *Edinburgh Review* 24 (November 1814): 1, 2.

30. Theodore Zeldin, "Ourselves, as we see us," *Times Literary Supplement,* 13 December 1982, 1435.

31. Drew Gilpin Faust, "Introduction: The Proslavery Argument in History," in Faust, ed., *The Ideology of Slavery: Proslavery Thought in the Old South, 1830–1860* (Baton Rouge, 1981), 1–20; Bertram Wyatt-Brown, "Proslavery and Anti-Slavery Intellectuals: Class Concepts and Polemical Struggle," in *Antislavery Reconsidered: New Perspectives on the Abolitionists,* ed. Lewis Perry and Michael Fellman (Baton Rouge, 1979), 308–36.

32. E. P. Thompson, *The Making of the English Working Class,* rev. ed. (Harmondsworth, 1968), 10–11.

Index

Rᴇᴛʜɪɴᴋɪɴɢ ᴛʜᴇ Sᴏᴜᴛʜ

Designed by Ann Walston.

Composed by G & S Typesetters, Inc., in Galliard.

Printed by the Maple Press Company
on 50-lb. S. D. Warren's Sebago Eggshell Cream offset
and bound in Holliston Aqualite.